New Neighbours
A Case Study of Cooperative Housing in Toronto

Housing continues to be one of the most significant problems facing communities throughout North America. Increasingly urgent are the demands for more affordable housing, elimination of public-housing ghettos, and more accessible housing for disabled persons. In Toronto, interest is focusing on cooperative housing as an alternative that may meet some or all of these demands. This study provides a close-up look at the realities of co-op living, based on extensive interviews with residents of two Toronto co-ops.

Both the co-ops that are discussed are private, non-profit, multiple-unit housing. Members are essentially renters who have secure tenure but no direct financial interest. They include people at very different income levels with diverse kinds of households, social and ethnic backgrounds, and levels of mobility.

Relying heavily on the words of the co-op members themselves, the book avoids academic discussion of abstractions such as democracy, participation, community, and quality of life. Rather it reveals how such concepts are talked about and put into practice in the daily co-op life.

The authors conclude that the diverse housing needs of cities today can best be satisfied through the creativity and energy of private citizens working together. Co-ops exemplify the advantages of resident control of housing, and offer a wide range of benefits to residents and their communities.

MATTHEW COOPER is Associate Professor, Department of Anthropology, McMaster University.

MARGARET CRITCHLOW RODMAN is Associate Professor, Department of Anthropology, and Director of the Graduate Programme in Anthropology, York University.

The authors are also co-editors of *The Pacification of Melanesia*.

NEW NEIGHBOURS

A Case Study of Cooperative Housing in Toronto

MATTHEW COOPER
MARGARET CRITCHLOW RODMAN

UNIVERSITY OF TORONTO PRESS
Toronto Buffalo London

© University of Toronto Press 1992
Toronto Buffalo London
Printed in Canada

ISBN 0-8020-5992-9 (cloth)
ISBN 0-8020-6925-8 (paper)

Printed on acid-free paper

334.1
C77n

Canadian Cataloguing in Publication Data

Cooper, Matthew, 1943–
New neighbours

Includes index.
ISBN 0-8020-5992-9 (bound)   ISBN 0-8020-6925-8 (pbk.)

1. Housing, Cooperative – Ontario – Toronto – Case
studies. I. Rodman, Margaret, 1947–
II. Title.

HD7287.72.C32T67 1992   334'.1'09713541C91-095664-2

TP

This book has been published with the help of a grant from the
Social Science Federation of Canada, using funds provided by the
Social Sciences and Humanities Research Council of Canada.

Contents

Figures

Preface

Research for this book began in January 1987. Beth Vallance, one of our graduate students, had just returned from an arduous year of fieldwork in Papua New Guinea, in conditions much like those each of us had experienced in earlier periods of research. She suggested that interesting fieldwork could be done much closer to home, for example in her own housing cooperative.

The possibilities of exploring a relatively little known, or anyway little described, alternative to the more conventional kinds of housing intrigued us. The crisis of affordable housing in urban Ontario and the need for viable alternatives had increasingly come to concern us. In the past Rodman had carried out research on housing, settlements, and social change in Oceania and Cooper on the sociology of cooperation in nineteenth-century North America. But neither of us had done urban research in a contemporary setting. The challenge of doing that intrigued us as well.

The co-ops we studied look much like the rental apartment buildings and condominiums in the Harbourfront area of Toronto, but they operated on very different principles. Most important, they were affordable for households with low or moderate incomes at a time when rental accommodation in Toronto was very scarce and expensive. They were non-profit, member-controlled enterprises which were meant to include people with a wide range of incomes, social and ethnic backgrounds, and physical abilities. Diversity, not homogeneity, was the goal.

Co-ops present practical models of resident involvement and democratic control. They show how people with very different incomes and backgrounds can find ways to deal with the diversity of their housing needs. One shows how designing a building to be fully accessible for someone in a wheelchair can benefit all residents. It can encourage the emergence of a community that integrates able-bodied people and those with physical disabilities and that improves the quality of life for everyone.

Critics have reproached co-ops because some people who are relatively well off benefit from the government subsidies they receive. The argument goes that available funds should benefit only those with the greatest need of affordable housing. To us, this reflects a lack of understanding of the social benefits of mixed-income communities. The history of public housing reveals all too well the problems that result from building homogeneous, low-income projects. The criticism also shows the public's continuing ignorance of how governments subsidize the private housing market. Direct subsidies always make easier targets than indirect ones.

Because this kind of alternative housing is so little known, we felt that our major aim in this book should be to describe how it works. In doing so we have relied heavily on the words that co-op members themselves used to talk about their experience. For the most part we have resisted the temptation to enter into academic debates about concepts like democracy, participation, community, and quality of life. Rather we have tried to show how they are talked about and put into practice in the co-ops' daily life. Through this descriptive approach we hope we have exemplified concretely the benefits of resident control of housing. At a larger level, we hope that these case studies contribute to the realization that citizen participation and democratic control are essential for the future of our cities.

McMaster and York universities supported the first two years of this project. A research grant from the Social Sciences and Humanities Research Council of Canada financed the final summer of fieldwork and gave us time free from teaching to write the book. We gratefully acknowledge the support of our universities and the SSHRCC.

Two articles we published in *City and Society* in 1989 and 1990 provided the basis for portions of chapters 3 and 10. Parts of other chapters grew out of conference papers we presented at the American Anthropological Association and the Society for Applied Anthropology annual meetings. We are grateful to journal reviewers and to colleagues at those meetings for their comments on our work.

We would like to thank a number of people involved in the co-op housing sector for sharing their insights and experience with us, especially Pat Ashby, Ashley Chester, Tom Clement, Mark Guslits, Fran Malandrino, Marianne Moershel, and Ralph West. Dan Fast was a constant source of patient help, insight, and wry humour. Michael Moir, archivist of the Toronto Harbour Commission, generously provided us with maps and photographs. Anne Adams, executive director of the Barrier-Free Design Centre, made helpful comments on chapter 6. Nancy Johnson, Janet McLellan, and Trish Wilson ably transcribed seemingly interminable interview tapes. Our greatest debt is to the members of Harbourside and Windward co-ops, who welcomed us into their homes and shared their experience with us.

On a more personal level, we want to thank Vicky Cooper, Bill Rodman, and our children for all their help, and especially for putting up with so many 'field trips' and so much talk about co-ops.

NEW NEIGHBOURS: A CASE STUDY
OF COOPERATIVE HOUSING IN TORONTO

CHAPTER ONE

Introduction

The quality of life in our urban areas to many people no longer seems to be what it was. Phrases like 'healthy cities,' 'green cities,' 'liveable cities,' 'humane cities,' or 'cities as if people matter' imply their opposites. Too many cities, especially large ones, today are less than healthy, not particularly green, less liveable than they were, and run as if anything but people mattered.

John Short captures some of these realities in the chapter titles of a recent book: 'Cities as if Only Capital Matters,' 'Cities as if Only Professionals Matter,' 'Cities as if Only Some People Matter.' Definitions of what makes a good city, he says, have come to be dominated by questions of economic growth and administrative convenience. Instead, he tries to develop a vocabulary for cities in which people do matter. 'My starting-point is to see citizens as the solution to, not the cause of, urban problems ... [B]etter cities can be created if all citizens are both *empowered* and *engaged*' (Short 1989: 2, 76; emphasis in the original).

Our book proceeds from that same starting-point. We focus on housing because it is a crucial problem in most cities today. We describe an alternative type of housing that residents democratically manage for themselves and that is affordable. Rather than look at a wide range of examples, we investigated two projects in detail. These are non-profit housing cooperatives in downtown Toronto opened in 1986. In both, citizens participated in planning and design, selecting members, and running the projects.

For us, improvement of the quality of urban life depends to a considerable degree on citizens taking greater control over the conditions that affect their own lives.[1] We do not see this as a panacea for all urban ills. Nor do we believe that cities merely are collections of neighbourhoods. In addition, we recognize that local control is not necessarily liberating or progressive. There are all too many instances in which local control has been exclusionary or worse. Nevertheless, we believe that greater citizen control can lead to real, if not necessarily revolutionary, change.[2] For one thing it fosters the diversity that makes cities interesting places in which to live. It focuses on real problems at a human scale. It forces developers to structure their plans so as to take local needs more seriously into account. The needs and preferences of residents and other stakeholders no longer are frills. They cannot be afterthoughts, taken into account only after the 'serious' economic decisions have been made.

Popular control makes planners realize that planning is more than a technical exercise best left to experts. Planning crucially implicates values, often conflicting ones. Those with a stake in the area being planned can best represent those values.

One reason for the apparent decline in the quality of urban life in recent years, we believe, is that too much of urban development has come to depend on the blind action of market forces. In our contemporary world, the 'market' has become an all-wise demiurge whose every utterance must be obeyed. Yet such a view systematically disregards the social damage that unrestrained markets can do and have done. It resembles a massive case of amnesia. Not all market participants are created equal. Economic (and related political) power strongly influences what gets built where, who benefits, and who bears the costs.

Housing and Needs

Contemporary cities have many problems – environmental deterioration, poor schooling, poverty amidst affluence, inadequate transportation systems, racial and ethnic conflict, rapid economic restructuring, unemployment, crime, to name only some of the most obvious. Not all necessarily occur in every North American city. Yet housing problems seem virtually universal. For the most part, such problems revolve around two general issues: *affordability* and *poorly met needs*.

Affordability

Affordability of housing, technically, refers to the ratio between income and the amount spent by households for shelter. Usually, housing that costs 30 per cent or less of gross household income is regarded as affordable. Some economists argue that since the Second World War housing in Canada generally has become more affordable (Miron 1988: 192–237). This resulted from the rise in real incomes compared with the costs of shelter. Naturally, others disagree (for example, Sayegh 1987: 17).

Whatever the general, long-term picture, it is clear that problems of affordability have become more important recently though not necessarily everywhere or for everyone. In the United States, the growing inequality of incomes during the 1980s severely affected the affordability of housing. '[T]he shortage of housing affordable by the poor reached crisis proportions as more poor people, with less money, sought fewer available apartments, of declining quality, at sharply rising rents' (Schwartz, Ferlauto, and Hoffman 1988: 3).

In Canada, the cost of housing in stagnant or declining areas did not rise especially rapidly in the 1980s. But in booming cities like Toronto, housing for all but the well-off became increasingly less affordable.[3] Many middle-income households in Toronto have serious affordability problems. Their needs rarely are addressed directly, perhaps because they are less dramatic than those of the poor. In both Canada and the United States, but especially in the latter, homelessness has become an ever greater scandal. We discuss affordability problems in Toronto in greater detail in chapter 2.

Poorly Met Needs

Housing needs vary enormously. As a number of writers have argued, a major problem today is that too much of North America's housing is designed for the 'traditional' nuclear family (for example, Hayden 1984; Schwartz, Ferlauto, and Hoffman 1988: 34–43; Franck and Ahrentzen 1989). Thus, the needs of many other households are poorly served.

Hatch (1989: x), for example, points to some assumptions that have influenced the recent development of housing: the as yet unmarried will not remain so; single parenthood is a temporary condition; and apartments are stepping-stones to the private house. These assumptions reflect several 'dangerous myths.' First, only one marital status is considered normal. Second, 'a perpetually rising economic tide' is assumed 'that will float all ships into the desired port: a private home.' A third myth is that the purpose of housing, in an individualistic and heartless world, is 'to generate protective islands, each complete in regard to human complement and equipment.'

Yet increasingly the 'typical' family of coresident wife, husband, and children has become the exception. Demographic trends suggest that much more housing will be needed that can meet the needs of single-person and single-parent households, especially of women. Furthermore, most of these single-parent households have low incomes. The proportion of the population that is elderly, particularly the so-called old elderly, continues to grow. People with disabilities increasingly live independently and require suitable accommodation.

Beyond these needs lie those of greater amenity and community. These include security, accessible social and community services, child care support, better design for residents' actual patterns of use and for people with special needs, reduced maintenance responsibilities, and the opportunity to interact socially with others. To this list we would add the need for residents to have greater input into the housing process.

Use Values versus Exchange Values

In thinking about the variety of housing needs and why they are not well satisfied, we find it helpful to distinguish between 'use values' and 'exchange values.'[4] Many would argue that decisions about the use of urban space have rested too heavily on considerations of exchange value – and that this helps to explain why many housing needs are poorly met.

By use values we mean the 'material and psychic rewards' people and households gain from housing such as shelter, privacy, work space, access to public services, a sense of identity, personal expression, and feelings of community, (Logan and Molotch 1987: 20; Pynoos, Schafer and Hartman 1973: 1). Housing is precious to its users in ways different from most other commodities perhaps because the practical needs met by housing are inseparably bound up with emotional ones. The exchange value of housing arises from its potential to generate rents or build equity for its owners. Thus, it refers to the value of housing as a commodity in the market.

In so far as housing and urban space have become commodities, they have both exchange and use values. Homeowners, for example, often appreciate their homes both for the shelter and comforts they provide and as an investment. These values do not necessarily conflict, but in practice they do increasingly in North America. Some scholars have argued that conflict between developers and their allies (particularly local politicians), on the one hand, and people concerned with the quality of urban life (residents and potential residents), on the other, explains much about recent patterns of development in North American metropolitan areas.[5] 'From the point of view of residents the creation and defence of the use values of neighborhood is the central urban question' (Logan and Molotch 1987: 99).

Through the working out of this conflict, urban space comes to take on the forms, uses, and meanings that it has.[6] Gottdiener (1985: 155) goes further to argue that 'the analysis of any local neighborhood must focus on the confrontation between use and exchange values – on the complex articulation between symbolic universes of meaning, capital accumulation and space.'

This way of thinking about urban areas implies that urban space is contested. It focuses on social and economic processes and the distribution of power. It points to the importance of understanding how people's needs are created, conceptualized, and represented. It raises questions about the creation, propagation, and manipulation of the meanings of urban space and built form. Thus, it encourages us to think about alternatives to our present patterns.

Housing Alternatives

'As the traditional economic "middle class" begins to shrink and household composition becomes more diverse, housing providers must develop new housing forms to accommodate these changes' (Franck and Ahrentzen 1989: xii). *New Households, New Housing,* the book from which this quotation comes, describes a variety of forms of alternative housing.7 From Europe, especially Scandinavia and the Netherlands, come examples of collective housing. Many of these projects, like some nineteenth-century American ones, include communal cooking and eating facilities. North American collective or shared housing tends to emphasize the economic more than the social advantages of collective living. For example, some projects for single people have units with small shared kitchens and living areas. The individual bedrooms are larger and each has its own private entry. Housing designed with single parents in mind has focused on their critical needs: affordability, security, accessibility of community services, social support, and convenience of maintenance. Many such projects are multiple-family housing with small units situated near important community services, especially public transit.

Several themes appear in *New Households, New Housing* that illustrate new ways of dealing with some of the poorly met needs we have mentioned. One is that increasingly housing must be designed to integrate different types of households within a single project – seniors, singles, single parents with children, childless couples, people with disabilities, and even 'typical' families. Furthermore, projects must include people at different income levels.

A second theme is that housing must be integrated with other uses. This is partly a question of the relation of housing to public transit, shopping, and community services, such as parks, schools, and recreation centres. Yet housing projects themselves can include provision for other uses, such as child care, work space, and commercial outlets.

Third is that residents must be involved in their housing. Such involvement can mean participating in the actual design and construction of their housing. It can mean sharing in routine maintenance chores. In some co-ops it can mean residents effectively managing all aspects of the project.

The final theme is that housing must provide for a better balance between individual privacy and the need for community. Alternative forms of housing can encourage sharing and community in different ways and to different degrees. Residents may share space, either in their own homes or in collective areas. They may share resources or in carrying out needed tasks. Built form and social organization must be designed so as to achieve the desired balance between privacy and community.

Central to this concern with housing alternatives is the failure of much of our present housing to meet the needs of a diverse and rapidly changing population. In our view, an explicit recognition of the primacy of use values over exchange values in housing will best ensure that these needs are met. That implies government support at several levels for alternative projects, for example, through financing schemes or changed zoning ordinances. But it does not imply direct government control. Rather, the diversity of needs can best be satisfied through the creativity and energy of private citizens working together.

The two housing co-ops we describe in this book represent just such an opportunity for ordinary citizens to take control of their own housing. They are private multiple housing that is nonprofit and self-managing. Yet they included people at very different income levels with diverse kinds of households, social and ethnic backgrounds, and physical abilities. Members individually had no equity or shareholding in the co-op. Rather, they essentially were tenants who had secure tenure and the right to participate in co-op management.

Canadian housing cooperatives provide a rare opportunity to analyse conflicts over use values in housing largely unobscured by consideration of exchange values. This is not to say that exchange value considerations have been entirely eliminated. Indeed, conflict within the co-ops sometimes developed around issues that did involve exchange value considerations, such as budgets or subletting. Yet these are issues that co-op ideology suggests should be assessed in terms of needs. Generally, though, in the history of the co-ops we studied, conflicts between exchange and use values were most important externally: first, in the creation of the co-ops and, later, in their relations with the neighbourhood.

Internal conflict between use and exchange values played a small role because of the institutional context in which the co-ops were developed. Built under federal government programs that provided financial guarantees and subsidies, they were non-profit and managed by their members. Through its decisions on, for example, maintenance, budgets, landscaping, the use of interior space, or whether one could keep a pet, the community directly affected the use values its members realized from their housing. Thus, through democratic member control, co-op residents had the opportunity to try to meet those needs that other kinds of housing have left unsatisfied.[8]

Harbourside and Windward Housing Cooperatives

Windward and Harbourside Housing co-ops are located near downtown Toronto in a redeveloped waterfront area known as Harbourfront. They occupy some of the most valuable and most contested land in Toronto.

Besides these two co-ops, their immediate neighbourhood on Bathurst Quay in 1989 also contained a park, two other co-ops, public housing owned by the City of Toronto, a disused grain elevator, a clothing factory, a parking-lot for people taking the ferry to Toronto Island Airport, and empty lots waiting for further construction. Housing was developed on Bathurst Quay when Harbourfront Corporation was required to provide affordable housing.

Much of the rest of Harbourfront consists of trendy hotels, condominiums, marinas, and upscale shopping areas. Ever since the federal government gave the land to the city in 1972 to be a waterfront park, development at Harbourfront has been and remains extremely controversial.

As non-profit cooperatives, Harbourside and Windward were established under a federal government program (section 56.1 of the National Housing Act). Among other things, this means that each unit was indirectly subsidized by Canada Mortgage and Housing Corporation (CMHC), the federal housing agency, through a grant that reduced the co-op's monthly mortgage interest payments. CMHC set the initial rents for the co-ops at the low end of the range of market rents for similar units in the area. These rents are called 'housing charges' in co-ops and usually include utilities. Members paid one month's rent as a security deposit; there was no other contribution or equity investment. The co-ops, as corporations, owned the property. Members individually had no shareholding or equity interest in it.

CMHC required each co-op to set aside a minimum of 25 per cent of the units for people in 'core housing need,' that is, who otherwise would have to spend more than 30 per cent of their income on housing. Such households received direct subsidies administered by the co-ops themselves. Over time, the amount of the grant for reduction of mortgage interest payments declines, while the amount available for individual subsidies increases proportionately. Forty to fifty per cent of the members of each co-op received direct subsidies.

Opened at the end of 1986, Windward consists of an eight-storey apartment building flanked by stacked townhouses, providing in all 101 residential units. The co-op had about 160 members and a total population of roughly 250. Harbourside opened in mid-1986. It contains fifty-four units, two-storey townhouses with one floor of apartments above, built around three sides of a courtyard. It had roughly 80 members and about 140 residents in total.

Neither Windward nor Harbourside stood out especially in the physical landscape. But Windward was a social landmark: the first housing cooperative in Toronto that was fully accessible for people with disabilities. Twenty-five per cent of the co-op's units were occupied by at least one person with a disability. Windward was designed expressly to integrate able-bodied people and those with disabilities. There are only two other entirely 'barrier-free' housing co-ops in Canada. People confined to wheelchairs could live wherever they liked rather than having to select from a limited number of accessible units and could use all of the building's facilities. Yet the building lacked the institutional appearance that would label it as housing for people with disabilities.

Harbourside was a family-oriented co-op. Some of Toronto's more than one hundred housing co-ops were designed to serve a particular kind of clientele, such as artists, ethnic or religious groups, and women (see Wekerle and Simon 1986; Wekerle 1988; Wekerle and Novac 1989). However, no such interest group had developed Harbourside. Compared especially with many suburban co-ops it was quite diverse socially.

Research Methods

We conducted ethnographic research at Windward and Harbourside co-ops from January 1987 until November 1989. The membership and boards of directors gave us permission to conduct the study and to have access to demographic data. We have used the real names of the co-ops in this book, but changed the names and altered some identifying characteristics of residents to protect their anonymity.

Our research plan was longitudinal. We followed the two new co-ops for their first three years, until they could be considered reasonably well established. The research was based mainly on intensive interviewing, as well as the collection of co-op documents, newsletters, photographs, etc. At each co-op, with the help of the co-op coordinator we selected a sample of households (approximately 20 per cent at Harbourside, 10 per cent at Windward) to follow that included a rough cross-section of residents.

In each of the three years of the study, one or both of us conducted a sixty to ninety minute, tape-recorded, semistructured interview with adult members of the households, as well as several interviews with the co-op coordinators. The initial interviews with members focused on their housing history, expectations of what life in a housing co-op would be like, and their experience with the co-op. During the second season we explored their changing views and continuing experience of cooperative living. The final round of interviews took place in the summer of 1989. We asked residents especially to evaluate their satisfaction with life at Harbourside and Windward and to reflect on their experience over the three-year period. The coordinators provided us with their views of how the co-ops were developing, the issues they faced, and many insights into how co-ops work. The interviewer prepared a written summary of each interview, while our research assistant transcribed the tapes.

In late September 1989 we conducted a mail survey of all members of both co-ops. A questionnaire was designed with input from the boards of directors, several co-op members, and staff (see Appendix). At both co-ops, committees concerned with trying to increase the level of member involvement assisted us in follow-ups. In fact, at Windward to create greater interest the co-op held a draw at a general meeting in October. The co-op gave a prize of $50 to a lucky member who had returned their questionnaire. The response rate at Windward was 66 per cent, and at Harbourside, 70 per cent. The data were analysed statistically and a summary provided to each co-op in November 1989.

In the following sketch we describe a meeting we attended at Harbourside co-op. It illustrates some of the themes of our research and gives a bit of the flavour of co-op living.

An Informal Meeting at Harbourside Co-op[9]

'Where do we want to be two years from now?' asked Nancy, who was chairing the meeting. She pointed to the top sheet of a flip chart that read, 'Welcome to the Social Audit.' Then she unveiled the next sheet, a drawing of flowers labelled, 'The Harbourside Garden.'

'Here's a good way to get started. Let's think about what we would like to be as if we were nurturing a garden,' she said, 'a garden being a good analogy for our co-op.' She went on, 'Talk to your neighbour: If you were a flower, what kind would you be?'

All twenty-two of the people present began to talk at once. Much laughter, some groans, then general hubbub. The upstairs meeting room in the community centre at Harbourside came to life. Even though the meeting coincided with the Grey Cup, the championship game of the Canadian Football League, more than a quarter of the co-op's members had come.

The meeting had been called to find ways to improve life at the co-op. First, Nancy and Rae, the organizers, planned to brainstorm suggestions for improvement with the whole group. Then the group would split in three to make concrete recommendations to present to the membership at the next general meeting.

We had been invited too. We had just finished our survey of Harbourside and had lots of data to share. Our computer set up on a table to one side of the room, we waited to answer questions. If someone wondered whether men or women felt they could influence co-op affairs more, for example, we could quickly cross-tabulate the data and give them an answer.

Nancy read from an Avon marketing manual she had come across: 'If I were planting a garden and I wanted to have a lot of healthy flowers, I would never think of giving every flower the same amount of water, the same amount of sun, and the same soil. I would be sure to cultivate every kind of flower differently. Does that mean that a rose or an orchid is any less because I have to do more with it?'

She called for members to tell her what the ground rules for the discussion should be. They volunteered that brainstorming should be non-judgmental, anything goes, no 'can'ts,' no 'buts,' no repression of ideas. Everyone was a different kind of flower and each flower has different needs. So everyone should be free to express his or her needs. The participants seemed quite familiar and happy with this way of doing things.

Then came a flood of suggestions. Nancy wrote the contributions on the flip chart. When a sheet was full, she tore it off. Rae stuck the sheets to the wall, first above the fireplace, then on the wall to the right. In the end, there were six sheets and thirty-seven recommendations.

They covered quite a range. Each began with the phrase 'In two years we will ...'

1 have a nicer garden
2 have a common understanding of the role of the board of directors
3 have a common understanding of the role of democracy in the co-op
4 be more representative of the community at large
5 have more integration of members living in townhouses and apartments
6 do better at facilitating greater member involvement, especially of new members
7 have seen an end to the idea of a ruling clique
8 have a welcoming committee for new members
9 have satisfactory security
10 have resolved the conflict with Karvon, the building contractor
11 have better neighbourhood amenities
12 see the Church Street bus run on weekends and evenings
13 have found a way of determining if noise between units is really a problem
14 have a fenced-in yard
15 have greater kids' participation
16 be rid of nasty stones in the courtyard (from the parking-lot excavation for the co-op next door)
17 have general meetings with 80 per cent participation (As Cathy, a long-time member, pointed out, 'If everyone came to meetings, this room would be too small.')
18 have found a solution to wandering cat problems
19 have a casual drop-in place within the co-op
20 have better community facilities
21 have several picnic tables
22 have a gazebo and swings in the courtyard
23 get new carpets for the halls
24 have garbage receptacles for garbage night

25 have garbage cans in the courtyard
26 have mail delivery directly to the units
27 have greater involvement with and knowledge of other co-ops
28 have a babysitting exchange
29 have a child exchange: 'You can have Alexander till he's 4!' (Pause
– Nancy: 'Anything else?')
30 'Greater consideration for your neighbours in some cases,' said
Judy (People laughed at the 'in some cases' part. Judy explained
that she meant more consideration about noise. Nancy: 'Going once
...')
31 Judy: 'I have to say I'd like to see people take greater responsibility
for their own front yards, their own places.' (She was asked if she
meant backyards too, but no she didn't. It was just front yards she
was concerned about because these are people's own responsibility.
As Nancy ripped off a completed page of the flip chart, a woman
shouted cheerfully, 'No, no, no! I want to see a woodworking shop,
a darkroom, and kitchens with two exits.' On went the list.)
32 have a woodworking shop
33 have a darkroom
34 have kitchens with two exits (A man called from the other end of
the room, 'If she can ask for a woodworking room, I can ask for
a jacuzzi!')
35 have a jacuzzi in every unit
36 resolve the smoking issue (Judy noted that Harbourside had a by-
law about smoking at meetings and socials but the issue had not
really been resolved.)
37 have general meetings where everyone feels comfortable speaking

Then Nancy pointed out the three areas the member involvement committee felt recommendations were likely to fall into:
board issues, people and participation, facilities and amenities.
She asked the audience to call out which numbers fell under
which heading. We sensed a high level of involvement. Many
people called out numbers. Probably half the people in the room
had made suggestions, even those who had not seemed engaged.
The group was ready to divide up. But Edwin proposed that

now would be a good time to ask us some questions. One that interested everyone came from Ian.

'I find it amazing that 25 per cent of the people who answered your survey were born in 1950–1. We'll have a big party this year.' General laughter. 'How typical are we? How do we compare to any group of people that you can compare us to? My understanding of Metro Toronto median family income is that it's around $38,000 ... So we're not normal I would think.'

'Well,' one of us replied, 'There's no question that education and income levels are higher than those of the general population. But, we have no comparable data on other co-ops, except for Windward. If you like, you could arrange with them to get access to their data.'

After some further questions and discussion the group divided up. People pulled their chairs together into three circles. Beer orders were taken. A few people got up to get coffee from the kitchen next door. Everyone settled in for more intensive discussion of the recommendations.

A Few Themes

The meeting at Harbourside gave people an opportunity to assess their community and to look for ways to improve it. It highlights some of their concerns: better neighbourhood amenities and co-op facilities, neighbours getting along with each other, some of the smaller irritants of life in multiple housing.

Beyond that it shows members asking to what degree the social goals of the co-op were being met. How well was it doing in trying to mix people of different backgrounds and economic levels? How well was member control working? Was the co-op sufficiently democratic? Such questions do not arise in high-rise rental apartment blocks or in neighbourhoods of single-family homes. Nor do they emerge in condominium developments. As alternatives to those other kinds of housing, non-profit co-ops have a more ambitious agenda.

The meeting also illustrates what has been called 'the symbolic construction of community' (Cohen 1985). Through meetings like this and gatherings of other sorts members come to define who they are as a group. They develop a set of terms and understandings which help them discuss their mutual concerns. But such processes also can involve all the arts of persuasion and even interpersonal conflict.

In the remainder of the book we take up some themes relevant to the co-op agenda.[10] First, though, we describe some of the conditions that made this, and similar meetings, possible. How is it that people who are essentially renters could take control of their own housing? In chapter 2 we discuss the institutional background, i.e., Canadian housing policy and the housing situation in Toronto.

At the meeting, issues arose about the use of the courtyard, the relationship between apartment and townhouse dwellers, and the need for better community facilities. The discussion hints at the importance of relationships between built form, the processes through which it is created or modified, and the people who use it. Chapter 3 takes up this theme by considering the social construction of Windward co-op, including how its site came to be used for housing. We focus on Windward in this chapter because of the greater complexity of the project and because of the problems of building integrated housing for people with disabilities.

The design of housing co-ops, however, is not simply a question of built form. In the Harbourside meeting, most of the meeting was aimed at how to improve the co-op as a community. Chapter 4 begins the discussion of the social design of co-ops, their shape as organizations and communities. It includes discussions of what the co-ops' goals should be and of the ideal images participants have of them.

One of the concerns expressed at the Harbourside meeting had to do with new members. The selection of members is a crucial process in housing co-ops: people get to choose the neighbours with whom they will then have to live. Member selection, of both original and later members, is discussed in chapter 5.

The meeting we have described took place at Harbourside. Thus, it did not touch on a theme of central importance to Windward co-op, which was created to provide an entirely barrier-free housing environment for people with and without disabilities. Chapter 6 therefore looks especially at the integration of people with disabilities and able-bodied people.

Non-profit co-ops are, by definition, affordable housing. They include many households receiving direct subsidies. Yet, as Ian suggested at the Harbourside meeting, a substantial proportion of Windward and Harbourside households have incomes greater than the median for Toronto. Mixing people of different income levels is supposed to prevent affordable housing projects from going the way of the notorious public housing projects of the 1950s and 1960s. In chapter 7 we discuss how well mixing economic levels works. Is it possible that co-ops, or at least these two, work best for middle-income households?

Many of the concerns raised at the meeting had to do with member involvement. How could the co-ops get higher levels of participation on committees and at general meetings? Could better ways be found to involve new members right from the start? Do social functions encourage member involvement? Questions of member involvement and community are discussed in chapter 8.

'Seeing an end to the idea of a ruling clique' and 'having a common understanding of democracy in the co-op' are recommendations from the meeting that underscore the significance of democratic member control for co-ops. This is what makes them alternative housing. Does the majority really rule? Do members control the operation? Is the process of equal, or even more, importance than the product? Chapter 9 considers the experience of Windward and Harbourside regarding these issues.

Chapter 10 considers some conflicts that have arisen at the two co-ops. Where are the lines to be drawn between individual and collective property and responsibility? The conflicts have to do particularly with the use of co-op resources and the realization of the use values of co-op living. It is the community that decides how these resources should be used, not the market. Thus, the use values members realize from living in the co-op depend quite directly on the community itself.

Finally, in chapter 11 we draw together the strands of the

story. The two co-ops we have studied are by no means representative of housing co-ops in Canada generally. But the issues raised we believe are general. We conclude that non-profit housing cooperatives deserve support as a viable alternative to the other forms of housing available today. They hold out the opportunity of restoring to citizens, even if only on a small scale, the ability to control an important part of their lives.

CHAPTER TWO

Housing Policy and Non-profit Cooperatives

In recent years, Toronto's newspapers have been filled with articles on 'the housing crisis.' Rarely does a day go by without a story about the new homeless, fractured families, the problems of rooming-houses, minuscule apartment vacancy rates, the cost of new housing, the NIMBY (not in my backyard) syndrome and affordable housing, developers and politicians, and the hopeful plans of housing experts. Government and social agency reports, too, pile up in libraries.

This is the context in which the co-ops we studied emerged. In this chapter we describe some relevant features of that background. Part of the story concerns the need for housing in a particular time and place. The rest tells how governments and private groups responded to that need. Rapid urban development, demographic change, increasing housing problems, and a plethora of government programs set the stage.

The Emergence of the 'World-Class City'

Kent Gerecke (1989) writes that Toronto has changed so much in recent years that we need a new vocabulary to understand what has happened. Even the changing application of its name shows how the city's power and influence have spread. Originally, 'Toronto' referred only to the City of Toronto, the present central core. With the creation of the Regional Municipality of Metropolitan Toronto (Metro) in 1953, the City and the surrounding areas (later grouped into five municipalities) joined in trying to solve some of their mutual problems. For census purposes, though, Statistics Canada defines the Toronto Census Metropolitan Area (CMA), which includes Metro and four neighbouring regions. More recently, the Province of Ontario defined the Greater Toronto Area, which coincides with the CMA. A senior civil servant was appointed to coordinate planning on issues such as waste management and transportation policy.[1] Today 'Toronto' may refer to any of these different levels.

One new term that has come to the fore is 'world-class city.' The world-class city measures itself against other world centres and is tightly integrated into the international economy. Other terms include gentrification, Manhattanization, foreign investment, reform, affordable housing, NIMBY and PIMBY (please in my backyard), homelessness, and flipping (Gerecke 1989).[2] For some writers the 'Manhattanization' of Toronto, the development of a polarized, two-class city, is revealed most starkly by the problem of the homeless. Not everyone would accept that Toronto already is such a city. But many see current development leading in that direction.

Barton Reid (1989), for example, argues that the idea of the 'corporate city' helps in understanding how this is coming about.[3] From 1945 to 1965, the 'emergent' period of the corporate city, urban land increasingly became a vehicle for capital accumulation. However, local, relatively small-scale developers predominated, especially in the suburbs. Corporate concentration grew between 1965 and 1975 (the 'mature' period) and the development industry increasingly dominated the process.

After 1975 the corporate city entered its 'dominant' phase. As Reid puts it, 'The new arrangement is that developers supply watered down urbanity to the middle classes, and the middle classes, in return, become the willing consumers of the new corporate environment.'[4] The professional classes and the development industry forged alliances based on their shared interest in real estate speculation. The built environment became increasingly commodified, as space and lifestyle became absorbed by the logic of corporate capital. As well, the property industry became closely integrated into the international financial system. This picture, although painted in rather broad strokes, helps to emphasize the concerns of those who feel that Toronto has become a playground for the affluent and selfish. People's feelings of their increasing powerlessness to control development may not be paranoia but have a realistic basis.

The Need for Housing

There are three widely used measures of housing need: affordability, suitability, and adequacy (Social Planning Council of Metropolitan Toronto 1985). The first often rests on the assumption that households should not spend more than a certain percentage, usually 30 per cent, of their gross income on housing.[5] Suitability refers to the availability of sufficient usable space, depending on the size of a household.[6] Adequacy measures the physical attributes of a dwelling, for example, its physical condition, access to bathroom and kitchen facilities, accessibility and needed modifications for people with disabilities. In this section, we will focus on affordability problems.

In the Toronto region in recent years one of the immediate reasons for the shortage of affordable housing was the dramatic rise in land values. This was then reflected in steeply increased house prices and rents. Between 1985 and 1989 the price of an average detached bungalow in Toronto rose by more than 150 per cent. By the first half of 1989 it would have taken 70–75 per cent of the pre-tax income of a family with the median household income of about $39,000 to carry such a house. That is, mortgage payments (after a 25 per cent down payment), property taxes, and utilities would have consumed three-quarters of their gross income. Since 1986 affordability, defined in these terms, has declined dramatically in Toronto. In fact, at best 20 per cent of Toronto families could have qualified for the mortgage on a modest bungalow.[7] But even this figure is based on a family having the wealth to put down 25 per cent of the purchase price. In

1989, the price of resale homes averaged about $275,000 and new homes about $350,000. Thus, a family would have needed between $68,000 and $87,000 for a down payment. Then, this median-income family still would have to spend 70–75 per cent of its income to carry the house.

As a study done by the Royal Bank of Canada put it, 'The Toronto housing market is becoming accessible only to high net worth, high income households and investors.'[8] Ironically, the children of those who have profited from the boom in housing cannot afford to buy houses of their own. In Toronto for the vast majority the Canadian dream of homeownership has vanished.

These recent rises in house prices, however, were only one phase in a longer trend. Average resale prices in the Toronto Real Estate Board market area (which includes neighbouring suburban municipalities as well as Metro Toronto) increased from $61,389 in 1976 to $138,925 in 1986, i.e., by 126 per cent. In the central area of Metro Toronto, the average in 1986 was $191,135. During that period, several contradictory factors affected whether households could afford to buy houses. Median family incomes rose by about the same percentage as house prices. But higher prices meant larger down payments, making it harder especially for first-time buyers. Mortgage interest rates soared from 12 per cent in 1976 to a high of 21 per cent or more in the recession of 1981 before dropping back to the 12–13 per cent level (Planning Department, Metropolitan Toronto 1987: 9–26). Nevertheless, in the City of Toronto itself homeownership increased between 1976 and 1986. The proportion of owner-occupied properties rose from 55.6 per cent to 63.7 per cent (in 1985). Some of this growth can be attributed to the building of condominium townhouses and apartments in the 1970s and 1980s. Most resulted, however, from the conversion of multifamily dwellings, especially ones occupied by the owner, back to single-occupancy status or to a smaller number of units. While such conversions are illegal today in large buildings, dwellings with fewer than four units may be converted. Gentrification of downtown neighbourhoods and, to a small degree, the splitting of immigrant families seem chiefly responsible for these changes. Thus, with the continuing decline of new residential construction in the City itself, there was a net loss of dwelling units (Planning and Development Department, City of Toronto 1986b).[9]

A snapshot of the situation in the City of Toronto in 1989 would have shown a shrinking stock of housing units, rapidly rising prices, decreasing affordability of housing, yet increasing levels of homeownership. '[W]e are witnessing the disintegration of residential ownership: the affluent are buying homes and condominiums, and the rest of us are dependent on government subsidized dwellings, co-ops, or what's left of the affordable housing stock.' 'Increasingly, Metro Toronto's booming economy is creating a city of two solitudes: potential home buyers and permanent tenants.'[10]

For renters, and especially at the lower end of the income scale, 'affordability has been steadily decreasing' (Planning Department, Metropolitan Toronto 1987a: 6). In Ontario generally, according to a study of homelessness commissioned by the Ontario government, in 1988 there were at least 254,000 households that could not afford adequate rental accommodation (Minister's Advisory Committee on the International Year of Shelter for the Homeless 1988: 40–42). According to the Metro Toronto Social Planning Council, by 1989 one in three renters paid at least 30 per cent of household income for shelter, and many spent 50 per cent or more.[11] This compares with 28 per cent of tenants who paid 30 per cent or more of gross income in 1981 (Statistics Canada 1981: Table 93-942).

Part of the problem is that the demand for rental housing has far exceeded the supply. One reason is that private rental unit completions have declined steadily since 1976. Rent controls, while ineffective in tenants' eyes because of continuing large rent increases, have deterred private developers from constructing rental housing. Poorly targeted government incentive schemes have led to the building of luxury condominiums but not affordable rental units. Private sector construction has been so low that social housing construction, while far from sufficient, has outstripped it since 1981.

Apartment vacancy rates tell part of the story. In Metro Toronto the vacancy rate has remained at or below 1 per cent since
1976. From 1986 to 1989 the rate ranged from 5 down to less
than 1 per 1,000 apartments. To make matters worse, according
to both landlord and tenant organizations the bulk of the available units seemed to be at the higher end of the market. With
the average rental of a vacant two-bedroom apartment at over
$1,000 per month in Toronto, that meant $1,200 per month and
up.[12]

Because so few apartments were available, tenants had to in-
vent various strategies to obtain or to hold on to housing. For
example, many apartments never came on the market but were
obtained through networks of friends or relatives. 'Word of mouth
has replaced newspaper advertisements as the search method of
choice.'[13] Some were obtained through the payment of (illegal)
key money demanded by landlords and/or by bidding against
other prospective renters.[14] Tenant associations became increasingly active in opposing condominium conversions, fighting
landlords against rent increases and for improvements, and
pressuring government to protect tenants more effectively.

Another result was growing waiting lists for assisted housing.
For example, the Metro Toronto Housing Authority, which man-
ages provincially owned public housing, had more than 45,000
names on its waiting-list in early 1989.[15] But turnover was low
and the wait was up to six years.

Most worrisome was the increase in homelessness. The Ontario government's advisory committee on the homeless reported
that approximately 200,000 households were caught in a cycle of
homelessness (Minister's Advisory Committee on the International Year of Shelter for the Homeless 1988). They saw a cycle
of three housing situations through which households at the low
end of the market might pass over the course of two or three
years. In one, people literally are without shelter; they live on
the streets. In the second, people use emergency shelters as permanent accommodation. In the third, households live in overcrowded, substandard, often illegal housing and/or pay more
than 50 per cent of their income for shelter. People caught in

this cycle move from one of these situations to another. Many more people than those living on the streets at any moment are at risk of being homeless.

'The housing crisis in Ontario has its greatest impact on the poor. Youth and single parents, who are mostly women, are particularly hard hit' (ibid.: 10). Low wages, the decline of factory employment, low rates of social assistance, the steady loss of traditional forms of low-cost housing, demographic changes, and faltering production of affordable rental housing have created the situation. As the committee on homelessness put it (ibid.: 28, 76): 'Homelessness has been exacerbated by public policy decisions in the 1970's ... to discharge institutionalized people and ... to stop building public housing .... [W]e are currently witnessing the result of fifteen years of neglect in the social housing field, by both the Provincial and Federal Governments.'

The costs of homelessness, though difficult to calculate, are enormous. Spending on shelters and other palliatives consumes large amounts of money but does not address the causes of the problem. Providing one bed in an emergency shelter costs $10,000 a year. The same amount would subsidize a household's rent in social housing (ibid.: 76). But the costs of homelessness extend well beyond the economic. Hunger and poor health strain the resources of health and social service agencies. Over 140 voluntary food banks help people who have been forced to choose between adequate shelter and food. Family violence and child abuse increase. Families may break up, children become uprooted.

Clearly, homelessness is not an individual problem but is rooted in the complex of demographic, social, and economic changes occurring in the city. The cycle of homelessness represents the other side of Toronto's growing prosperity: poverty amidst affluence.

Some Economic and Social Trends

Several economic trends have affected the housing situation in Toronto. One is the increasing concentration of economic activity in the larger cities in Canada. In general, the larger the city, the higher the level of household income. Disproportionately greater market size results from the combination of large populations and high incomes. For example, the Toronto CMA (which includes Metro Toronto and the surrounding regional municipalities of Halton, Peel, York, and Durham) has twenty-six times the population of Trois Rivires, Quebec, the twenty-fifth largest urban area. But its market size is fifty-three times greater (Simmons and Bourne 1989: 40–2). Toronto, as the largest market area in Canada, is also the greatest magnet for job seekers.

Increasingly, Toronto's economic role is played out on a larger stage. International capital movements and monetary policies affect the level of economic activity in Toronto more strongly and rapidly than was the case thirty years ago. The high interest rates of the early 1980s, for example, helped to produce the worst recession since the 1930s. Jobs and homes were lost. Construction, especially of rental housing, dropped drastically.

The employment situation and changes in the sectoral composition of the economy crucially affect housing demand. Recent job growth has occurred almost entirely in the service sector, such as trade, finance, professional services, and government. Between 1983 and 1988, for example, Toronto gained 400,000 jobs, 80 per cent of which were in services. Yet many are concerned that 'the city's work force is being Manhattanized as middle-income jobs in the manufacturing sector are lost, replaced by higher-level office jobs and lower-level ... service occupations.'[16]

As Simmons and Bourne (1989: 48–51) show, the Toronto economy has become increasingly diverse. Manufacturing, finance, government, and various services have followed sometimes quite different paths. Thus, the growth of employment has varied widely. From 1976 through 1987, it was positive in every year except for 1982–84. Total employment, as well, increased from 1976 to 1981, then fell during the recession, only to increase rapidly from 1984 to 1987. Unemployment has remained much lower, generally, than in other parts of Canada, contributing to Toronto's economic attractiveness.

Real average household income in the Toronto CMA rose 4.3

per cent between 1981 and 1986. This compares with a drop of 1 per cent for the twenty-five largest cities in Canada during the period (ibid.: 41). But the Toronto region's economic success has been accompanied by declining real incomes for the poor, especially but not only those receiving social assistance. As well, a greater proportion of the poor tend to be young, single, and female. Many are working but at low-wage jobs that cannot support households in the city with the highest cost of living in Canada.[17]

Demographic change also underlies many of the changes in the demand for housing.[18] In recent years, the rate of population growth in the Toronto region has exceeded that in both Canada and Ontario. Many smaller places in Canada, especially resource-based towns, have suffered declining populations. Rapid growth has mostly occurred in larger urban areas. 'Canada is not only highly urbanized, but it is increasingly focused at a small set of locations' (ibid.: 26).

The Toronto CMA has grown because of immigration as well as natural increase. While the Toronto CMA was about the same size as Montreal in 1976, by 1986 it was 17 per cent larger (ibid.: 35). However, most growth within the Toronto CMA took place outside of Metro Toronto. Between 1971 and 1985, the four regional municipalities grew by 77 per cent while Metro Toronto increased only 3 per cent (Planning Department, Metropolitan Toronto 1987b: 5–11). Yet after having declined for twenty years, population in the older parts of the city began to grow again after 1981 (Simmons and Bourne 1989: 42–48).

An important feature of demographic change in Toronto is that the number of households keeps growing. In Metro Toronto, between 1971 and 1986 the number of households increased by about 30 per cent although population grew by only 3 per cent. The population of the City of Toronto declined by 14 per cent during that period yet the number of households grew by 14 per cent.

Another significant aspect is that households continue to grow smaller on average, especially in the City itself. Between 1971 and 1986, average household size in the Toronto CMA declined from 3.4 to 2.8. In Metro Toronto, it shrank from 3.2 to 2.7. However, in the City of Toronto it dropped from 3.0 to 2.4, showing the growing prevalence of one- and two-person households (ibid.: 45–7). Moreover, projections suggest that by 2011 household size will decline to 2.1 (Planning Department, Metropolitan Toronto 1987b: 9–11).

The Planning Department of Metro Toronto (ibid.) argues that smaller average household size will result from several factors. As the population ages, there will be an increasing number of empty nesters and single-person households. Furthermore, the number of large households will decline as children grow up and leave home. High rates of household formation among single people and continued high divorce rates also will contribute to the decline.

Given the demographic change that already has taken place and is likely in the future, the demand for housing in Metro Toronto will remain high. Much of that demand will be for smaller-sized housing units. More diverse and smaller households will need more suitable housing. Ironically, much of the existing housing stock will be under-used. An ageing population means a large number of existing single-family houses occupied by one or two people. Furthermore, while the central city's population decreased by 14 per cent between 1961 and 1986, the amount of residential floor space grew by 34 per cent. Each resident of the central city now occupies 54 per cent more floor area than in 1961.

Social and economic trends in Toronto paint a complex picture. Over the past fifteen years or more, the city became richer, more diverse, more powerful as an economic magnet. Land and housing prices soared. Population in the central areas began to increase again. The number of households increased even more, especially small ones. Yet the consequences of Toronto's growth also are with us, including a growing division between the well-off and the poor, food banks, and homelessness.

Government Responses to the Housing Problem

The current housing crisis in Toronto is not a storm that has appeared suddenly in a clear sky. 'The crisis in housing today is not a crisis, it's an institutionalized economic problem,' according to New Democratic Party MP Jim Karpoff.[19] If the present crisis is only the latest episode in a long-running story, it is fair to ask how government has tried to deal with it. While some would argue that government should not involve itself in the provision of housing at all, in fact Canadian governments at several levels have done so for many years (Rose 1980; Bacher 1985; Sayegh 1987: 121–212; Miron 1988: 238–67).

D.V. Donninson, a British housing expert, points out that Western governments generally have approached housing policy in three ways (Donninson and Ungerson 1982). The 'assisted free market' approach aims to stimulate the flow of mostly private funds into housing but does not concern itself with the distribution of the housing produced. By contrast, the 'social market' approach makes government's principal role 'to come to the aid of selected groups of the population and help those who cannot secure housing on the open market' (Donninson 1967: 96). 'Comprehensive' housing policies, found in Sweden for example, reduce the distinctions between market and social sectors by making government responsible for guiding most housing production according to defined policy objectives, research, and careful planning.

John Bacher (1986: 11) argues that Canadian housing policy, beginning at least in 1935, has been the 'very inverse' of the comprehensive approach. 'Rather than being the product of a careful analysis of the nation's housing needs ... housing programs were devised in response to goals largely unrelated to ... providing Canadians with an improved standard of shelter in a better living environment. Study of confidential files 'reveals a pattern of drift from crisis to crisis, with government throughout appearing more eager to create ingenious schemes relying on business interests to reduce the public's demand for a more socially sensitive housing policy, than to heed evident social housing needs.' Whatever the motives involved, over the years government has employed both the assisted free market and social market approaches. Clearly, though, support of the private sector always has come first.

Barbara Wake Carroll (1989) provides a helpful outline of

postwar trends in Canadian housing policy. There have been three distinct but interrelated phases, she argues. All too often, policies adopted in one phase created problems which later policies then tried to correct. During the 'development phase,' between 1945 and 1968, federal housing policy focused on stimulating economic growth through the creation of construction jobs and promotion of the building industry in response to rapidly expanding demand for housing.[20] Policy makers assumed that the private sector could provide the needed housing, especially new detached single-family dwellings, most efficiently and rapidly. The housing problems of low-income households would be solved by filtering as the more affluent vacated their older, smaller, cheaper homes for new ones.

Initially, the federal government carried most of the program costs through direct delivery and financing by the Canada Mortgage and Housing Corporation. Later CMHC gradually withdrew, passing on the direct costs to the provinces and the building industry. Generally, these policies succeeded in reaching their major goal: the housing stock almost doubled. But unintended consequences emerged. Programs to provide more serviced land encouraged high capital cost programs. As standards of 'adequate' housing rose, the sizes of houses and lots increased. Thus, the programs helped to accelerate low-density development in the rapidly growing suburbs and the decay of inner cities.

Urban renewal seemed the panacea for inner city problems. Cities could easily find money to raze older buildings but not to rehabilitate or find new uses for them. Urban renewal displaced many low-income people who then were resettled in large-scale public housing projects.[21] If nothing else, these projects did provide housing and had the advantage of 'utilizing the increased capacity of the development industry' (ibid.: 65).

From 1968 to 1978 Canadian housing policy entered what Carroll (1989: 65–9) calls a phase of social reform or social development. The Trudeau government introduced comprehensive, rational planning to meet new pressures on housing markets from the coming of age of the baby boom generation. High rates of household formation and heightened expectations of material prosperity fuelled the demand for housing. As well, the political climate of the late 1960s resulted in urban reform movements that raised concerns about social and environmental issues, especially about the problems created by urban renewal and public housing schemes.

Overall, policy focused on community involvement, neighbourhood revitalization, coordination of the work of different levels of government, and flexibility of response to changing conditions. Neighbourhood improvement, residential rehabilitation, non-profit and cooperative housing programs joined the existing programs (although the urban renewal program was suspended). During this phase provincial governments increasingly became involved in housing and other social programs, both through cost-sharing arrangements with the federal government and through their own schemes (see below).

Yet unintended consequences again undermined the success of many of the housing programs. For example, after rapid inflation in housing prices the Assisted Home Ownership Program (AHOP) was introduced in 1973 to help lower-income Canadians buy first homes. AHOP provided high-ratio mortgages and interest reduction grants in an effort to make 'easy money' available to lower-income households. Subsequently, the grant program was replaced with second mortgages that were interest free and resembled graduated payment mortgages. Developers pressured CMHC and municipalities to lower standards and speed up approvals after CMHC set a maximum price for the 'modest' homes it would subsidize. Both supply and price rose but quality fell. 'Lots became smaller, assured levels of amenities lower, land prices higher, and, increasingly, new urban housing took the form of highrise buildings or row condominium units' (ibid.: 66). Increasing mortgage rates in the late 1970s coincided with the end of the period of interest-rate assistance. This forced large numbers of AHOP-assisted homeowners to default and abandon their houses because their incomes had not increased sufficiently to absorb the higher payments. CMHC thereby became one of the largest owners of housing units in the country.

AHOP exemplifies the assisted free market approach generally favoured by Canadian governments. While the social market approach also was employed its prospects became entangled with those of AHOP. The demise of AHOP put pressure on the non-profit and cooperative programs. Changes in these programs in 1978 were 'affected by a desire to utilize the inventory of unoccupied projects, to deal with unemployment in the construction sector, and to reduce the pressure on rental markets' (ibid.). These programs had aimed at the rehabilitation of inner city properties. Yet when CMHC began to accumulate inventories of ex-AHOP projects it encouraged non-profit groups to purchase them. Thus, many of the new non-profit projects were suburban. Moreover, only a small portion of this housing actually went to low-income groups.

The non-profit and cooperative programs had been intended to stimulate self-help activity. Unfortunately, many citizen groups had difficulty planning and implementing housing schemes. Instead non-profit agencies owned by governments, housing resource groups, charitable organizations, and churches became the primary delivery mechanisms. They already had institutional support and the capacity to implement programs. Thus, the goals of encouraging community development and building local organizational capability virtually disappeared. During this period, in sum, 'the variety of influences and complexity of goals in the housing sphere were such that program objectives changed frequently and unintended consequences of these housing policies created significant problems for the future' (ibid.: 67).

The most recent phase, from 1978 to the present, is one of attempted financial restraint.[22] With the general swing to the right politically, especially after the election of a Conservative government in 1984, considerations of macroeconomic policy increasingly affected housing policy. Rapidly rising inflation in the late 1970s was followed in the early 1980s by the worst recession in fifty years. Economic expansion began again in 1982 but unemployment and interest rates remained high and the federal budget deficit headed skywards. Block municipal grants replaced federal land, sewage treatment, and neighbourhood improvement programs.

CMHC's planning now emphasized disentanglement, privatization, and cost containment. Private lender financing replaced the direct federal lending programs for housing. As well, tax incentive schemes were introduced to support the construction of new homes and private rental projects. The provinces and larger municipalities assumed much of the direct control of housing delivery. Adoption of a new housing strategy by the federal government in 1986 (CMHC 1986a) meant that only five federal housing programs remained in existence: the traditional mortgage insurance, residential rehabilitation, non-profit and cooperative housing, rent supplement, and housing for native people (ibid.: 67). CMHC largely turned over control of these programs to the provinces in 1986. After forty years of active involvement, the federal government had virtually withdrawn from the implementation of housing policy.

Government restraint policies affected housing tenure patterns and the distribution of income over the period from 1974 to 1984, according to J. David Hulchanski and Glenn Drover. They conclude that restraint led to the decline of direct housing subsidies, which are highly visible. But off-budget tax expenditures to aid the private sector increased dramatically. As a result, households became increasingly polarized into homeowner and renter groups. Furthermore, higher-income homeowners and investors in private rental projects benefited most from governmental restraint (Hulchanski and Drover 1987).

Cooperative Housing Programs

Canadian housing policy generally has favoured private sector solutions to housing problems. Neither the principle of housing as a commodity like any other nor the 'myth of market efficiency' has been challenged. But most commentators recognize that the market has failed to meet the needs of low- and many middle-income households.

Non-profit co-ops have emerged as an innovative way to try to meet these needs (Laidlaw 1977; Selby and Wilson 1988; CMHC 1990b). However, without government programs probably only a few non-profit housing co-ops would exist.[23] From the early 1940s through the 1960s several federal task forces recommended that the government should promote cooperative housing. Joan Selby and Alexandra Wilson (1988: 5–6) propose two factors to explain the lack of government response.[24] First, developers and government officials opposed cooperative housing as alien to the Canadian tradition of homeownership and inimical to the interests of private developers. Second, the cooperative sector lacked the needed organizational capacity.

During this period, however, a small number of housing cooperatives already had been organized privately. In Nova Scotia during the 1930s, building co-ops emerged based on provincial government loans and member contributions of cash or labour. After completion of the project, members owned their own homes. Similar projects appeared in other provinces, resulting in more than 20,000 such units by the late 1940s.

'Continuing' cooperatives, that is, ones in which active members jointly own the entire project but have no individual equity, began with a student housing co-op at the University of Toronto in 1934. However, it was not until the 1960s that cooperative organizations and trade unions got together to organize the first non-student continuing co-ops. Willow Park, the first, opened in Winnipeg in 1965.

The success of the few pioneering continuing co-ops led to the creation of the Co-operative Housing Foundation (today, Federation) of Canada in 1968. Churches, the Canadian Labour Congress, the Canadian Union of Students, and the Co-operative Union of Canada joined in the effort and in lobbying government for a co-op housing program. In 1970, the federal government made available a $30 million loan fund for five pilot projects.

In 1973 amendments to the National Housing Act created the non-profit and cooperative housing program. Finally, alternatives existed to the rigid system of market housing for those who could afford it and public housing for everyone else (Bacher 1986: 15). This program involved 10 per cent capital grants and 90 per cent mortgage loans repayable over fifty years made directly by CMHC. Grants for start-up costs, rehabilitation of existing housing, and rent supplements (with costs shared by the provinces) also were available. Over the next four years, about 240 co-ops with 10,000 units appeared (Selby and Wilson 1988: 10). However, by 1978 the program had come under attack.[25] Relatively large federal capital contributions, disparities in provincial ability to participate in cost-sharing arrangements, open-ended subsidy programs, intergovernmental friction, and the emphasis on low-income groups all had weakened support for the program. Only a concerted effort on the part of the cooperative movement, churches, the labour movement, tenant associations, and other community organizations averted its demise. Parliament again amended the National Housing Act in 1978 to make the program work more efficiently. The basic rationale of the program, however, remained to provide modest, affordable housing at minimum cost for low- and moderate-income households.

The new non-profit and cooperative program (called the section 56.1 program, after the appropriate section of the NHA)[26] entailed a mix of direct federal funding and loan guarantees (CMHC 1981, 1983). Thirty-five-year mortgage loans from private lenders for 100 per cent of capital costs replaced direct government loans. As well, CMHC provided start-up funds, money for rehabilitation of existing buildings, and grants to community resource groups to help develop projects. It also required that projects house people of different income levels, some of whom would pay rents geared to their incomes.

For each co-op, CMHC provided a total grant based on the difference between the monthly amortization payment on the mortgage at market rates and what the payment would have been at 2 per cent (up to a maximum of $500 per unit). Rents were set at the low end of market rents for the area.

Two sorts of subsidies became available to co-ops. CMHC paid the difference between the true economic rent and actual rents to the co-op as a general subsidy.[27] Thus, even though most members paid market rents, all members of the co-op indirectly were subsidized. Money left over (that is, the difference between the total grant and the general subsidy) formed a pool to provide direct rental subsidies to at least 15 per cent (later 25 per cent) of member households. For these households rents were subsidized down to 25–30 per cent of income. Each co-op administered its own subsidy pool.

The new program was well received. Between 1979 and 1985, about 900 new projects added 34,000 units to the co-op stock (Selby and Wilson 1988: 11). Windward and Harbourside were developed under this program. However, during this period soaring interest rates rapidly increased government costs and pressure developed to cut back. Evaluation of the section 56.1 program showed that it had made important contributions to the stock of affordable rental housing, but it did not effectively reach those most in need nor was it a cost-effective way of producing assisted housing. Furthermore, the programs had met only a tiny percentage of the need for assisted housing CMHC (1983). The program was terminated in 1985. Projects developed under it, however, remain in effect.

In 1986 the new federal housing policy turned over delivery of social housing programs to the provinces and targeted assistance exclusively to those most in need. The new federal cooperative housing program was classified as market rather than social housing. It featured private thirty-year index-linked mortgages guaranteed by CMHC.[28] Payments were indexed annually at a rate 2 per cent below the change in the national Consumer Price Index. As well, rent supplements made it possible to let 30 per cent of the units to households that otherwise would have to pay more than 30 per cent of their income for housing (CMHC n.d. [1986]).

The effect of the 1986 co-op program was to transfer responsibility further to the provinces, some of which expanded their own co-op programs. Financial restraint and a predilection for market solutions led to a failure to meet the program's stated goal of producing 5,000 new units per year. Only about 10,000 new federally sponsored units were produced between 1986 and 1988. Funds for the program were reduced by 25 per cent in the 1989 federal budget, reducing the number of new units produced to about 2,000. 'In effect, the government has cut out the heart of housing co-ops in Canada,' lamented the Co-op Housing Federation of Canada.[29]

A major review of the 1986 program was carried out in 1990 (CMHC 1990b). Generally, the evaluation found that the federal co-op programs had produced a sizeable stock of good quality housing in a cost-effective manner. The co-op sector and community organizations lobbied desperately to save the program. The federal minister responsible for CMHC, a long-time supporter of co-ops, managed to persuade his government to continue the program at about the same levels of support.[30]

Co-op housing programs, like housing policy more generally, have changed repeatedly in Canada, even in their short life-span. Yet the co-op sector has shown its ability to produce good housing at reasonable cost if given the chance. During the 1980s, co-ops accounted for from 27 per cent to 59 per cent of social housing starts.[31] As Vivian Campbell, former president of the Co-op Housing Foundation, put it, 'After 20 years and 60,000 co-op units across the country under our belts, we've proved the concept works well.'[32]

Provincial and Municipal Initiatives

It is no secret that large numbers of people who have low or moderate incomes cannot afford adequate housing without some form of assistance. In Toronto this problem has existed for years; many would argue that recently it has become worse. In this section we describe attempts by the Ontario and municipal governments to provide housing in Toronto.[33]

Canadian housing policy always has taken homeownership as its main goal. In theory, the market, if allowed to operate without hindrance, should provide appropriate housing for all. But the market has not worked well for those at the lower end of the income scale. Hence, the need for social housing, subsidized and/or provided by government.

Shortly after the end of the Second World War, the City of Toronto began the first major project aimed at meeting the growing need for low-cost rental housing. Rapid population growth, overcrowding, and deterioration of the older housing stock had produced calls for slum clearance and urban renewal. The result, begun in 1948, was Regent Park North. After the existing housing was cleared, over 1,000 units in low-rise apartment block and row houses were built.

From then until the early 1970s, several public housing projects appeared. Although Regent Park North was developed by the municipal government, most later projects depended on cost-sharing arrangements among federal, provincial, and municipal governments. In 1964, following amendments to the National Housing Act, the government of Ontario set up the Ontario Housing Corporation to build and run its public housing projects. The Municipality of Metropolitan Toronto founded the Metropolitan Toronto Housing Company Ltd. (MTHC), which built for senior citizens.

Between 1965 and 1975, more than 28,500 public housing units were developed in Metro Toronto, mainly on large suburban tracts (Social Planning Council of Metropolitan Toronto 1984: 3–8). Most of these projects, especially the ones built on downtown sites, were built at much higher densities than Regent Park North. By the late 1960s, however, public attitudes had turned against large-scale public housing projects. Opponents decried the damage done to communities and the city as a whole when neighbourhoods were razed. Redevelopment displaced many individual households as well. Increasingly, public housing projects became low-income ghettos, 'warehousing' the poor. Thus, in the early 1970s provincial and municipal social housing policies began to emphasize smaller-scale, mixed-income projects. The federal government as well began to support the improvement of existing neighbourhoods and rehabilitation of the older housing stock.[34] Slum clearance and urban renewal disappeared from the agenda to be replaced by concern with neighbourhoods, community level planning, and social integration (Planning and Development Department, City of Toronto 1985).

In 1973, the City of Toronto created Cityhome, its own public housing company. As well, the city's Official Plan was amended in 1976 to include policies and targets intended to stimulate the development of social housing. The City's policy envisioned private sector involvement and provided incentives, especially by allowing developers greater densities in return for their providing assisted housing (ibid.: 56–9). Importantly, the new planning policy also aimed to create an urban environment that was human in scale. It encouraged diversity. Neighbourhoods should contain a mix of uses and also a mix of people.

Several new neighbourhoods were developed by the City on formerly industrial sites. The goals were to stabilize central city population by providing new housing and facilities that would re-create typical Toronto neighbourhoods. That meant, among other things, that there would be families, 'enough well-off people to ensure economic viability, and a mixture of housing, business and some light industry.'[35] The first, close to the downtown core, was the St Lawrence neighbourhood. Its initial phase opened in 1979; by 1990 it contained approximately 3,500 housing units. About 2,000 of these units were non-profit, social housing, much of it cooperative. About one-quarter of the tenants paid rents geared to their incomes. The St Lawrence neighbourhood generally is regarded as a success, particularly by residents.

A second major new neighbourhood was the Frankel/Lambert development. Planned beginning in 1976, it houses about 2,000 people in 850 low-rise units. Evaluation of this project showed that not all the planning objectives had been met. For example, given the aim of building mostly ground-related housing, the high cost of land meant that densities are great. Simon and Wekerle (1985) refer to this as the 'miniaturization' of the typical Toronto neighbourhood because street widths and open space were reduced to accommodate other goals.

Despite many accomplishments, the City did not meet its assisted housing targets for the period from 1976 to 1986. Only 13,875 of the 20,000 units targeted for the city were built. In the central area of the city the program resulted in a smaller percentage, 7,924 out of 15,000 or about 53 per cent, actually being completed (Planning and Development Department, City of Toronto 1987: 1–2). One reason for the shortfall was that the private sector did not participate to the extent anticipated. Nevertheless, in its 1986 report the City's Housing Policy Review Committee recommended greater reliance on the private sector for the provision of assisted housing (Planning and Development Department, City of Toronto 1986a).

In 1983 the Council of Metropolitan Toronto estimated a need for an additional 30,000 assisted housing units. Metro Council set a target of 2,000 units per year but has not been able to meet that goal. Its MTHC builds projects outside the City of Toronto, at first only for seniors but now especially for singles and one-parent families.[36] By the end of 1985 MTHC had a stock of almost 17,000 units, mostly for seniors. Shortages of funding, difficulty in finding sites, and community opposition to the construction of assisted housing have lowered the rate of production (Planning Department, Metropolitan Toronto 1987a: 1–2, 38–41).[37]

The government of Ontario re-entered the social housing field in the mid-1980s. The Assured Housing for Ontario program, announced in late 1985, aimed to 'make basic, affordable housing available to all' through improved housing supply, a new rent review system, cooperation between government and the building industry, and the use of government owned lands for housing (Ministry of Housing, Ontario n.d. [1985], n.d. [1986], 1986). Much of the concern with affordable housing, however, has focused on assisting the private market.[38]

In 1986 the Ontario Ministry of Housing entered into an agreement with the City of Toronto to redesign its non-profit programs. The new program aimed to target housing assistance more effectively. But it also had other goals. One was to ensure socio-economic integration in each project. Other goals were to increase the likelihood of community acceptance and of integration of the project in the community.

In most earlier City projects 25 per cent of residents paid rents geared to income while the remainder paid at the low end of market rents for the area. As market rents increased rapidly, however, low end rates in new projects became barely affordable for moderate-income households. Thus, large gaps had developed within the projects between the highest-income assisted tenants and lowest income market rate tenants.

The 1986 agreements required a mix of tenants to bridge the gap: 40 per cent on deep subsidy, 40 per cent on shallow subsidy, 20 per cent paying market rent. By early 1990, 938 units had been built. Preliminary evaluation of this program suggests that such a mix of tenants has produced administrative difficulties and potential adverse effects on the residents' quality of life (Cityhome 1990).

Introduced also in 1986, Ontario's cooperative housing program initially involved cost sharing with the federal government. Later, a strictly provincial program was added. In both cases, Ontario required a higher proportion of units to be let on a rent geared to income basis than did the federal government. Co-ops also were allowed to increase that proportion beyond the required 40 per cent. In at least one co-op developed in the period all units were rented on this basis.[39]

Co-ops, though government supported, are privately developed. Under the several federal and provincial programs, the number of co-ops in Metro Toronto grew from 10 in 1975, to 74 in 1984, and 104 by 1989. In 1975 there were approximately 800 units of cooperative housing; by 1989 the total exceeded 9,000.[40]

As impressive as this growth appears, it must be seen against a background of funding cuts, high development costs, and a shortage of available sites. Officials of the Co-op Housing Federation of Toronto report getting some 15,000 requests a year for units in Metro Toronto.[41] Even with this unfulfilled demand and the fact that co-ops averaged less than one hundred units and were well integrated into the community, they faced a mixture of public ignorance and resistance. To the extent the public knew about them at all, it seemed to think of them as being just like the rather notorious large public housing projects.[42]

Although there have been real accomplishments in the social housing area, problems have continued to mount. Politically, in the late 1980s the Housing Ministry became one of the most sensitive portfolios in the Ontario government. One reason was the widespread public perception of excessively close ties between the provincial Liberal government and the private development industry. Another was the number of programs that never got off the ground or that failed to meet their targets. Between 1985 and 1989, there were three different ministers of housing who put forth two major strategies, Assured Housing for Ontario and Homes Now, and a plethora of programs.

The Homes Now program, introduced in May 1988, promised 30,000 new non-profit units, about half of them to be built in Metro Toronto. Three billion dollars in low-cost financing from Canada Pension Plan funds was provided to municipal and private non-profit organizations and to co-ops.[43] By December 1989, 28,000 units had been allocated. In about 70 per cent of them rent would be geared to the tenant's income.[44]

Most of these new units will be located in two new neighbourhoods developed by the City of Toronto on formerly industrial lands. Ataratiri neighbourhood will contain about 7,000 units on a site to the east of the St Lawrence neighbourhood. The other will be built downtown on lands formerly used by the railways, adjacent to the Skydome stadium and CN Tower.[45]

So far, this program has been a real success. Yet in August 1989, the new housing minister declared his belief that the only long-term solution to the housing crisis would be to give tenants the opportunity to become homeowners. His ideas all centred on supporting the private market.[46] With the election of a New Democratic Party government in 1990, it appeared more likely that social market approaches would be tried.

Two aspects of these provincial programs require further comment. First, along with the recent shifts in federal policy discussed earlier, they went against the trend toward mixing people of different income levels in housing projects and neighbourhoods. By the late 1960s it was already clear that concentrating low-income people in projects, especially dense high-rise buildings, led to resident dissatisfaction, poor community relations, high rates of vandalism, and other social problems. Second, both recent federal and provincial housing policies have tended to devolve authority to lower levels of government, while at the same time constraining their ability to act. Municipalities, for example, have been required by the Ontario government to set aside land so as ensure a better supply of affordable housing. Yet no funding was provided to service the land.[47]Furthermore, as Barbara Wake Carroll (1989: 72) has pointed out, municipalities have less ability to raise funds than do other levels of government. Legally, they are creatures of the province with limited capabilities. In addition, they are the most vulnerable to pressure from private interests.

From Background to Foreground

In this chapter we have described some of the background against which to view the co-ops we studied. The picture includes demographic and economic change in Toronto, but also growing housing problems. Non-profit co-ops have emerged as one response to these problems. To some extent, that is because government programs and planning opened a political space for their development.

Now we focus on the foreground. Clearly, there were many people in Toronto who needed affordable, suitable, adequate housing. There were non-profit housing resource groups with the expertise to implement projects. The section 56.1 federal co-op housing program made building Windward and Harbourside co-ops economically feasible; it also constrained what they would be like.

What the picture still lacks is a physical space, buildings, and the actual groups involved in developing the projects. In the next chapter, we take up these topics.

CHAPTER THREE

The Social Construction of Cooperative Housing

Creating housing cooperatives implies constructing or rehabilitating buildings. As well, it implies designing an organization. How projects come to have the physical form they do is not as simple as it seems. Built form and site plan often can reveal the social processes through which they came about. As well, built form strongly affects the quality of life of those who live in it. In co-ops it especially influences the building of community.

Windward and Harbourside co-ops reflect social processes that are producing new kinds of urban residential space. As Smith (1984: 85) points out, 'We do not live, act and work "in" space so much as by living, acting and working we produce space.' In this chapter, we consider some of these processes and their consequences.

To understand the development of Windward and Harbourside one must place them first in a wider physical and social setting. Thus, we begin with the larger area known as Harbourfront and proceed to Bathurst Quay, where the co-ops are located. Then we consider the co-ops' own sites. At each of these scales in the development process different, often conflicting, interests came into play.

We focus on Windward because it was the more complex project. Many of the challenges it faced and the problems it encountered were ones that Harbourside shared. But we feel that Windward is especially interesting as a fully accessible building and as a project that involved a variety of interest groups.

In exploring the interplay between different interests, we ask how that shaped the physical form of the resulting building and the social composition of the new co-op. Changing circumstances also affected the co-op's formation. We consider how built form reflects the different meanings people bring to things. The relationship between the cooperative form of social organization and the organization of space for an integrated community of able-bodied people and those with disabilities is particularly interesting.[1]

Building Windward Co-op

Green gabled roofs with varied levels and setbacks give Windward housing cooperative a post-modernist look. Its appearance is in keeping with the upscale hotels, condominiums, and shops on the ninety redeveloped hectares of downtown Toronto's lake shore known as Harbourfront. Windward consists of 76 apartments in an eight-storey building flanked by 25 stacked townhouses, providing in all 101 residential units. The first members moved into the co-op in December 1986, but the building was not fully finished until early spring 1987. Its official opening was in September 1988.

Windward stands out because it is the first fully accessible and fully integrated housing cooperative in Toronto. At the time it opened, only a handful of entirely barrier-free co-ops in Canada housed a mix of mobility-impaired and able-bodied residents.[2] One unusual feature is that people confined to wheelchairs could choose to live wherever they wanted. All units are fully accessible to people in wheelchairs; so are all the building's common facilities. Residents with disabilities who required additional modifications to their units could request these prior to construction.

Building Windward co-op took at least two years longer and cost at least $500,000 more than anticipated. This lengthy process did not simply *occur* in space but *produced* space. Windward's brief history shows how the varied understandings, agendas, and resources of different interest groups intersected to produce a particular project. These groups included a non-profit housing resource group, the Harbourfront federal crown corporation, the City of Toronto, an advocacy group for housing for people with disabilities, the co-op's first board of directors, and, ultimately, residents of the co-op itself.

The Windward project also helps point up something important about the redevelopment of Toronto and other port cities. The waterfront can be likened to an urban 'frontier.' Its redevelopment fundamentally depends on external forces, interests, and actors (Desfor, Goldrick, and Merrens 1988). The course of waterfront redevelopment thus reflects more pervasive changes in the city and in the larger political economy. If part of the revitalized waterfront is for people and provision of housing is a goal, *who* should live *where* and in *what type of housing* become contentious issues.

Space at Harbourfront

Harbourfront has been the focus of controversy for at least the past fifteen years. Questions of the scale and kind of development that should take place, including the amount of parkland, persist with no signs of abating. The issue has been a genuine political football, passed back and forth among the federal, provincial, metro, and city governments.

The land that is now Harbourfront was created from landfill dredged out of Lake Ontario (see Fig. 3.1). Before the First World War, the old shoreline lay about one-quarter mile inland from where it is today. The new lands were developed into port facilities by the Toronto Harbour Commission, a federally appointed body. Just behind the port lay the railway yards, roundhouses, and Union Station. But as container ships became more common in the 1960s, the old port facilities fell into disuse. New port facilities were developed in the eastern part of Toronto harbour. The central part of the waterfront was deserted and rapidly became derelict. In 1972, the Trudeau government expropriated the area and gave it to the people of Toronto as an election campaign present.

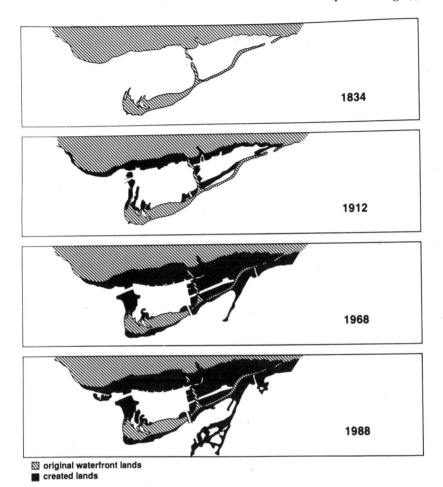

original waterfront lands
created lands

Figure 3.1
Map of Toronto's waterfront showing natural and man-made changes to the shoreline. Adapted and reprinted with the permission of the Royal Commission on the Future of the Toronto Waterfront.

Initially, the federal government envisioned a long stretch of green space along the waterfront with a mix of cultural and recreational activities. The Harbourfront crown corporation was created to redevelop and administer the area. Its board of di-

rectors saw it as 'an urban meeting place with a waterfront flavour, providing opportunity to display, enrich and share the diverse cultural traditions of the people of Toronto' (Harbourfront
1978). The early park plan gave way in 1980 to a scheme ap-
proved by the Toronto City Council and the Ontario Municipal
Board that 'would bring the city to the water's edge.'[3]

According to Desfor, Goldrick, and Merrens (1988: 100–2;
1989), the Harbourfront plan was a response to the interaction
of complex political and economic forces affecting the redevelopment of the waterfront. Toronto's economy had become more
oriented toward services in the 1970s and 1980s, especially finance and information processing. Furthermore, high-order in-
formation-based services tended increasingly to concentrate in
the central area of the city. Thus, the city's occupational structure
also changed, with the rapid growth of managerial, technical, and
administrative jobs.

Many of these relatively affluent white-collar workers preferred to live near where they worked. Thus, extensive gentrification occurred in older, working-class districts near the central
area and many expensive condominium projects went up. At the
same time, established middle-class residential areas were able to
win exclusionary zoning regulations to protect themselves against
redevelopment. The upshot was rapidly rising land rents
throughout the central area and adjacent parts of the city. One
of the few areas that could be redeveloped was the waterfront.
Given the general level of land rents, for developers only the
construction of high-density, luxury commercial and residential
space made sense economically.

In this wider context, Harbourfront Corporation sought to
define both its own mission and a new meaning for the area. It
soon became apparent that Harbourfront lacked the financial
resources to fund its ambitious plans. In order to defray the
development and maintenance costs of its own facilities and the
multimillion dollar cost of some 4,000 cultural events annually,
Harbourfront Corporation became a developer. It leased rights
on its property for the private development of rental apartments,
condominiums, hotels, marinas, and shops (see Fig. 3.2). Such

Figure 3.2
Central Harbourfront area. Harbourfront Corporation leased rights on its property for the private development of rental apartments, condominiums, hotels, marinas, and shops.

revenues went into a fund that had reached about $30 million by the late 1980s. Along with commercial fees and receipts from events, interest on the fund was supposed to pay for Harbourfront's programming.4

Trouble had struck first in 1981. With the worst recession since the 1930s, developers became leery of investing in waterfront development. To fund its programs, Harbourfront entered into agreements with a developer to construct three large apartment towers: two of thirty-one storeys and one of nineteen storeys. As the buildings went up, the public and politicians began to complain that the 'site was becoming an ugly concrete canyon.' Besides the ugly high-rises, luxury condominiums, hotels, and upscale shopping facilities began rapidly to occupy the area (see Fig. 3.3).5 As Colin Vaughan (1987: 54) said: 'Harbourfront foun-

Figure 3.3
Politicians complained that high-rises were turning Harbourfront into an ugly concrete canyon.

dered on three key decisions: the need to break even financially in seven years; Harbourfront's partnership in development on the site; and the construction of that east-west highway down the centre.' The first forced excessive development at breakneck pace. The second created a conflict of interest on Harbourfront's part between planning and profit-generation goals. Finally, the road heightened the scale of development.

Stephen Dale (1990) summarized Harbourfront's early history: 'Buffeted by antagonistic currents ... Harbourfront was shaped by conflict and defined by compromise, as several levels of government vied for position on a shifting constitutional landscape; as the grandiose conceptions of an affluent age met an incoming tide of fiscal conservatism; as an emerging urban reform movement faced off against an entrenched federal bureaucracy.'

In 1987 a panel of architects was asked to draw up recommendations to salvage plans for the area. Their work was constrained in that 50 per cent of Harbourfront already had been spoken for. Essentially, they concluded that Harbourfront should be urban in character rather than pastoral. While there should be less-intensive development, a continuous wall of buildings still would be acceptable (Baird/Sampson Architects 1987).[6] But events overtook the panel. Also 1987, first the city and then the federal government froze all projects already planned. Responding to public concerns, in 1988 Toronto City Council revised its official plan for the central waterfront, the area including Harbourfront and adjacent lands (Royal Commission on the Future of the Toronto Waterfront 1989: 54–92). The new plan aimed to extend mixed residential, commercial, and institutional development in the central waterfront. Public access was to be improved as were the aesthetics of development. Unfortunately, the city did not stick to its own planning guidelines. Developers, for example, were allowed to build the required assisted housing part of their projects off site rather than integrating them into their waterfront developments (ibid.: 88).

In 1987, a federal royal commission was charged with reviewing development along the Toronto region's entire waterfront. Former Toronto Mayor David Crombie, well regarded for his concern for neighbourhoods and quality-of-life issues, was appointed the sole commissioner. In an interim report issued in the summer of 1989, the royal commission recommended that the Harbourfront Corporation should get out of property development and management.[7] Meanwhile, however, the City of Toronto entered into a deal with Harbourfront to lift its freeze in return for cash and additional parkland on the site.[8] When the city freeze was about to expire in December 1989 and before the new deal could take effect, the Ontario government stepped in with its own indefinite freeze.[9] At about the same time, the Toronto Harbour Commission, disregarding the concerns of other bodies or nearby residents, decided to expand facilities at and the number of flights from Toronto Island Airport.[10]

Overlapping jurisdictions have continually bedevilled waterfront planning. Harbourfront's land is *federally* owned; constitutionally, harbours are under federal jurisdiction. But land use planning is a *municipal* responsibility. However, because municipalities in Canada legally are creatures of the provinces, the *Province* of Ontario also has an interest. Through several provincial ministries and agencies it regulates municipal affairs and planning. Just to complicate the situation further, in this case there are two municipal levels involved: Metro and the City of Toronto. At the time of writing it was unclear how or when these development issues actually would be resolved.[11] Public confidence in planning for the waterfront was at an all-time low. For some, Harbourfront had succeeded in turning a derelict waterfront area into a neighbourhood that is interesting, diverse, and filled with people at all times of the day or night. Yet for others Harbourfront had come to embody the public's worst fears about the city. For one resident it had taken an opportunity for waterfront parks and turned it into 'an investment opportunity for private developers and wealthy speculators.'[12] 'The story of Harbourfront,' one critic wrote, 'is the story of Toronto in the eighties right down to the last, quivering grab for profit and power.'[13]

Slightly less than two-thirds of Harbourfront's retail, residential, and office space was allocated for housing in the 1980 plan.[14] (Residential and office densities were reduced following the 1987 architects' report, but they remain contentious issues.) But most of this housing consists of expensive condominiums, as do projects in the immediately adjacent areas. Nevertheless, Harbourfront was required in its plan to provide affordable housing. As Dale Martin (quoted in Dale 1990: 83), member of Metro Toronto Council for the downtown area, put it: 'The official plan says fifty per cent of housing should be for the bottom fifty percent of the population. Harbourfront has a thirty per cent commitment ... What we've seen is Harbourfront attempt to get out of that ... commitment, and as a result we're at around ten per cent of the units being affordable. That's simply not good enough for publicly owned land.' Most of the space Harbourfront allotted for this housing is peripheral, on Bathurst Quay, as far as possible from the central area of upscale hotels, condos, and shops.

Remaking Bathurst Quay

Most of Bathurst Quay was a derelict waterfront industrial area like the rest of Harbourfront (see Fig. 3.4). Landfill operations created the quay in the 1920s. From 1926 until 1968, Maple Leaf Stadium, named after the minor league baseball team that played there, occupied the area where Harbourside co-op now stands (see Fig. 3.5). One of the earliest industrial occupants was the Canada Malting Company, which located there in 1926. It produced malt for Toronto's breweries, like Molson's just north of the quay which still adds a yeasty scent to the air. The monolithic elevators still fill the eastern pier. Toronto Island Airport was built in 1938, connected by ferry across the Western Gap with Bathurst Quay. The airport has become increasingly busy in recent years with the growth of business and commuter traffic (see Fig. 3.6).

During the Second World War, Bathurst Quay became the site of barracks and a training camp for the Norwegian Air Force. The barracks later were used for emergency wartime housing. After 1954, the site fell into disuse until the mid-1970s. Then Harbourfront turned what had become a dump into adventure and creative playgrounds. Today, the playgrounds too have disappeared, replaced by Little Norway Park which commemorates the wartime training camp.

No one lived in the Bathurst Quay area before the co-ops arrived in the 1980s. Since 1986, Windward, Harbourside, two other housing cooperatives (Arcadia and Harbour Channel), and two Cityhome projects (non-profit, assisted housing provided by the City of Toronto) have all been developed. With a total of 660 units, these projects had a population estimated at just over 1,500 in 1989 (Bradbee 1989: Appendix A, 6, 7).

Previous uses of the area had provided no infrastructure for the development of a residential neighbourhood. In fact, some of the few existing facilities that might serve residents have been razed. A Montessori school at the edge of Bathurst Quay was closed to make way for proposed high-rise condominiums, as was a restaurant on the waterfront. At the time of our study, there

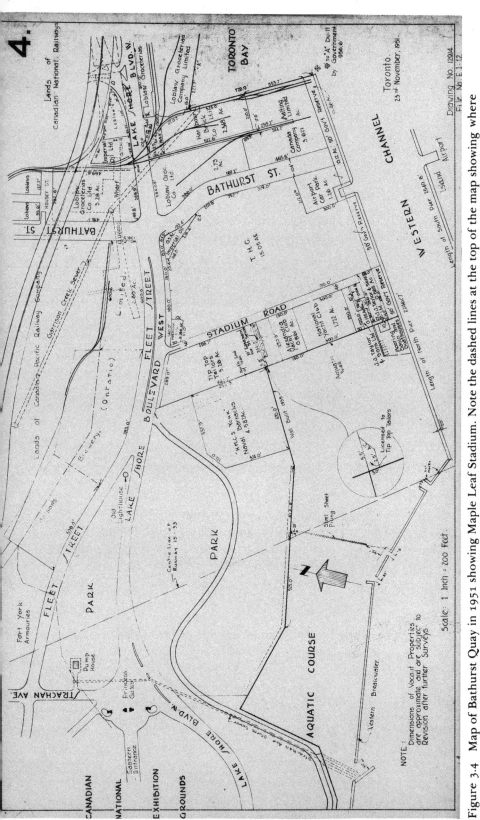

Figure 3.4 Map of Bathurst Quay in 1951 showing Maple Leaf Stadium. Note the dashed lines at the top of the map showing where the Queens Wharf once stood on the water's edge. Photo courtesy of the Toronto Harbour Commission   Archives, PD 2/1/474.

Figure 3.5
Photo of Maple Leaf Stadium facing south on Bathurst Quay. Harbourside co-op was one of several residential projects to occupy this site in the 1980s. Harbourside members proudly claimed that the site of home plate was on their co-op property. Photo courtesy of the Toronto Harbour Commission Archives.

were no schools, no churches, no restaurants on the quay, and the only shops within a 15-minute walk were the beer outlet at Molson's brewery and a gourmet convenience store across from the Admiral Hotel in Harbourfront's central area. Public transportation was available, but limited.

To the north, the neon sign on the roof of Tip Top Tailors lit up the night sky above the quay. Dylex Corporation, which owned Tip Top Tailors, played a role in the development of Windward co-op because of shared rights to underground parking on the co-op site. Just to the west of the site were several empty lots. The yacht clubs that used to occupy them were moved

Figure 3.6
Toronto Island Airport facing north across the Western Gap in 1962 to Bathurst Quay. Windward co-op was built on the northern edge of the Gap in the 1980s. Photo courtesy of the Toronto Harbour Commission Archives.

westward in 1988 to accommodate more proposed condos. While the lots officially were not part of Harbourfront, they were caught in the various freezes on waterfront development. The proposed construction of these condos provoked conflict among the developers, Bathurst Quay residents, the City of Toronto, and the prospective condo owners, who had paid large down payments on their units even before planning approvals were obtained.[15]

During our three years of interviews co-op residents became increasingly concerned with how the neighbourhood was developing. Continual changes in policy on the part of the various interested government organizations made it hard to know what was happening. Neighbourhood associations developed to defend resident interests. Many residents came to feel that they were under siege.

The Windward Site

Windward Co-op's building site presented its own difficulties, two of which are important here (see Figs. 3.7 and 3.8). One relates to the use of space required by Harbourfront, the other to Bathurst Quay's history as reclaimed land. Both difficulties also affected the building of Harbourside co-op.

First, Harbourfront Corporation required that a public access route cross the Windward property. Torontonians have vigorously defended the right to walk along their waterfront. Citizens' groups have been very critical of the high-rise condominiums at Harbourfront, in part because these buildings threaten to close off the lake shore to those not lucky enough to live there. They also criticized the paucity of parking facilities in the area; Windward's garage was intended to provide some public spaces. Thus, it was at least symbolically important to be able to draw a public path through the Windward site.

For people using this access route the view would be the 'backstage' of the co-op. Hence, the right of public access potentially conflicted with residents' use of the co-op grounds. For them it was a semiprivate space, part of their home. The solution was to define the exterior space at Windward in such a way as to discourage the public from passing through, while not actually denying them access. The co-op buildings form three sides of a courtyard, open to the public path that passes between Windward and the Cityhome building to the north. Through landscaping and the orientation of patios and benches, the space clearly welcomed residents and discouraged intruding outsiders (see Fig. 3.9).

Harbourside faced similar difficulties with its courtyard (see Fig. 3.10). Its townhouses are built around three sides of a courtyard; Arcadia co-op forms the other side (see Fig. 3.11). As far as Harbourfront Corp. was concerned, Harbourside's courtyard was parkland. Thus, there had to be public access. As well, Har-

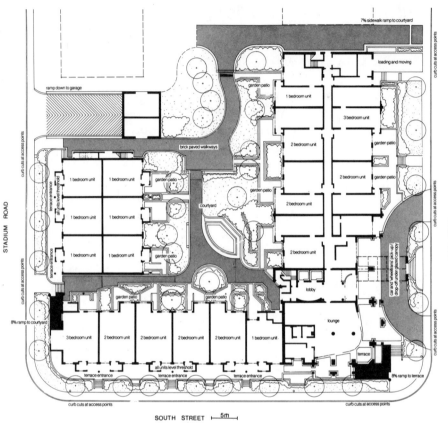

Figure 3.7
Windward co-op site plan. Note paved walkways north of the co-op which complied with Harbourfront's requirement of public access while maintaining residents' privacy. Site plan courtesy of Roger Du Toit Architects.

bourfront had to approve the landscaping. But this space too has been made semiprivate. Few passers-by, seeing the narrow entrance to the courtyard from the street, would assume that it is public land.

A second difficulty with the site was the high water table. Bathurst Quay is reclaimed land filled in behind bulkheads that extend into the lake. The site thus posed problems for an apart-

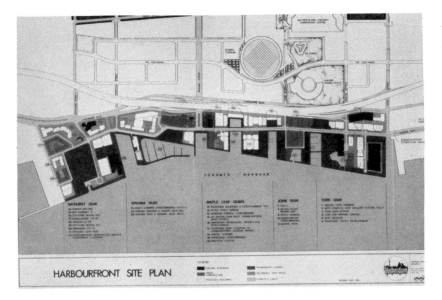

Figure 3.8
Harbourfront site plan showing Bathurst Quay development at far left. Reprinted with the permission of Harbourfront Corporation.

ment building, especially since it needed an underground garage. One proposal to solve this problem involved raising the level of the street by several feet. This would have been expensive for the city and was rejected. The need for accessibility exacerbated existing problems with the site. For example, vans for residents with disabilities require higher floor-to-ceiling clearance and a higher door, but deepening the garage was impossible because of the water table. Trying to find solutions to this kind of problem added to construction costs and delays.

Converging and Conflicting Social Interests

In 1981, Harbourfront issued a proposal call for a co-op to be constructed on the site that borders the west side of Little Norway Park. This marked the beginning of a building process that brought together diverse interests: Lantana (a non-profit housing resource group), Intecity (an advocacy group for housing for

Figure 3.9
Windward co-op courtyard. Although Harbourfront required a public path through the site (far right), landscaping and the orientation of patios and benches made the residents feel welcome while discouraging outsiders from intruding.

people with disabilities), Harbourfront, the board of directors for the co-op, CMHC, the Canadian Paraplegic Association, the architect, the contractor, and potential providers of attendant care for the residents, among others.

Lantana, Intecity, Harbourfront, and the co-op board receive the most attention in this chapter. In particular, we want to show, first, how Lantana's response to the availability of the Windward site reflected changes in political and economic aspects of the housing situation in Toronto. Second, we explore how Harbourfront and Intecity, partly through the board, shaped the physical and social form that Windward was to assume.

Lantana

One response to the proposal call came from Lantana Nonprofit Homes. Housing resource groups aim to provide technical and

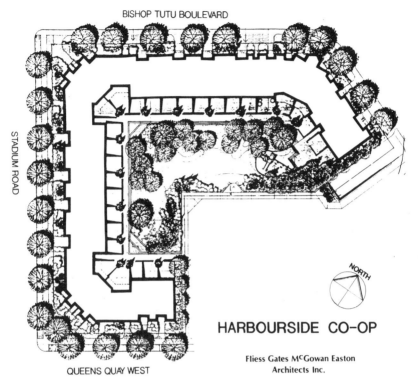

HARBOURSIDE CO-OP

Fliess Gates McGowan Easton
Architects Inc.

Figure 3.10
Harbourside co-op site plan. This courtyard, like Windward's, had to include public access while seeming semiprivate. Site Plan courtesy of Fliess, Gates, McGowan, and Easton Architects.

professional assistance to people who want to develop non-profit housing, including co-ops, for low- and moderate-income earners. The resource group guides clients through the development process from the earliest stages of incorporation through post-occupancy member education. In the past, this process began with the resource group's response to an existing group – for example, church members who want to build non-profit housing for seniors. But the development process has changed course. First, CMHC and the provincial government changed the proposal call system to an annual competition so that resource groups had

Figure 3.11
Harbourside co-op's stacked townhouses are built around three sides of its courtyard. The green concrete exterior space behind Arcadia co-op is visible on the left.

to identify sites farther in advance. Second, building sites were so difficult and expensive to acquire in Toronto that resource groups often tried first to obtain a site and then to find or even organize an appropriate sponsoring group. In this way, resource groups tried to provide as many non-profit homes as possible under increased political and economic constraints.

Lantana's strategy of site-first development in responding to the Harbourfront proposal call reflected the exigencies of building cooperative housing in Toronto in the 1980s. The resource group had no particular client group in mind but hoped to attach itself to any appropriate project.

One implication of site-first development was that the resource group has much more control over identifying and shaping the group of people who sponsored and later occupied a co-op. Toronto resource groups were committed to incorporating people with special needs into projects wherever possible. As well, CMHC required that at least 5 per cent of all units be wheelchair accessible. Other government programs provided financial incentives for building special-purpose units that encouraged resource groups to increase their involvement in this area. Client groups created or identified by the resource groups, then, were in a weak position to argue against sharing their housing with people with special needs; nor could they object to the social mix fundamental to the housing cooperative movement, which drew together people from different income levels.

Despite the mandate to construct housing for low- and moderate-income people with special needs, resource groups did not always find it easy to identify potential users or to find occupants for these units. They could gain a clearer idea of who the users might be and what exactly their special needs were by establishing links with special-purpose interest groups representing people with disabilities, for example. But the advocacy group that responded to the proposal call to develop Windward differed from others concerned with housing people with special needs. It was concerned far more with the idea of integrated housing for people with disabilities and able-bodied people than with practicalities.

Intecity

A small group that grew out of the International Year for the Disabled, Intecity was largely the creation of a single organizer and had few links with the disabled community. Intecity's vision was of an 'integrated city' without the impediments of traditional architecture where people with disabilities could live with non-disabled people. Because 1981 was the Year for the Disabled, Intecity's ideas may have especially appealed to Harbourfront as a theme around which to build a cooperative project. But the group's lack of experience led Harbourfront to 'marry' Intecity to Lantana, with the expectation that the resource group's expertise would transform the idealism of Intecity into a functioning housing co-op.

Intecity's idealism contrasted not only with the practical orientation of other special-interest groups for people with disabilities, such as the Canadian Paraplegic Association, but also with Lantana's increasingly pragmatic approach to site development. A Lantana staff member commented to us that Intecity's was 'a positive and exciting approach, but it wasn't based on door widths and grab bars. It was based on freedom and power; those were the terms they used, and they're wonderful terms, but it's hard to build a building with those things ... You need to talk about turning dimensions and wheel-in showers.' Yet Intecity's influence is evident in the design of Windward as a building and as a social group. Expressing the concept of an integrated environment so that it took the form of a fully accessible housing cooperative took place largely through the first board of directors, as will be discussed below. Acceptance of full accessibility as the way to realize Intecity's goal of integration determined many aspects of the building design.

Harbourfront

Harbourfront further shaped the project. It imposed stringent design criteria on the building, even specifying details about the quality of exterior finishes and landscaping. These standards were more appropriate for the expensive condominiums in the central area of Harbourfront than for the social housing projects out on Bathurst Quay. Social housing cannot exceed maximum unit prices (MUPS) set by CMHC. For Windward, though, this requirement made it difficult to meet Harbourfront's demands. Windward managed to satisfy Harbourfront's design criteria better than the other co-ops on Bathurst Quay. But the price was cost overruns of at least $500,000.

The decision to make the building fully accessible to residents in wheelchairs helps to explain why the design criteria were met. On the surface, accessibility seems to have nothing to do with the aesthetics of the building's appearance. None of Harbourfront's guidelines concerned accessibility. But, we suggest, part of the meaning of Windward as fully accessible, integrated housing for able-bodied people and people with disabilities is expressed in the standard to which the building is designed (see Figs. 3.12 and 3.13).

Harbourfront wanted to make Windward special (this orientation also was evident in the decision to focus another Bathurst Quay co-op on artists). The selection of Intecity with its vision of an integrated city laid the groundwork for a special building. As the first fully accessible housing cooperative in Toronto, Windward became a model project. Such a social landmark in a showcase setting at Harbourfront seemed to the co-op's board of directors and the architect to deserve an attractive building. Once the decision to make the building fully accessible had been reached, meeting Harbourfront's aesthetic criteria became high priority.

Board of Directors

Competition between interests on Windward's initial board of directors was one reason that Windward became a fully accessible building. Intecity's concept of an integrated environment necessarily included able-bodied people as well as people with disabilities. A majority of the members of the board were able-bodied. For them, affordable family accommodation on the waterfront came first and accessibility was secondary. Disagreements ensued among the able-bodied board members and those with disabilities. But by the end of the first year, the concerns of members with disabilities dominated the situation and full accessibility became the board's central objective in its dealings with the architect. The active participation of people with disabilities in the development of the project may have encouraged the co-op's success.[16]

Full Accessibility, Bathrooms, and the Building Process

Windward lacked the institutional appearance that would label it as housing for people with disabilities. The institutional ele-

Figure 3.12
Part of the importance of Windward co-op as fully accessible, integrated housing is expressed in its appearance. Such a social landmark seemed to deserve an attractive building.

ments that it did have were similar to those of other high rises, for example, in the double-door entry design and long corridors. Within the constraints of urban high-rise living, the environment was homelike. For in housing that integrates people with special needs into a community 'the degree to which homelike qualities can be achieved is assumed to be related to the degree of normalization that can be created in the design' (Robinson et al. 1984: 13).[17]

Maintaining the atmosphere of a home became more difficult, yet no less important, with the inclusion of an attendant care component in the project. Originally, 15 per cent of the units were to be allocated to mobility-impaired co-op members. But the people with disabilities whose need for affordable housing was greatest in Toronto at the time were those who also needed assistance from an attendant in order to live on their own.

Figure 3.13
Harbourside co-op is more conventional in appearance than Windward, but its low-rise design and small size (fifty-four units) encouraged social interaction among members.

Participation Apartments was given the job of providing attendant care in Windward. They used one of the building's units full time as a base of operations and lounge for people with disabilities. In order to make the project viable for Participation Apartments, the co-op had to allocate twelve units for members who needed attendant care. When added to the other members with disabilities who could live fully independently, the attendant care component brought the proportion of households that included a member with disabilities to about 25 per cent when the co-op opened.

The principle of full accessibility meant that every unit in the building had to be accessible to people in wheelchairs although only 25 per cent of the units were occupied by households with a person with disabilities. Units occupied by people with disabilities were indistinguishable from others along the corridors, unlike other accessible housing in Toronto in which 'the international wheelchair symbol is displayed on the doors of the adapted units' (Cluff and Cluff 1982: 2). Someone in a wheelchair could go anywhere and live anywhere that an able-bodied person could.

Bathrooms can be seen as the practical key to implementing this principle in Windward. Accessible washrooms, even in the apartments of able-bodied people, were the essential condition from which the interior design of the rest of the building followed. In the words of a consultant with Lantana: 'once you could establish a washroom in every unit that was accessible, almost everything else followed because it meant that you had to have the path to that washroom accessible. That path had to take you down corridors and into apartments, then through corridors inside the apartments. Then the doorknobs had to work, the light switch had be within reach, the sink had to be accessible, and so on.'

Many of the design features needed to ensure full accessibility should not have increased unit costs. For example, a light switch installed low enough to be reached from a chair should cost no more than the same switch installed at a height convenient to a standing person. Lower peep-holes in front doors, electrical outlets raised a few inches, and lower rods in closets could all be included as design modifications. If decided on early enough, such features would not increase costs substantially although sometimes there was the added cost of having to install both high and low versions, particularly of peep-holes. But these features did increase costs at Windward, partly because these non-standard features were not part of computerized, off-the-shelf plans. The special accessibility features available at Windward included:

- Ramped and wheelchair-accessible entrances
- Automatic door opener with electronic remote controls at main entrance – There are plans to install this system on the courtyard door to enable wheelchair users to enjoy the garden, as soon as finances permit

- Wider doorways and hallways through the common areas and each home
- Low control panels on elevators
- Lower light switches and thermostat controls
- Higher electrical outlets
- Lower 'peep' holes in unit doors
- Lever door handles on doors instead of door knobs
- Courtyard planters at a reachable height for people in wheelchairs
- Infrared safety beams to prevent elevator doors from closing on wheelchairs
- Low windows with large window space to allow better visibility to wheelchair users
- Roll-in showers where requested
- Cut-away areas under bathroom vanities, kitchen sinks, and countertop stoves
- Countertop stoves and wall ovens to make access easier to wheelchair users
- Side by side refrigerator and freezer units
- Wing handles on taps
- Easy-roll drawers in kitchen
- Lower kitchen counter heights where requested
- Sliding closet doors to facilitate access
- Extra large bathrooms to facilitate wheelchair use
- Sunroom built into living area to provide more wheelchair space
- Accessible balconies level with apartment floors
- Parquet floors instead of broadloom to make wheelchair use easier
- Second-floor corridor from elevator to upper townhouses to provide access to all townhouses
- Townhouses include accessible washroom facilities on their first floors and a special upper and lower floor closet which would permit the installation of a lift
- Extra large parking spaces in underground garage for wheelchair users
- Emergency power for both elevators in case of electrical power failure

Such an unconventional building could not be handled as a

turnkey project, that is, one that is entirely developed by the resource group rather than a residents' group and then marketed by the former. Turnkey projects were advantageous for a resource group because they shortened the development process and avoided the problems of acquiring a site, obtaining approval from CMHC, and finding architects and builders experienced with social housing. General contract projects, an alternative to turnkeys, required greater supervision from the resource group and the architect.

Windward's architect had some experience designing for people with disabilities, but none with social housing and so was unfamiliar with the cost limitations involved. The complexity of the project soon become apparent. Payment of the architect's fee was deferred because of delays involving CMHC and Harbourfront, and because the original architect had left the firm. The architectural firm, we were told, eventually abandoned some 'high minded principles in favour of getting the building done.' In particular, the architect had to deal with multiple pressures from CMHC, Harbourfront, Lantana, and Intecity, among others, all of whom wanted different things from the building.

Some deficiencies in the building reflected communication problems in the supervision process. A Lantana consultant summarized the chain of miscommunication: 'A fair number of modifications never got transferred. You can never establish whether the architect didn't revise the spec, or took it back to his office and gave it to some junior person who didn't revise it either. Or maybe they did revise it, but maybe the drawing never got to the site. Or maybe it did get to the site, but maybe the construction group never got it in the right trays. You have a chain of communication here which in the best of times would result in problems, and this was not the best of times.'

When the building was tendered the construction market was slow. 'The builders were hungry,' a board member told us; 'the trades were siting around with nothing to do.' But by the time construction actually began, the market was booming and it was difficult for the relatively small contractor to get subtrades to work on the project. This led to more delays and cost overruns.

Some design features inevitably increased construction costs. Yet, as well as benefiting residents with disabilities, they increased the attractiveness of the building to other potential occupants. This was important because of the income mix integral to the co-op's member selection process and essential for Intecity's goal of an integrated environment. The co-op was to include residents who paid full housing charges, as well as people (both able-bodied and with disabilities) with directly subsidized rents. Full housing charges in co-ops were set equal to the low end of the rental housing market in the neighbourhood. But even the low end of Harbourfront area rents was high compared with other parts of the city. To attract households that could afford to pay as much as $1,044 per month (in 1987) for a three-bedroom apartment, Windward had to be aesthetically pleasing.

Large areas of glass were one of the features that added to the building's appeal for those paying full housing charges. Windows had to be set low enough to give a view of the city to people in wheelchairs. They also had to be high enough to satisfy able-bodied residents. The resulting walls of windows added greatly to Windward's attractiveness. The fact that an expressway and a railway line cut Harbourfront off from the city, while detrimental to Harbourfront's plan of bringing the city to the waterfront, pleased some co-op residents because of the view. One market rent occupant commented: 'I think what I like more than anything is the fact that it's in downtown Toronto and yet it feels like I'm living on the outside of the city. To be able to sit back and look at the whole thing from my home is exciting for me.'

Wider public corridors and interior halls, as well as larger rooms, gave the building a sense of spaciousness that all residents enjoyed, whether or not their household included a person with a disability. This sense of space was expensive to achieve, although it may well have been worthwhile.[18] Additional funding had to be arranged beyond the 12 per cent by which CMHC increased the MUP for wheelchair-accessible units. In order to increase internal space within MUP constraints, many balcony spaces were transformed into more or less fictional sunrooms after lengthy discussions with CMHC.

All of the construction bids submitted on the building came in over budget. Ultimately, all the bidders' suggestions about how to cut costs were combined and attached to the lowest bid. But the firm selected was a quality builder which found it hard on principle to cut corners. Cheaper materials often were not substituted for more expensive ones. Chipboard did not replace plywood in closet subfloors, for example.

Because of the requirement of full accessibility, many features common to all units in Windward, such as light switch locations, could not be taken 'off the shelf.' By extension, none of the units themselves could be fully standardized. A social tenet important to the cooperative was that any member with a disability could choose to live anywhere in the project (except that those needing attendant care had to live in the high-rise). Residents with disabilities could request special modifications of their units to suit their particular disability – for example, a wheel-in shower was an option – so each completed unit potentially was different from every other.

Probably the worst case of miscommunication on the project resulted in modifying the wrong units. People's specific requirements for additional modifications to their units were noted. Windward's first coordinator described what happened. 'They specified the particular countertop heights and wheel-in showers and various things like that, and they designed apartments to [these people's] needs. But part way through the process, the consultant renumbered all the apartments and failed to provide this information to the people who were building in the modifications. [So they] modified the wrong apartments at a cost of roughly $10,000 per apartment. [Some] people who had selected those apartments now found they would be living in modified apartments and they weren't disabled! Some were willing to swap around, but one or two were not willing, so we wound up modifying other apartments at a significant cost.' Moreover, the building included an unusually large number of different unit layouts, partly because of the varied roof lines, setbacks, and windows. One consultant at Lantana commented: 'It's a complicated building. We usually standardize things, which is attractive to architects and it probably doesn't make much difference to the people living there. They don't spend a lot of time going from apartment to apartment saying, "How boring! Your apartment is the same as mine!"' But there were at least twenty-five differences among the 101 units at Windward that were variations on fifteen different layouts. These variations complicated supervision of the construction process. Because of the complexity of the building as a whole some design flaws – for example, lack of access to the underground garage for overheight vans – were overlooked until it was too late to find quick or inexpensive solutions.

Residents with disabilities whose units needed modifications, such as special tubs or showers, could choose to live anywhere in the building. Thus, no units could be completed until the members with disabilities had themselves been chosen and had selected where to live. The freedom to live anywhere in the building, then, carried a price tag: the cost of mistakes and of 'extras' late in the construction process; extra time to finish the units; and the potential for miscommunication because of added complexity.

Despite the concern at Windward with independence for residents with disabilities, the goal of full accessibility remained elusive. This added to the frustration of all parties with increased construction costs and delays. The first wheelchair residents to occupy the building, around Christmas 1986 had difficulty even getting in the front door. When Windward won an Access Award from the City of Toronto in early 1987, some residents with disabilities called a local newspaper to object. They felt the award was inappropriate so long as they faced such problems as cupboards that were too high, steps between their patios and the street, and doors to the parking garage that they could not open. Since then, the grade of the ramp leading to the front door has been modified, an appropriate elevator control panel has been installed, and other changes have been made so that, by and large, Windward now more closely approximates its fully accessible image.

One lesson that Windward taught those involved in the building process was that 'people with disabilities' is a label that covers a wide variety of abilities with different design consequences. CMHC design standards were inappropriate for many of the residents with disabilities. Yet it was difficult to devise new standards for housing them in the course of a construction process that was in many ways not standardized itself.

The whole question of customizing units for people with disabilities in social housing was unresolved. Some people with whom we spoke considered allowing such people to select any unit in the building to be an expensive 'luxury' while acknowledging that they might consider it a 'right.' One development consultant at Lantana offered this advice: 'We're not really building custom units for individuals in wheelchairs any more than we're building custom units for anyone else ... What you have to come up with is more flexible design – for example, a kitchen with a variety of different counter heights so that people have a choice of where to work or where to eat.'

In cooperatives, developing a sense of community is crucial. Cooperatives stress the importance of meetings, not only as a way for members to participate in the running of the co-op but as situations in which people interact and build a sense of community with neighbours. Thus, meeting rooms are important contact points as are the laundry area and the courtyard. All of these facilities were designed in Windward to be areas for sociable circulation, not destinations, a concept that flowed from the notion of accessible pathways.

The pathways through the building created by the principle of full accessibility in turn created the possibility for greater social interaction. Residents with disabilities could socialize not just with each other but with able-bodied people. Members of Windward, with disabilities or without, could invite friends in wheelchairs who lived elsewhere to visit them in their homes. By and large, as we discuss in chapter 6, Windward members responded positively to the opportunity for able-bodied residents to interact with neighbours who had disabilities.

Bringing Things Together

For Harbourfront social housing on its lands was a political necessity but the site allocated was as far from its central area as
possible. Furthermore, Harbourfront imposed criteria for the
appearance of the building and required that its courtyard be
accessible to the public. Intecity had a vision of a completely
integrated environment for people with disabilities and able-
bodied people, but it was the founding board of directors, Lantana, and the architects who decided what that actually meant.
On the board differences existed between the members with disabilities and the others which were resolved through 'civilized
competition.' For Lantana and the architects the sometimes competing claims of economic necessity and social goals influenced
design decisions. The contractor was subject to rapidly changing
economic circumstances and communication problems that affected how plans became reality.

A proposal call for Windward went out in 1981, but the co-
op did not open finally until late 1986. During that time the
changing political and economic climate affected the major actors
in many ways. Harbourfront found itself embroiled in continual
controversy with the City of Toronto and the federal government
over its development plans. Changing economic conditions were
crucial for Lantana: first, high interest rates and depression in
the housing market, then rapid inflation and a boom, thus a
severe shortage of affordable housing. Lantana came to prefer
site-first development whenever possible. Cost overruns at Windward caused, in part, by a strengthened construction market produced losses for Lantana when it attempted to provide its usual
full range of services. Thus, according to one informant, Lantana
could not afford to train new members adequately in managing
the co-op. Nevertheless, the firm remained committed to com-
pleting this part of the project as well as the physical construction.

By and large, Windward residents had little prior experience
with cooperative living and many of them felt rather abandoned
by the resource group. The co-op, and its board of directors,
faced a large debt burden because of the cost overruns and suf-

fered internal dissension over how to deal with the problem. Because of the length and complexity of the project and because the contractor had difficulties in getting adequate tradesmen in a suddenly booming construction market, Windward had many building deficiencies, including the lack of many accessibility features. These contributed to the cost overruns.

Finally, the actions of the various parties to this development at any particular time reflected both their own agendas and their earlier experience with the project itself. There was a dialectic between experience and understanding from which later action flowed. This was particularly true for Lantana, the co-op's board, and Intecity. Intecity itself eventually disintegrated, 'consumed by the co-op,' as its members perhaps saw that their expertise and energy were not equal to the task. Windward's board of directors opted for full accessibility early on, but to achieve their goal they had to learn to manoeuvre through an obstacle course set up (and changed from time to time) by CMHC, Harbourfront, Lantana, and the contractor. While Lantana's experience was gained at considerable financial and emotional cost to the firm, staff members considered the project a success as a model for fully accessible housing. So did the Province of Ontario, which presented Windward with a Premier's Award of Accessibility in 1987.

Thus, to understand the building of Windward Co-op we have explored some of the complex connections among site, social processes, and built form. As the different parties became involved, given their own agendas, ways of conceptualizing the issues, and changing circumstances, the project took on a life of its own. Furthermore, even when the project was completed, changes in the wider neighbourhood continued to affect it as they did Harbourside as well.

Yet constructing the co-ops did not consist only of building. A viable organization also had to be set up. In the next chapter we describe briefly how Harbourside and Windward were organized. We also take up debates over appropriate co-op goals and ideal images of community.

CHAPTER FOUR

Co-op Organization and Goals

Establishing a housing cooperative means constructing a small society as well as a building. While Windward and Harbourside were not separatist, utopian communities they did aim at the growth of community among their members. Like any such groups embedded in a larger society, the co-ops were to some degree conditioned by outside forces. Yet how they developed depended importantly on their own actions in light of their goals. Furthermore, the goals of co-op members often incorporated rather different ideal images of what a community should be like.

In this chapter, we begin by describing how the co-ops actually operated. Then we turn to a debate that took place in the co-op housing sector over appropriate goals. Finally, we consider some images of community held by co-op members and activists. The images implied different prescriptions for what the co-ops and their members should do if they hoped to realize their ideals.

Resident Management: How It Works

Harbourside and Windward co-ops are medium-sized projects. Still, they managed assets worth perhaps $5 and $9 million respectively. Their annual operating budgets have run between $675,000 and over $1 million. Such organizations cannot be managed the way a household might be run. A brief sketch of how they were organized is therefore necessary.

Windward and Harbourside were incorporated under and

regulated by the Co-operative Corporations Act of Ontario (1980). As well, they were bound by the terms of their contractual agreements with Canada Mortgage and Housing Corporation, under section 56.1 of the National Housing Act.[1] Thus, legal and contractual requirements set the broad parameters of co-op organization.

Each co-op had to have a board of directors, made up of seven members in good standing, that was legally responsible for its affairs. While other committees might be set up, legally they were creatures of the board. Furthermore, each co-op had to adopt a set of by-laws regulating its operations. The by-laws specified the co-op's objectives; defined and regulated its membership, directors, and officers; detailed general meeting procedures; laid out how it was to conduct its financial affairs; defined the rights and responsibilities of the co-op vis-à-vis members, e.g., with respect to eviction. Furthermore, upon becoming a member one had to enter into an occupancy agreement which set out the members' obligations to the co-op. Members agree to:

- pay all housing charges promptly and in full
- attend general meetings of the members
- give time for participation in co-op affairs
- be responsible for all other occupants of the unit, including guests
- keep the unit well maintained
- comply with the terms of the subsidy agreement, if the member is receiving housing charge assistance (i.e., rent subsidy), e.g., in providing annual evidence of income to the co-op

The rights of members also were detailed, such as the right to

- enjoy the use of the unit, and to come and go freely
- use common areas of the co-op
- have access to all decisions except confidential ones of the board of directors
- be notified of and attend any meetings at which the member's rights are to be discussed

- attend and vote at all general meetings, as well as request a general meeting
- sublet the unit for up to six months, with the co-op's permission
- apply for a subsidy

The by-laws and agreements were detailed and legally enforceable documents. Fortunately, Windward and Harbourside were able to adopt agreements based on samples provided to them by the resource groups that had helped them develop the projects. More recently, the Cooperative Housing Federation of Toronto rewrote such documents in plain (or anyway, plainer) English. The federation was especially proud of this achievement because it helped make it easier for all co-op members to participate in running their co-ops.

As lengthy as the by-laws were they could not go into many important policy areas in great detail. Further policies were necessary to spell out how the co-ops would deal with, for example, members' rights to keep pets, their access to parking, or the provision of subsidies.

Much of the everyday business of Windward and Harbourside was conducted by hired staff. Windward originally had a superintendent and a coordinator. In 1989, an assistant coordinator was hired to help out. At Harbourside there was one coordinator. Most of the routine maintenance work was contracted out. Co-op coordinators play a range of roles, from property manager to community organizer. As we will discuss later, how the coordinator chooses to interpret and play his or her role can make a real difference to a co-op. Suffice it to say here that the very title, 'coordinator,' signals how different this position can be from, for example, the manager of a condominium.

At each of the co-ops a number of committees was set up to deal with important aspects of their affairs. The basic model for committee structure was provided by the resource groups. Harbourside co-op had committees concerned with finance, member selection, maintenance, the newsletter, social affairs, member involvement, and landscaping. From time to time, ad hoc committees were set up to deal with issues like making improvements to the stairwells, fire safety, and a disputed budget. As well, one member turned out a weekly newsletter for the co-op on his own.

At Windward, the major committees were concerned with finance, member selection, maintenance, the newsletter, social affairs, member education, parents' concerns, and gardening. In 1988–89, another committee was formed to try to secure outside funding for additional modifications to the units of members with disabilities. As well, there was a group of volunteers who were on call when the building superintendent was off. Each committee reported to the board of directors. For several years, the coordinator and members of Windward were concerned about how well the committees and the board worked together. An organizational task force spent considerable time in 1988 and 1989 trying to sort out the problems of liaison.

Thus, Harbourside and Windward adopted a bureaucratic model of organization. In chapter 9 we will discuss how member control operated at Windward and Harbourside during the three years of our study. However, the co-ops had both economic and social goals, particularly the growth of community among their members. For some people, though, it was clear that highly rationalized, impersonal bureaucratic structures ran directly counter to the aim of community formation. In the next section, we discuss some debates about the appropriate mix of goals for housing co-ops.

The Goals of Cooperative Housing

The main goals of Canadian cooperative housing were spelled out by Alexander Laidlaw (1977: 48), one of its founders: collective ownership, adequate housing at cost, non-profit operation, democratic control, and creation of community. Often the latter two ideals are extended to include the support and empowerment of disadvantaged members of the co-op. George Melnyk pointed out that all cooperatives have both idealistic goals of 'ending exploitative relations through self-help group action' and pragmatic goals of successful economic activity. The interplay between idealistic social and pragmatic economic goals has propelled the development of co-ops and the cooperative movement in a liberal democratic society like Canada (Melnyk 1985: 28–30, 102). In Toronto during the late 1980s the relative importance of these goals became a contentious issue. Given the acute need for affordable housing, how much should the co-op housing sector continue to stress its social goals? Should it try simply to build as much affordable housing as possible? An uncertain economic and political climate created pressure to develop social housing projects as quickly as possible.

Clearly, this issue cut both ways. Providing good-quality, affordable housing on a non-market basis met the socially desirable objective of housing those in need. Yet, if the non-profit housing resource groups that develop co-ops devoted most of their resources to housing provision they would have little left for community development. In new co-ops this trade-off can be reflected in insufficient training for members in management and organizational development.

A related debate questioned how important member participation is for the success of co-ops. What is it actually good for? How should the trade-offs between efficiency and democracy be evaluated? We discuss these issues at Windward and Harbourside in chapters 8 and 9.

In summing up one aspect of the current debate, the Cooperative Housing Federation of Toronto (1988a: 4) suggested that: 'Co-ops should think carefully about *why* they want members to participate. Is it because there are so many really necessary things to do? Or because participation is believed to reduce housing charges? Or because it's in our by-laws and policies? Or to share burdens equally? Or because it's educational? Or??'

Peter Tabuns, then a co-op coordinator and housing activist, argued that the commitment of co-ops to voluntarism contributes to several common problems: cynicism (especially about other people's contributions), waste of time and resources, territorial disputes among committees, petty corruption, degeneration of underemployed committees, overextension of the few with leadership abilities, poor maintenance and personnel policies leading to poor management, and insularity of the co-ops. He claimed that volunteer labour in running co-ops is trivial in holding down housing costs, $10 per unit per month in the three co-ops he knew well.

'Given the negative impact on community life and the minimal impact on housing costs, there seems little reason to have the essential functions of the co-op carried out by volunteer labour' (Tabuns 1986: 12–14). Democracy, according to Tabuns, does not require frequent general members' meetings or elaborate committee structures. Most actual management, including budgeting and member selection, should be done by hired staff. Co-ops could better reach their goals, both social and economic, by simplifying their structure, using more professional management, and reducing member participation.

The issue was joined by another co-op activist, Don Young (1987: 11), among others. 'I can't help feeling that by stripping the organization down to the bone, the soul of the co-op is lost. Involvement of members ... [is] what co-operatives are all about.' On one question Young went even further than Tabuns. For him, voluntarism actually *increases* costs. So, from a property management perspective, it should be discouraged. But he questioned whether efficiency should be the sole or main objective of co-ops. He argued (ibid.: 12): 'It is through participation itself that members are educated. Given the chance, they can grow by leaps and bounds as they meet the challenge, make mistakes, and, yes, sometimes squander resources. Democracy, and especially direct democracy, is far from an efficient system. Sacrifices have to be made so that everyone can achieve his or her full potential and, in so doing, as far as possible, allow everyone to reach the same level rather than surrendering authority to experts.'

It would be easy to exaggerate the differences between Tabuns and Young. Both thought that co-ops should provide good-quality, affordable housing democratically managed by their residents. The differences had to do with the relative weighting of social and economic goals. Young opted for community development and member improvement at the cost of efficiency. Tabuns thought that efficiency would encourage the growth of more pleasant communities.

By implication, this debate also spoke to the larger hopes of people in the co-op housing sector. If their chief objective was efficiency in providing and managing housing, then they would have to give up their pretensions to being a 'third sector,' neither private profit oriented nor public. Co-ops would become like public housing projects; professionals would manage the property. Ironically, increased resident participation in the management of public housing projects has recently been seen as a way of overcoming some of their problems (e.g., Cityhome 1990, Monti 1989).

However, for people like Young (1987: 13), co-ops were 'a noble experiment in the realization of human potential and should always be in search of new approaches to communal living.' The organization of co-ops should encourage both the realization of human potential and the growth of community. It should foster the links between them.

These debates over goals and the need for member participation to some degree reflect the position of co-ops more generally in Canadian society. While producer and consumer co-ops are large and well established, they have become ever more professionalized. Many have become virtually indistinguishable from similar private sector companies. Levels of member participation are very low and consist mostly of buying from them or selling to them.

Housing co-ops are the major form of cooperative that is still expanding in Canada. The co-op housing sector still has some characteristics of a social movement. It tends to value more highly social goals of community and member democracy than do, for example, the Prairie wheat pools or credit unions.

The differences that emerged over the trade-offs between co-op social and economic goals, such as democracy vs efficiency, in our view reflected at least in part the attempts of co-op activists to shore up and, if possible, expand the role of co-ops in providing housing. After all, there was little government support for their development. And the public at large, if it thought of them at all, saw them either as public housing or as communes.

Members' Goals for Harbourside and Windward Co-ops

The perspectives and concerns of co-op members overlap with but are not necessarily identical to those of coordinators or other housing professionals. We surveyed members of Harbourside and Windward co-ops about what they saw as proper goals for their co-ops. They were given a list of thirteen goals and asked how strongly they agreed or disagreed with each of them (see Appendix).

In both co-ops there was considerable agreement; more than 50 per cent of the respondents agreed or strongly agreed with all but one of the goals.[2] Members especially favoured the co-ops striving to provide good-quality, affordable housing. There was least agreement on housing people really in need or helping members improve themselves. At both Windward and Harbourside fewer than half agreed that 'the co-op should make it a priority to house people who really are in need.' Members with incomes below the co-op median were much more likely to agree than members with higher incomes. While more than half agreed that 'the co-op should do all it can to help members upgrade their skills and training,' only 19 per cent at Harbourside and 18 per cent at Windward strongly agreed. At Windward, while almost half of all men and women agreed with this statement, more men (35 per cent) than women (24 per cent) disagreed with it.

Members did appear to agree that community development was an important goal for Windward and Harbourside. There were several survey items that dealt explicitly with community development goals. More than 70 per cent of respondents in both co-ops agreed that: .

- Developing a genuine sense of community is one of the most important goals this co-op should have.
- The co-op should be run in a completely democratic fashion; for example, all major issues should be debated and decided at general members' meetings.
- The co-op should strive to have almost everyone participating in co-op activities and community life.

- One of the co-op's chief goals should be to support its members when they are in trouble or when emergencies arise.

These are rather general statements of ideals. Most members agreed that building a sense of community *is* desirable and that member involvement should be encouraged. Yet while the co-ops' economic goals were relatively specific and measurable, their social goals were diffuse and ill defined. Thus, even at such a general level, how member involvement relates to community formation remained controversial, partly because what a community *is* was itself unclear.

Three Frames of Reference for Co-ops

One way of conceptualizing the different approaches to what a co-op community is and should be was offered by Ralph West (1989, personal communication). He was Harbourside's first co-ordinator and, more recently, has worked on developing co-ops for the resource group Chris Smith and Associates. West argued that housing co-op members seem to have three quite different frames of reference. These frameworks relate to the ideal organization and community that members would like to have. In his view, which of the three they have stems mostly from their background.

People with a *traditional* frame of reference tend to believe that a co-op community will develop organically, much like that in a small town. There should be few rules for doing things. Leadership, normally by men, depends on the personal qualities of individuals. Men and women should play appropriate but different roles in the co-op. People should learn their jobs through experience but competence is respected. Anyone with the same values and the willingness to help out should be accepted as a member. The main incentive for people to participate is thought to be a diffuse sense of responsibility to the community.

For people with a *business* frame of reference the primary concern is with the viability of the co-op as an enterprise. Thus, leadership should depend on expertise and demonstrated competence. In the interests of reliability, staff rather than members should do many of the necessary tasks. People should participate because of the benefits that will flow to the co-op, and thus to themselves. People with this orientation, according to West, tend to be impatient with the other perspectives. For them, having an economically viable co-op of which one can be proud is a sufficient aim. Fostering community and promoting equality among members are worthwhile goals but far from necessary.

Finally, those with a *social democratic* frame of reference value highly universal principles of 'humanity,' 'equality,' and 'equity.' They tend to favour a more bureaucratic form of organization, in which there are universal standards and many rules. Authority in the co-op resides in the membership which delegates it to people holding particular roles. Ideally, all members should be empowered through education and experience to take on the necessary tasks involved in running the co-op. This may require the co-op to support members having personal, financial, or other difficulties. Members should be recruited who share these values. All should participate in community affairs from a sense of social responsibility rather than self-interest. Periodically, the group should try to set goals and assess how well it is doing.

The nature of different co-ops, he argued, depends on the interplay and mix of people with the different frames of reference: 'My impression is that no individual holds exclusively to any single model, and that in the absence of any clear understanding of what their co-op environment is, or is intended to be, they are routinely merged in odd ways by members seeking to persuade each other to their perspective on individual issues.' Most members have not thought systematically about their own or other peoples' frames of reference. West thought that improved conflict resolution processes in co-ops might require ways of forcing people on 'differing sides to grasp the other person's experience so that they can incorporate the needs which flow from it in their decisions.'

Images of Community

Many other people associated with Harbourside and Windward

co-ops also had thought about what their communities should be like. To some degree what they thought depended on how they imagined the community. They seemed to have images of community that they could hold up from time to time and compare with their observations.

One of the chief questions that arose at both co-ops was how member involvement relates to the growth of community. Three rather different views on this question emerged from our interviews: the traditional, the social democratic, and the 'new age' (for want of a better term). There also are people with an orientation similar to the business one described by Ralph West; but for them the question of community development is of much less interest. Rather than make a composite of the voices of many different members, we report at some length the views of two very articulate Windward residents and Windward's former co-ordinator.

The traditional view likened the co-op to a small village or neighbourhood. Michael Lord told us about growing up in a medium-sized Ontario city, where he had lived in the same place for his first twenty-five years. His ideas of how people's informal involvement with each other helps create community reflected that experience:

> Coming from a small place, it seemed like the community was where you grew up. All the neighbours knew who you were – if your folks had to be out at noon, you would have lunch with the neighbours. And it was one of those sorts of things. So, I guess it was a community, where, within the one-block radius, you knew the names of all the people who lived there, and they had been living there for at least a decade, and you knew which of them were in rough shape, and which of them were in better shape – and you knew what their moms and dads did.
>
> It just seems funny to come to Toronto and see that the city is so large, and there's so much turnover in terms of where people are living, that there has to be some kind of deliberate effort to establish community.

He extended these views to his experience at Windward:

Seldom will it be that I'll walk across from one side of the courtyard to the other, without at least two or three people who I have seen before – whose names I *may* not know – stopping and remarking about whatever issue happens to be there. So, it's a kind of social undercurrent that causes you to realize that you're living *with* these people, and how their thinking and feeling *is* important. Because these are the people you'll have to rely on if things are going to get done.

So the more aloof you are, the more hostile the community you're guaranteeing for yourself. The more friendly you are with people, you're *moving* in the direction of assuring that people are going to be friendly when they see *you*. And that you're going to feel like you're living in a little village, or a little community – not feel like you're living in one isolated unit. Which is the way that it feels living in the different apartments and flats that I've lived in in Toronto.

The quality of life [at Windward] is good by Toronto standards, but by the standards of the small town, it doesn't feel like you're in a home. It does feel like you are, well – it feels to *me* like being in a unit of [a] development. And, of having these challenges to try – in whatever way possible – to make it feel more like a community where you've lived for a long time. It's mainly the gentleness of the social interaction that contributes to that – so that you won't live adjacent to somebody for *too* long before you strike up a conversation with them, or they with you. And, there is a genuine sense of 'How do you feel about the music that I play late at night?' [in other words, of real concern for each other].

In so far as it concerned community formation, the traditional view mainly required a certain quality of interaction. Individuals would know and care for each other, though not necessarily well or deeply, because of long association and some shared interests. But it did not necessarily entail any particular changes on the part of individuals or in the organization of the community. The other two views pick out organizational and individual change as crucial elements.

Dan Fast, coordinator of Windward from its inception through

1989, strongly put forward the organizational view. For him, it was crucial that the co-op develop adequate organizational structures and that its members acquire the relevant skills:

> I think that there's a difference in kind between a co-op [and other housing] that has to do with the sense of community. And that the sense of community is related to the fact that they [i.e., the members] share the sense of responsibility about the place. They know that they're in the driver's seat. They sometimes sweat in the back of their minds – 'Gee, I wonder ... I hope that somebody's watching out for the building.' They sometimes realize the degree of responsibility that's theoretically on them: they've got a $7 or $8 million structure that they're technically responsible for. And this translates into the other kinds of committees of the essential type – like the finance committee and the membership committee, and so on. And I think that that's where you get your sense of community. I think it's directly related to the structural nature of the organization. That without that, you wouldn't have that sense of everybody knowing each other.

For Fast, organizational tidiness was not an end in itself, however. It promoted greater levels of participation:

> Now, they could maintain sloppy committee structure, and still have all that [i.e., a sense of community]. I think that the desire to get the committees in order is just a little add-on of my own, that has to do with a sense that they can't operate efficiently, and get things done, unless they do things in an organized fashion. And, if they don't operate efficiently ... a *lot* of people are not going to be interested in helping. And if those people don't help, the committees will founder, and eventually – it works its way down to being like any other six- or ten-year-old co-op, where all they've got is the finance committee and the board ... you know, and the people out there cutting the grass. And, at that point seventy or eighty per cent of the members are *not* really participating – and they've got a fight on their hands every year to try and get enough people to form a board of directors.

Fast's views reflected, among other things, his years of experience as a political organizer and his personal predilections. 'Committee organizing is a hobby of mine and was my chief interest in hiring on at Windward.' He recognized that others in the co-op sector, as well as many members of Windward, saw the issue rather differently. 'The "right answer" [for the co-op sector] is that a sense of community doesn't come from meetings but from little things like going out and buying sugar for each other or from social events.' But for him the important thing was that participation on committees helps members to get to know each other and to gain confidence in their own abilities: 'People in a new co-op meet people through meetings. The requirement to come to committee meetings provides added impetus for developing community. Through participation in committees people loosen up and feel free to talk in general meetings. What made me feel good was to see people who hadn't known each other discussing good old co-op issues. That gave me a warm feeling. I still feel that ultimately for them [shy members] the answer is participation. They'll meet people. They'll break the ice even if it takes three years for them to get around to it. It's by dragging them into a committee that you get to that.'

Fast's position, thus, was essentially humanistic and social democratic. The good of the members outweighed organizational concerns. But good organization was crucial to realizing those human values. Furthermore, social engineering would bring about needed change in individuals.

Greg Yarrow, former president of Windward's board of directors, saw his perspective as at once complementary to and diametrically opposed to that of Dan Fast. A consultant on organizational development, Yarrow found the social democratic view overly narrow.

People don't get motivated by formal structure. I think that they have to know that their individuality – their errors, their mistakes, and just their humanity – will be recognized in a system. And ... structuralism is *boring* stuff ... ultimately dehumanizing.

Organizations, I think, are fundamentally pathological. Structure ... disorients. People end up saying things because of their position. They say things to other people that human beings would never say to each other. You know ... as human beings, sitting on the dock at the cottage, you'd never say to each other. But no, in the office, they feel that they have to say it, because ... of some 'ism,' or idea or image in their mind, about how an organization ought to work. And they don't know the damage they do – the psychic damage they do – to people.

Yarrow (n.d.) felt sufficiently strongly about this that he published an article about 'community' in the Windward newsletter. First he defined what he meant by community, based on a book by M. Scott Peck (1988). Communities are groups of people 'who have learned to communicate honestly with each other, whose relationships go deeper than their masks of composure, and who have developed some significant commitment to rejoice together, mourn together, and to delight in each other, make others' conditions [their] own.'

Community making for Peck has four stages. In the first, *pseudocommunity*, people avoid conflict by denying individual differences. They pretend that they all believe in the same things, such as the values of cooperative housing. *Chaos* is the second stage. Differences surface but the group attempts to obliterate them 'out of the motive to make everyone "normal".'

According to Peck (in Yarrow n.d.: 8–9), there are two ways out of this chaos. One is into organization, but 'organization and community are incompatible.' The other is *emptiness*, the third stage. In this process people empty themselves of 'expectations and preconceptions; prejudices; ideology, theology and solutions; the need to heal, convert, fix or solve; the need to control.' Finally, then, we reach the fourth stage, *community*. 'When its death has been completed, open and empty, the group enters community.'

Yarrow concluded with this prescription for Windward: 'Should we accept our responsibility, we must begin at several interconnected levels at the same time. Community-building begins at home. In our own hearts and minds we must build a community based on paradox: that includes the truth of our strengths as well as our weaknesses; our wholeness as well as our brokenness; our independence and our interdependence. At the same time we must do the same with our spouse and family; our friends and neighbours, and with every group we are involved with which would benefit from the peace and wisdom of community.'

In this view, for true communities to grow the individuals that make them up must undergo profound change. They must achieve a transcendence of self that one associates almost with Buddhist ideals. Or they must make enduring the fleeting periods of 'communitas' people can experience, for example, during shared adversity or in certain religious rituals.[3]

These three perspectives, if taken seriously, point in very different directions, as the history of intentional communities would show. The traditionalist asks little of a community except that through long, informal interaction its members should come to know and be concerned about each other. Members become involved with each other but 'community' remains amorphous. The social democratic approach plans rationally to create a structure that will encourage social ties and change individuals. Here, members become involved with the structured community first. Then they connect with each other. As they do so, their attitudes change and their level of confidence rises. Finally, the 'new age' tells people to give up structure and self, to encourage chaos out of which true community will emerge. Involvement of members will contribute to community if individuals relate to each other as whole persons, not segmentally.

Conclusion

In this chapter we have discussed how Windward and Harbourside co-ops were organized and have presented three images of what the co-op community should be like. People's actions and their attempts to understand others made use to some degree of these frames of reference. The history of these co-ops was partly a product of the interplay of these models. No single frame of reference or ideal image could characterize what either co-op actually was like. What happened at Harbourside and Windward and what that meant to participants were contested in terms largely of these orientations.

These co-ops were not utopian societies, however; nor were they isolated. Rather, they were essentially single-purpose associations providing housing in a large city for people who had many other ties and interests. Whatever the relationship between member involvement and community building, the motivation of members remained a key issue.

From the street neither co-op appeared particularly unusual architecturally in present-day Toronto; nor did the organizational structure, which followed a highly formal bureaucratic model. The goals of community formation and the processes of democratic self-management make co-ops stand out among other types of housing. In the next chapter we take up a key process in housing co-ops, the selection of members.

CHAPTER FIVE

Choose Your Neighbour Well

'Don't Shoot the Dog, Shoot the Owner!'

INTERVIEWER: *Can you tell me a little about the member selection process? What was the interview like?*

NORMA: *It was the most nerve-racking interview of my life. Well I guess because it was so important to get in, I wanted to say the right things. Of course there is no right thing.*

KEN: *I didn't find it as bad as Norma did mainly because I was apprehensive about coming here in the first place, much more so than Norma. Like, I wasn't involved in all this. So I found it fairly easy. They asked questions and I would answer. If they don't like your answer, you can't do anything about it. [They asked] 'What do you think about people who don't clean up after their dogs?' And I said 'Shoot them!' I mean, it was the first thing that came in my mind so I said it. It came out. 'What? Shoot the dogs?' [they asked.] And I said, 'No. Shoot the owners!' You know the dog doesn't know any better, so really, the dog doesn't know naturally to clean up after itself, shoot the owner. They thought that was quite good.*

INTERVIEWER: *Well, what do you think they're looking for? I mean not necessarily in that test, but in selecting people to move in here? Are they looking for a particular kind of family or ...?*

KEN: *I think they're looking for an attitude more than anything, more than a certain type of family, a certain attitude if they're going to get along with everybody [and] be responsible. There were various interview questions like 'Do you have strong prejudices?' I didn't know it at the time but one of the people that came out to interview us was in a mixed racial marriage and one of the questions was 'What do you think about racial differences in a co-op set up just for Blacks or just for Ukrainians?' He no sooner got it out and I said, 'No!' It was a very quick answer. And he said, 'You're very quick about that.' And I said, 'I think it just creates ghettos.' And he liked that.*

When Ted moved to newly opened Harbourside co-op he joined the member selection committee. An experienced member took him aside and gave him some advice. Look, [she said] you may not know it, but you have a great opportunity in your hands. You can select who is going to be your neighbour ... [But] keep in mind that once they're in, they're almost impossible to remove ... So take your time and make sure.

How do co-ops 'make sure'? In this chapter we explore some of the issues raised by member recruitment at Harbourside and Windward co-ops. One of the key features of Canadian housing cooperatives is that members get to choose their own neighbours. Ordinary homeowners or tenants in conventional rental housing do not have such an opportunity, though many might wish for it. In this chapter, we argue that the member selection process is an important element in co-op members' sense of control over their housing. Initial member selection crucially shapes the character of a new co-op. Most of this chapter is concerned with initial recruitment at the two co-ops. The selection of new members in already established co-ops involves similar issues although it need not affect the co-op as seriously. We deal with later recruitment towards the end of the chapter.

Applicants were accepted into the co-ops through a selection process which, while standardized to some extent, depended on selection committee members' assessments of who would make a good co-op resident. Successful applicants were those who seemed likely to be financially responsible, willing participants in running the co-op, and good neighbours.

Yet member selection was complicated by several facts. One is that while these co-ops sought harmony based on a sense of community or like-mindedness among members, they were predicated on heterogeneity. They made new neighbours out of people who could afford to buy a home and those who could pay only a limited rent.

Another is that the process itself was fraught with ambiguity. The information available to the selection committee was partial and sometimes unclear. The criteria by which applicants were judged often were vague or difficult to apply. Committee members might have been biased.

As well, the selection process depended to some extent on committee dynamics. This was true both within the selection committees themselves and between them and the boards of directors. For example, committee members developed tacit understandings among themselves that underlay their decisions. Rifts in the committee at Windward seriously affected its ability to work productively. Conflict between the committee and the board led to a stalemate on acceptances.

In considering initial member selection we focus on those applicants deemed *unlikely* to make good members and therefore rejected. Such cases highlight more than acceptances do the complexities involved in making selection decisions. Clear reasons had to be given for rejecting an applicant whereas acceptances did not need as detailed justification.

Participants in making these decisions were trying to create mixed-income residential communities that work. They recognized that difficult decisions often had to be made, ones that appeared to contradict the co-ops' commitment to egalitarianism, openness, and providing housing for those in need. Yet such decisions did not necessarily express simple conflict between ideology and practice.

Selectors were gatekeepers who controlled access to one of contemporary society's most important consumption goods. On a larger scale, access to the major means of consumption powerfully affects people's life chances and political alignments, and helps to shape cultural and personal identity (Pratt 1986, 1987; Saunders 1986). But selection decisions did not necessarily reveal a struggle between people positioned differently in terms of their relationship to the means of production or consumption. Selection committee members at Windward and Harbourside, as a group, did not differ in social class or range of incomes from applicants or in whether their housing was directly subsidized.

Rejection decisions often revealed negotiation taking place over the meanings of the use values of housing. This became particularly clear because the exchange value of housing was not at issue here. No one was concerned about the resale value of his or her unit. One thing these decisions point up is that enjoyment of the use values of multiple housing depends in good measure on one's neighbours.

They show especially that part of the process of constructing a community involves defining what a *good member* is. Highly charged terms like *commitment, giving, volunteering, neighbour, home*, and *cooperative* come into play. Such symbols helped selectors to create an image for themselves of what their co-op and its members should be like. For example, a good neighbour must achieve a delicate balance between being sociable and helpful and respecting others' privacy and property. As well, they allowed members to compress the wide range of applicants' personal characteristics, experience, and needs into easier to handle wholes. The symbols also served within the community as rhetorical means with which to justify decisions.

Choosing Members

To be a member of a Canadian housing co-op is to be at once tenant, co-owner, and neighbour (Poulin 1984: 21–2). Those selecting new members must bear in mind the differing implications of these roles. A good tenant pays the rent on time and follows the rules prescribed for use of the property, while a co-owner participates in management and takes decisions that affect its future disposition. A good neighbour must somehow integrate appropriately into the group.

Co-ops work out for themselves how to choose households whose members will meet these desiderata and how to deal with difficult cases. Usually, the founding board of directors of a co-op decides on a member selection policy, and establishes a committee to do the actual work. In recent years, planning and implementing such policies have been materially affected by consultants working for housing resource groups who have considerable experience in the co-op housing field. They train selection committee members in interviewing applicants and even provide sample interview schedules. But the founding board establishes the actual criteria and, in at least an informal way, how they are to be weighted.

A pool of applicants could be developed in two ways. One was that resource groups market new co-ops. Because of the housing shortage in Toronto, resource groups often employed site-first development since appropriate sites were a good deal scarcer than people looking for affordable housing. They found appropriate building sites, planned the project (at least roughly), and then tried to form groups. When people called the Cooperative Housing Federation of Toronto, for example, they were given lists of co-ops that had open waiting lists and of new ones being formed. They could then apply to one or several co-ops that seemed suitable, based usually on a combination of location, availability, cost, and less tangible factors that might have to do with the reputation of the co-op for harmony or neighbourliness.

A second way was found mainly in co-ops with a special focus where the pool of applicants would be at least partly recruited through the founding group or appropriate interest groups. A seniors' co-op, for example, developed in association with a synagogue sought some of its members among Russian Jewish immigrants. Windward found some of its disabled residents through the Canadian Paraplegic Association, although the association had not been involved in planning the project. Applicants to Harbourside largely were recruited through the resource group involved.[1] Public sessions were held at which prospective applicants received information about the co-op and how to apply.

Having secured a number of applicants, the selection committees then set to work. Applicants were interviewed, often following a prepared schedule, by a team which later reported to the committee. Rejected applicants might ask to be reinterviewed and, if rejected again, might appeal to the board of directors.

In his study of sixteen co-ops in Quebec, Poulin noted sixteen criteria sometimes employed in membership decisions. These included household size and composition, age, ability to pay the rent, earlier experience with collective management, reasons for wanting to join, particular skills, housing need, willingness to participate, low income, capacity to integrate into the group, and intention to remain in the co-op for a long time (Poulin 1984: Annexe IV, 10). He grouped these into three types of criteria: those linked to the co-op as an enterprise (solvency, particular skills), by the claim of a right to housing (housing need, low income, aid to stigmatized categories of people), and as an association (e.g., interest, experience, capacity to integrate).

At Windward co-op, selection policy, besides aiming for at first 15 per cent, then later 25 per cent members with disabilities, incorporated two somewhat unusual features. One was to stress voluntarism and community participation. Successful applicants, including ones with disabilities, had to show that they had contributed to the wider community in ways that went beyond their jobs. Good intentions did not count. However, participation in community activities that took so much of the applicant's time that he or she seemed unlikely to contribute to the co-op weighed against acceptance, indicating a persistent tension between commitment to various levels of community. The second feature was to interview applicants in their homes so as to see them in their own 'habitat.' This made the selection task that much more difficult and time consuming for the volunteer committee members.

In sum, as a member involved in selection from the very inception of Windward put it: 'What we were looking for were people who had either been at a co-op or had been active in the community at some point, had given freely of their time, people that we felt would be cooperative or cooperators in general, who would be good at being a neighbour, a friend, whatever, who could afford to pay the rent, who had a good credit history. There was a range of different things involved. The bottom line was, would they make a good neighbour?'

Selection policy at Harbourside co-op initially was concerned with deciding how to allocate subsidy funds. As at Windward, applicants were interviewed in their own homes. Actual selection decisions employed many of the criteria mentioned above but none seemed to be given especial weight at least as a matter of policy. Besides determining that the applicant was financially capable (including those applying for subsidies), there was an attempt to find people variously described to us as likely to be 'good neighbours,' 'cooperative,' or 'like-minded' in some sense.

Both co-ops successfully filled their units shortly after opening. Most members said that the selection process was a success. In our 1989 survey, we asked if members thought that the selection process had 'chosen the right kind of people for this co-op.' At Harbourside, 85 per cent of respondents answered 'often' or 'almost always,' the two highest of five possible choices. Windward respondents were more equivocal. Sixty per cent chose the two highest categories; the top three categories included 85 per cent.

Seventy-six per cent of Windward respondents and 65 per cent of Harbourside ones had moved into their co-op within its first six months of operation. Thus, arguably, in answering the survey question as they did they were merely approving themselves. However, at Harbourside more respondents (95 per cent) who were not pioneer members chose the two highest categories than did early members (77 per cent). There was no such difference at Windward.

Importantly, both selection committees contained members on subsidy as well as those paying full (i.e., market) housing charges. The composition of these initial committees did not follow a conscious decision to include people from different income levels. Rather it reflected the make-up of the early boards of directors.

The complexity and length of the Windward project meant that actual selection went on for almost three years. Because of the continual delays in planning and construction, the selection committee at times felt pressed simply to fill the co-op. Each time it seemed that the interest adjustment date was near (and thus that revenue would be required to meet mortgage payments) the committee scrambled to fill the available places. Some had already been filled but previously accepted applicants had given them up. Nevertheless, committee members said that they maintained the rigour of the selection process.

Acceptance and Rejection

Many applicants were rejected, often because they could not demonstrate sufficient community participation. At Windward, by December 1987 there had been 361 applications for 101 units. Of these, 205 applications were accepted, of which 55 later were withdrawn and 49 remained on a waiting list. Rejected applications totalled 44, while 112 other applications never were completed, were withdrawn prior to a decision, or the co-op lost contact with the applicants. Rejections, then, comprised 17.7 per cent of the selection committee's actual decisions. Unfortunately, we could not obtain comparable data for Harbourside.

According to one housing consultant involved with Harbourside, many rejected applicants were told that the co-op did not see them as able or willing to make the necessary commitment of energy or that they seemed unlikely to benefit from the co-op lifestyle. Not everyone accepted this explanation, of course. Some later were reinterviewed and appealed to the boards of directors or took their cases further by complaining to their alderman or member of parliament.

Describing one rejected applicant (perceived as a 'yuppie' concerned only with living near the waterfront), a member of Harbourside said: 'And I was convinced, just talking to him after he'd got that rejection letter that we had made the right decision. This guy just didn't even understand what it meant to be cooperative. Intellectually he grasped the concepts we were expounding but he was basically just not the right kind of person.'

As we have suggested, difficult cases, especially rejections, show best how co-op members worked through the ambiguities, vagueness, and even contradictions in their task. Clearly, not everyone could be accepted; the need for housing was great but space was extremely limited. Moreover, the opportunity to choose one's neighbour encouraged selection committee members to weigh the merits of applicants in particular ways. Selection committees had to be discriminating without discriminating in a legal sense, as well. Ideals sometimes had to be set aside, reinterpreted, or balanced against other goals to achieve a functioning community.

The very vagueness of the criteria made the selection task difficult, opening the co-ops occasionally to charges of unfairness. Too, the slipperiness of some of the criteria made selection committees sometimes seem subjective in their judgments. In many cases, it was hard to know if someone is 'just not the right kind of person.' Committee members could not always pinpoint what it was in an applicant's demeanour, history, conversation, and/ or home that worried them.

The committee's experience with earlier cases inevitably shaped its later work, so that it might alter its standards in practice or reach decisions based on tacit understandings among its members. Once the co-op had opened, later selection decisions (for example, after a resident had moved out or if a member married) reflected, as well, the committee's evolving sense of what the co-op was like as a community, including its internal politics. This lived reality may have been clear to the committee members. But it remained largely implicit and was not formally taken into account, yet might provide the real reasons for their decisions.

We organize the following discussion of rejections according to the three general types of criteria employed in arriving at the decision: the co-op as enterprise; the co-op as association; the co-op as social housing, or in Poulin's terms the claim of a right to housing. None of the cases falls entirely into one of these categories. Indeed, in many the decision reflects conflict among two or more of the criteria.

Those making the selection decisions had not only to evaluate the relative importance of various criteria. They also had to assess how accurate their view of the applicant was likely to prove as a guide to his or her future conduct. The cases show committee members having to balance their assessments of applicants' strengths and weaknesses. Thus, they show to some degree the interpretive process through which such decisions were made.

The Co-op as Enterprise

People who were otherwise well qualified for acceptance into a co-op might be rejected because of doubts about their finances. For example, one couple who were members of another co-op applied to Windward and performed well during the interview. Their experience in the other co-op and as active members of their community suggested that they would work hard and give their time freely to Windward. They had, in the opinion of the interviewers, 'great potential' as neighbours and co-owners. But as tenants this self-employed couple was less attractive. They did not always pay their housing charges on time in the other co-op, nor were they forthcoming with what Windward considered to be 'credible income verification.' They were rejected; demonstrated financial soundness seemed to be crucial.

At both co-ops an applicant's demonstrated ability to pay housing charges on time was critical in selection decisions. People requesting subsidies and those paying full housing charges alike had to have good credit records. Moreover, they had to appear open and forthright in disclosing their financial affairs.

The Co-op as Association

To succeed in the selection process, applicants had to create the impression that they were community oriented. This was not simply a question of their actions as volunteer workers but also of their attitudes toward the co-op as a nascent community in its own right. Indeed, for some interviewers their attitudes and the likelihood of their contributing to the co-op could be judged from the relationship between two individuals. The formation of community begins at home. An interviewer observed, in recommending rejection, that one couple had 'not even formed community with the two of themselves. They [were] two independent, career-minded single people.'

All household members were expected to attend the interview, partly so that interviewers could gauge the quality of their domestic relationships. The apparent tone of these relationships suggested how applicants might fit in to the co-op. If they were not good neighbours to each other, how could they be expected to be good neighbours to others in the co-op?

In some cases, one applicant might seem likely to make a good neighbour, while his or her partner failed to convince the selection committee. Interviewers reported that one woman 'would be an acceptable neighbour' if she were applying just with her two children. But they could not recommend acceptance since she was applying with a partner the committee felt would not contribute to the co-op. Concerns that the partner would be a liability as a neighbour outweighed the potential contribution the woman might make in that domain.

The case of one single mother illustrates the importance attached to the committee's assessment of an applicant's likely commitment to the co-op. Willingness on the part of applicants to give time and concern to the co-op was taken as a good sign. This young woman had no history of volunteer experience to temper the committee's feeling that she would display 'no strong sense of commitment or involvement in [the co-op].'

As well, this case shows that how the applicant presented herself made a real difference. The interviewers reported: 'This applicant is a bit young and immature. Yes, she is friendly, pleasant, etc., but that's not enough ... She did not "sell" herself [as someone being interviewed could, e.g., at a job interview]. She did not make any great effort to tell us why she should be in the co-op, why she would be an asset to running Windward ... She gave the impression that she was interested in what the benefits of being in a co-op were, without making any effort to tell us that she was willing to give something, to make an effort herself.'

The language used by the interviewers to describe this case is revealing. Terms drawn from the market-place like 'sell,' 'asset,' 'benefits,' 'give something' threatened to make the applicant a commodity. At least metaphorically, she had to express herself in terms of exchange, that is, what she could offer the co-op in return for acceptance. Ironically, the less assertive applicant who did not manifest the style and language of the market-place might be rejected because she seemed unlikely to 'give something' to the co-op. Use of such terms shows the difficulty some co-op members had in finding ways of talking about cooperation. Too many of the models our society provides us with for talking about human relations take market relations as the norm.

Some applicants apparently saw the co-op as a potential landlord, based on their experience as renters. In the interview situation, they thus focused on those aspects of the co-op that were most narrowly concerned with housing. Yet interviewers thought of the co-op as much more than just housing and they did not see themselves as landlords. Looking for enthusiasm and commitment to community from the applicant, they might have misconstrued the applicant's behaviour and misunderstand her attitudes.

Special skills and the applicant's willingness to contribute those skills to the co-op could influence the selection committee's decision. For example, a physician willing to be on emergency call for residents with disabilities at Windward was accepted and even allowed to have a unit larger than that to which his household size entitled him. Yet a registered masseuse unwilling to consider giving her services for free to such residents was rejected. To the committee members she seemed mostly concerned with the benefits she and her son could gain from the co-op and not with what she could contribute. For the selection committee members, perhaps thinking of the co-op as being like an extended family, members' skills should be given freely, not treated as commodities. But the masseuse evidently felt that her skills were her livelihood; they were a commodity with exchange value. The committee members did not deny this but felt strongly that she should make them available without charge for the use of needy members.

In these new co-ops, the selection process created a unique opportunity to form what one member described as a 'community of like-minded people.' The commitment to include applicants in need of subsidized housing and, in the case of Windward, people with disabilities may have weakened somewhat the strain towards homogeneity. But the nostalgic ideal of the community of like-minded people can have a negative side. One disgruntled (but successful) applicant felt that the co-op's selection procedure tried to 'perpetuate its own,' if only because members felt more comfortable with people like themselves as neighbours. Yet different members meant different things by the phrase 'like themselves.' Some meant community oriented and tolerant of ethnic diversity, others a willingness to devote many hours to meetings or house proud or being a 'professional.'

The Claim of a Right to Housing

Cases in which applicants had a clear need for housing yet seemed weak in other areas posed special difficulties for selection committees. This sort of case can present particular problems for co-ops and their members. Institutionally and individually they are sincerely concerned with providing affordable housing. Furthermore, as noted above, co-ops receive subsidies, both direct and indirect, toward this end. Yet, selection committee members always must strive for a viable co-op, one that functions reasonably harmoniously, maintains and improves the property, and, not the least, pays its bills. Those in greatest need of affordable housing may not seem to be those most capable of contributing to the viability of the co-op.

Trying to reach these sometimes conflicting goals of housing those in need and maintaining a well-run co-op required Windward and Harbourside committee members selectively to emphasize certain criteria in rejecting some applications that, on other counts, appeared quite positive. Long discussions and considerable emotional involvement resulted from this tension. In the end, though sometimes with regrets, they seemed generally to opt for protecting the co-op. For example, Windward rejected one single mother who was living in an adults-only building and concealing the presence of her two sons from the landlord. The selection committee acknowledged the woman's housing need but felt she was not suited to Windward. The applicant 'did not know enough about co-op living, and we did not think that she was eager to find out. Even though she is in need of affordable housing, we believe this project is not for her.'

We lack further documentation on this case. But, at the least, it illustrates how the interviewers required applicants visibly to demonstrate an interest in and a willingness to learn about co-op living. They had to show that for them the co-op would be 'not just a home.' Otherwise, they were viewed as being interested 'only in housing' or as likely to be 'just tenants.' The co-op's need for involved, active members outweighed the woman's obvious need for housing.

Another case illustrates difficulties selection committees encountered in dealing with people in housing need who belong to stigmatized groups. A single mother with a history of health problems appealed Windward's rejection. She occupied a room in a boarding-house and wanted desperately to find a place where she could live with her young child. In her initial interview, she created the impression that she would be unable to communicate with other co-op members. She seemed not to listen or to heed suggestions. The interviewers' doubts about her mental stability were supported by references from people who knew her.

In responding to the woman's appeal, the co-op cited her health problems. They observed that Windward included residents with disabilities but not those with other health problems which might limit participation. Disability thus was defined to include physical conditions but not mental ones, for example, the developmentally mentally handicapped or people with psychiatric problems.

Some applicants who had physical disabilities and were in need of appropriate housing were disqualified. Attitude toward co-operative living was important. One man who was very unhappy in another co-op was turned down when he applied to Windward because of his lack of involvement in the co-op where he was living and because he seemed unwilling to 'turn his energies in a positive direction.' Another person, a quadriplegic, was rejected because of a lack of volunteer work. Still another was felt to be interested in Windward only because it was convenient to the athletics club around which his social life revolved.

A more complex case concerns a man of twenty-one, a quadriplegic as a result of an accident, who appealed his rejection at

Windward. The applicant was living in hospital and clearly needed affordable, accessible housing, which he wanted to share with his mother and sister. But his mother did most of the talking at the initial interview. His whole life, according to her, had been athletics prior to his accident. The young man seemed to the selection committee to be hesitant, shy, and apprehensive. Thus, the committee felt he was unlikely to get involved in the co-op. The fact that applying was his social worker's idea was taken as further evidence of his lack of enthusiasm for participating in Windward. The committee concluded that while he was 'needy of an accessible unit and seems to want to help out ... that's as far as it goes.' Here, again, potential contribution to the co-op, as inferred from the interview, seemed to outweigh demonstrated need for appropriate housing.

An Extended Case

The next case concerns a young single mother who was rejected by Harbourside co-op. We present it at greater length, first, to allow for a deeper exploration of several issues. Second, it gives a sense of the difficulty selectors had in resolving conflicts between applicants' needs for housing and the co-op's need for members who would participate and cooperate.

It should be borne in mind that nearly half the members of this co-op are on subsidy, including many single mothers. The speaker was a single woman who lived in the co-op. She began by noting that the young woman in question was one of two rejected applicants who had complained to their member of the provincial parliament. The interviewers thought she would not be likely to give much time to the community.

> I really didn't believe that she was going to be anything but a tenant. In her case, I mean, her situation was really bad. She was actually living at home but she was about nineteen or twenty and had just had a baby and the father [i.e., the applicant's father] had taken a really negative attitude towards that and so he had essentially sort of isolated her from the [home].

And you feel really badly about rejecting people like that ... but anyway the father had isolated her from the home ... She still had her room because she had nowhere else to go. From what she was saying, she didn't feel comfortable eating with them, and sometimes they didn't even bother to cook for her or set a place for her, things like that.

The interviewers felt torn. They recognized the applicant's need not only for a home but for a sense of belonging. Yet they had severe doubts about whether they wanted her as a neighbour and about whether she would participate in the co-op.

The case raises questions about how co-ops can put an important ideal into practice: namely that an improved, supportive environment makes personal growth possible. Many co-op members and resource group consultants believe that housing can make a crucial difference to people's lives, especially for women. But it is difficult to decide which powerless person will benefit from such a changed environment and which will not.

Although the speaker thought the applicant would be just a tenant, not a true co-op member, she wanted her to have every chance of being accepted. She was concerned also that the applicant should feel that she was dealt with fairly. The selectors reinterviewed the applicant at her parent's home.

The night we interviewed her [first] wasn't the best situation. But we felt that because of her situation we wanted to give her every possible chance and so she should be reinterviewed. And that was in fact what the committee did. But on the reinterview they still rejected her.

The actual conditions of the second interview strongly influenced the decision. On the night of the interview there was a party of some kind going on and a lot of noise and so on and the baby kept crying. And because of the party, well, she had the baby originally sleeping in her room, I guess, so she said that the only place that she could interview was in the kitchen, which frankly was a pigsty. I mean there were dishes in the sink that had to have been there for a week, for sure.

So one of the things, and this is where ... being the right kind of person comes in, one of the things we asked her about was ... who looks after the place, who does the cleaning, ... the housework, ... and it turned out she did nothing. And granted, on the one hand, she wasn't being made to feel very much at home or very welcome, but the fact that she'd been content to continue living in those conditions, I mean you know, and not doing anything about them, really bothered me.

For the interviewers, visiting the applicant's own bedroom was the *coup de grâce*.

And we happened, from my perspective, to be lucky enough to see the bedroom too, because the baby kept crying and originally she brought him into the kitchen, but there wasn't really any place for her to sit down. She was sitting on a stool that was sort of fibre matting or something like that, most of which had rotted out, so she was sitting on a hole largely and she couldn't really deal with the baby properly. So we ended up going into her room, which was slightly better than the kitchen but not a whole lot. But we were really, really concerned about that because you didn't see her taking the kind of pride in her home ... that we wanted to see.

Thus, the applicant's declared willingness to contribute to the co-op seemed untrustworthy in the sense that she seemed just to be saying what she thought the interviewers wanted to hear.

And then as I say there was the fact ... when people tell you, when she said, oh yes, she'd be willing to help in the co-op and so ... But when somebody is living in those conditions and isn't even sort of cleaning up, you know, her own environment, I find it hard to be convinced that you're going to suddenly do all of these wonderful things in the co-op.

In this case the committee recognized the applicant's real need for better housing. But she was judged not to be taking sufficient responsibility for her environment and herself. Yet she was living with her parents, who clearly did not want her to be there. Because the committee interviewed her at home, they were able to see things they never would have known if the interview had been conducted at the co-op or the offices of the resource group. From what they saw at her home they inferred her character and, even though she was only nineteen or twenty, concluded she could or would (it is not clear which) not change. Committee members felt bad but did not regret their decision.

Interpreting Rejection

The cases of rejection we have discussed in this chapter raise questions about interpretation, conflict over use values, and class differences.

First, those charged with selecting new members continually had to grapple with an interpretive question: would an applicant make a good member of this co-op? While they had a broader view of the situation than did the applicants, members of selection committees knew all too well that their information about potential members was limited. They had to interpret what they saw and heard; measure what an applicant said in an interview against his or her history of community service; read the applicant's demeanour and home as a set of signs. Skilful applicants in a tight housing market might try to say what they think the selection committee wanted to hear. They could easily provide 'correct' answers to standard interview questions about, for example, their willingness to participate in co-op committee work.

So those involved with the selection procedure at Harbourside and Windward opted for a richer, more rounded strategy which they felt was better suited to choosing one's neighbours. Yet at the same time they employed fairly specific indicators (such as, amount of community work) to guard against excessive subjectivity and perhaps to provide a defence for their choices. The practice of interviewing people in their homes exemplified this tension. It contextualized and enriched the more formal material gathered in the selection process yet objectified and externalized selection criteria. Disorder in a home was more easily identified and defended as a basis for rejection than the vague feeling that an applicant was a disordered person.

Also, choosing to interview applicants in their homes points to the importance that those involved in the selection process placed on pride of place over other use values. This raises again the issue of interpretation. By and large, good neighbours were assumed to be tidy people. A concern with 'keeping the place up' was evident in the selection process (and was a persistent theme in our interviews with residents) despite the lack of exchange value in the co-op that often is argued to underlie conventional homeowners' interests in maintaining their property.

Homes were more than a window into the character of the applicants, they were assumed to shape that character. Homes and household objects 'constitute an ecology of signs that reflects as well as *shapes* the pattern of the owner's self,' as Csikszentmihalyi and Rochberg-Halton (1981: 17) put it.

In the extended case above, the interviewers construed disorder in the home as evidence for their interpretation of character. Dirty dishes in the sink, a chair whose matting had rotted away, a noisy party going on, the baby crying, nowhere for the mother to sit with the baby while talking to the interviewers, all signalled a person who had no pride of place. As well, they seem to have signified that she would or could not change. Perhaps if she had visibly taken some control over her parents' home, her participating in the co-op might have seemed more likely. Dishes 'that had to have been there [i.e., in the sink] for a week' spoke louder than words.

The interviewers interpreted the home as a system of signs that not only reflected but had shaped and continued to shape the applicant's character. Along with the rest of the situation, this made the interviewers feel she was unlikely to change. The messy home and her not doing the housework sounded an alarm for them. Physical disorder and social disorder (even if not of one's own making – for example, the noisy party) implied personal disorder. To be a good neighbour and a productive co-op member, a disordered person is 'just not the right kind.'

Another issue raised by these cases reflects the way the co-ops were organized. They were run democratically but on a middle-class bureaucratic model, with many committees, officers, meetings, memos, and the like. Must 'the right kind of person' possess the experience and skills required by that model? The reluctant answer, at least in these co-ops, was a qualified 'yes': reluctant because this meant accepting more people who could afford other housing than some in government and the cooperative movement would prefer; and qualified in that 'yes' meant heterogeneity but did not mean excluding those in real housing need.

The housing shortage in Toronto was such that co-ops could be very selective. This allowed them to accept only the applicants in need of affordable housing they deemed most likely to participate in the co-op. Those who were most dependent on government assistance to pay their housing charges often lacked the opportunity and time to develop the skills to be effective committee members. To ensure that a co-op is neither run exclusively by people who are affluent enough to pay for their own housing nor run poorly by lower-income residents without sufficient cooperative or bureaucratic experience, the selection process can be used to 'cream off' the potentially subsidized applicants most likely to contribute effectively.

The issue of bias in favour of middle-class skills troubled people in the cooperative sector. One consultant who worked on the Windward project noted, 'Interviews themselves are biased towards articulate people, people who are good at writing exams, people who read from the literature that they are given or pick up from ... the orientation meeting, anyone relatively astute can figure out exactly what answers [the interviewer] wants.' Later, he wondered: 'But if they had some organizational experience, yes it does make a bit of a difference, however, who are you excluding by that? You are probably excluding a higher portion of lower-income people or ... people with a different background, who are not necessarily, but I suspect proportionally, who may not be as involved in service clubs. Single mothers with children for example are not likely to have the time to be involved. You may cream off the very best, the most articulate, the most energetic ... people from [the] lower class ... That's a concern of mine.'

Many of those involved in the cooperative housing movement have felt that the way to deal with this problem is to transfer the needed skills to those who lack them. They have felt that the co-op environment can provide this opportunity. But of course this can only be done after people have moved in. It does not improve people's chances in the selection process. They argued that the selection process could be less rigorous because co-op members would learn to participate in their housing. Whether they have ever participated in other kinds of volunteer work would not matter.

Some went so far as to say that it might be better to have no selection process at all. Perhaps the criteria for acceptance have little bearing on whether a person will prove to be a good co-op member. And perhaps cooperative 'know-how' can be developed in any population. But even those in the cooperative sector who held this extreme position acknowledged that 'you can and should legitimately exclude some people some of the time.'

Other consultants argued that the need for affordable housing was so acute that perhaps concern with the amount and quality of member participation should be put aside. They should build as much housing as possible and be much less concerned about the ideals of voluntarism, community, and cooperation. Still others wondered if perhaps there are not different ways to organize co-ops so that people feel they have control of their own housing or if there are better ways to transfer the needed skills (see chapter 9).

Later Member Selection

There are important differences in the member selection process between new and established co-ops. Some of these are evident in contrasting Windward and Harbourside in 1989 with member selection at the time of initial occupancy. One difference, obviously, was that the volume of acceptances declined as the co-op filled. Second, maintaining a waiting-list, which was crucial during the construction period and initial rent-up, continued to be important to the financial viability of each co-op. Another difference is that in the later years selection committees made use of their experience with earlier cases and a diffuse sense of what the co-op was like as a community. This had positive and negative aspects which we will discuss.

A final difference is that, after three years, in both co-ops the member selection committee's sense of its own importance was stronger than ever. At Harbourside this led to concern with careful replacement of committee members to ensure fairness in the selection process. At Windward, it was connected to tensions between the board of directors and the committee.

The volume of business that the member selection committees in both co-ops handled declined once the rent-ups were complete. But the committees remained crucial to the co-ops as enterprises. They had to maintain active waiting-lists so that a new occupant would be ready to take over a unit as soon as an old member moved out.

Each co-op kept an external and an internal waiting-list for units of all sizes. As well, at Windward the lists noted the degrees of modification that applicants with disabilities required. One problem at Windward was that virtually all the one-bedroom units were allocated to people with disabilities. There was little turnover among these units. Many applicants had to be rejected simply because it was so unlikely that the one-bedroom units they needed would be available.

The internal list consisted of members already living in the co-op who wanted to move to other units. Generally, these had priority over applicants from outside the co-op. The lists were divided into applicants who could pay full housing charges and those who required subsidies.

Keeping good waiting-lists was a juggling act. If the lists were too long, applicants would get discouraged and drift away by the time a vacancy occurred. If the lists were too short, the coordinator would have to scramble to fill a vacant unit.

By 1988, a major problem had arisen with member selection at Windward. The board of directors was dissatisfied because the

committee had failed to process applications. This was connected
to a disagreement between the committee and the board on subsidy policy (see chapter 7). From the coordinator's viewpoint:

> One of the big accusations against the committee was they weren't
> doing any interviews. The waiting-lists were getting shorter and
> shorter, and – I don't know – nobody was left on those waiting-
> lists. We were getting vacancies, and we were having to fill vacancies
> practically on the spur of the moment – find an applicant, interview
> him, and move him in.
>
> It got to the point where the president of the co-op in a general
> meeting sort of snidely referred to the membership committee as
> the culprits in the whole affair, when he asked all the members,
> 'If you've got any friends, can you get them to apply? We need
> somebody real quick, we've got a vacancy coming up.' You know,
> and this in the midst of the worst housing crisis in the country.

It was especially hard to find occupants with disabilities for
Windward's modified units who did not need housing charge
assistance. Dan Fast, Windward's coordinator, was tearing his
hair out in the summer of 1988:

> I've been complaining for practically a year to [the member selec-
> tion committee] that we were in trouble if a modified apartment
> became vacant. They just kept believing that it would never hap-
> pen. So now we have a vacant modified unit. The problem with
> filling it – you'd figure with the problems of housing for disabled
> people it wouldn't be hard to fill – but we don't have any subsidy
> money to provide. We have a fixed subsidy pool. It's allocated
> completely already to households on permanent subsidy. So I have
> to find a person who is handicapped who doesn't need subsidy and
> needs a particular set of modifications that that apartment has.

When we spoke with Fast a few months later, he told us what
had happened next:

> I contacted the networks in Toronto and handicapped people and

said could you find somebody that could afford the full rent and they found – I got a call from Victoria. I also had a call from Winnipeg and in both cases it was a couple that was getting married right at that moment and planning to honeymoon as they motored across the country to Toronto.

In both cases [one of] the couple was in a wheelchair and in both cases they had jobs already offered to them in Toronto. They were looking for a place to stay and they needed a modified unit. Right at the same moment.

And so Victoria got here first. They got the unit. Although the other one looked like a more likely bet. They had a return address and a phone number back in Winnipeg. Victoria, I had to deal with a phone booth. They were going to be at a phone booth at certain times so I didn't have many expectations about that one. But they turned out great and are very active in the co-op now. They got that unit. The other ones arrived later, called up and said, 'We're in a trailer camp, what can you do for us?' I said, 'Sorry the unit went.'

After the co-op was fully occupied, members worked with more clearly established, although not necessarily entirely explicit or fair, criteria. Thus, when they did assess applicants, they could do so more rapidly and easily. Both the Harbourside and Windward committees developed a working rapport among their members. By 1989, they had worked together longer than any board of directors. They thought they knew the co-op well. As one Windward committee member commented, this seemed to encourage conflict with the board. 'There seems to be a natural struggle for power between the member selection committee and the board of directors because of the committee's stable sense of what the co-op is like.'

Not only did the committees have a strong sense of what each co-op was like, they had high hopes for the development of community. As a consultant with Lantana (the resource group that developed Windward) observed, member selection committees, especially initial ones, tend to be composed of people deeply committed to the co-op project. They have high standards and high expectations. 'They are often looking for more than I think is necessary, both in the selection process and after they move in. They are quite frequently the ones who are the most into policing participation. They feel a certain amount of responsibility, and that is communicated to the people: "We brought them in and now look at them! Why aren't they all participating the way we did?" '

As the committees became more experienced they also became somewhat callous, leading to concerns about 'pigeonholing' and impression management. The Lantana consultant commented on this tendency:

I don't think that [the member selection committee at Windward] was discriminatory. But there is something that happens, not only to them but perhaps to any member selection committee ... They can become fairly tough and sob stories don't necessarily work.

Sob stories often may be just that. But they may also sometimes be truth. So the member selection process is always one that, frankly, most people who walked into it near the end, after a group has become fairly experienced, would be a little shocked by. Because it sounds gossipy. You sit there and you say, 'Okay. Who's this fellow? How many people? Where do we put their kids [in that unit]? What do they live like? Were they brats? Did they behave? What's their income? What's their credit rating? Have they been bankrupt?' It can sound like a grilling process.

Apart from everything else, apart from the degree to which this may or may not be appropriate, it also depends on the interviewer. If you're a good interviewer and relatively self-confident, you come back to the group and you don't waste time on description. You say, 'This is a great family of three – a single mother, two kids. The kids are really together. One of them wants to be a lawyer.' You know you sow [the seeds] ... The whole group says 'Fine, good.' They get in on the basis of the recommendation.

If it's an interviewer ... who is timid or equivocal [the results are different]. 'Well, gee, she said she has participated in this but that was five years ago. He said he wanted to go to law school but, you know, he's having difficulty with history so I think that's probably a pipe dream. And the younger kid, you know, is a nice kid but I thought that he was probably into booze. [So] maybe I'll recommend them and maybe I won't.' Well the group is going to sit there and say, 'Oh, no, this sounds too dicey!' So the process is not one of absolute justice.

At Windward, some complained about injustice of this sort. As committee members became more experienced, they grew tougher, more perfunctory, and more subjective. One case in particular led to charges of personal bias. The sister of one of the founding board members applied for membership in Windward in 1988. She was rejected. We were told that

> The applicant happened to be the sister of one of the real big shots on the board of directors – a fellow named [Chad Quentin] – and Chad was not only involved in the [Windward] project from way, way back, but ... he handled himself in a very powerful way through the whole history of the project. Chad's sister applied. And the people on the committee that they wanted to do the interview were two of the old guard who have always been diametrically opposed to Chad, and hated his guts.
>
> What happened was that they interviewed the sister and they made a report back to the committee to the effect that she was a bad applicant. The way [one of the interviewers] made the report, she kept dripping venom every time she referred to how this was Chad Quentin's sister, as though everybody in the room should appreciate that this [relationship] was enough to explain everything. It was all in the tone of voice.

The committee voted to reject the applicant. Quentin's sister responded to the rejection angrily. She sent a three-page letter in which, as one person involved in the case put it, 'She lambasted the co-op and decided maybe she didn't want to live there after all!'

The board of directors overruled the member selection committee's rejection on the grounds that the applicant had not received a fair interview. It directed the committee to reinterview the woman and not to include the person who had made the initial report on the interviewing team. After the second interview, the team reported directly to the board. They recommended acceptance. She went on the waiting- list. By the end of our study she had been offered several units but had turned all of them down for a variety of personal reasons.

This episode drew the board's attention to the possibility of serious bias in the way the member selection committee was handling cases. In the coordinator's words: 'The board of directors decided they had to deal with this membership committee. [It] was going to have to be told – taught – about such things as not allowing personal bias to enter into the thing. At this point the committee chairman resigned (for reasons only partly connected to this case). The board appointed one of its own members as a watchdog on the selection committee. And the president began reconsidering the committee's role in the co-op. As one co-op member commented, it was time to face 'some leftover issues that were never dealt with – about power, autonomy, [and] credibility.' We discuss this period of Windward's development in more detail in chapter 9.

At Harbourside, relations between the board and the member selection committee never were as tense. But the committee had a strong sense of its own importance there as well. By 1989, its members were concerned to replace themselves. They felt that it was unwise to remain on the committee for more than about three years. They accepted the co-op sector's view expressed at a 1988 forum on member selection we attended: committees should frequently replace members. Otherwise they tend to become rigid. But they also recognized that the member selection process was a crucial part of the co-op's control over community formation. Rather than simply allowing anyone who expressed an interest to join the committee, retiring members tried to shape things informally. They encouraged people who they felt were fair minded. Those who had difficulty keeping matters confidential or who had 'right wing' views were discouraged.

Conclusion

The selection process itself, we feel, contributes to the successful formation of cooperative communities that transcend people's different positions in the housing market. Perhaps because of the concern in the selection process with participation, those who were most involved in running the two co-ops included both subsidized and non-subsidized members. Cleavages along such lines did emerge in other contexts but the lines on many issues were drawn in other ways as well.

In this chapter, we have explored some of the conflicts, ambiguities, and interpretive difficulties that confronted selection committee members as they decided that certain applicants were just 'not right' for their cooperative. We have tried to address these issues by placing the cases in a context that makes the decisions understandable but does not reduce their complexity.

The essential context was the attempt to imagine a community, one in which one's own access to and enjoyment of housing might conflict with the consequences of an open-door policy based on need. Disorderly people and people who are not 'house proud' potentially affected one's enjoyment of one's own housing, especially in multiple housing. People who do not participate make the burdens of those who do greater. People who do not pay their rent put the whole co-op in danger.

Social class, both of committee members and of applicants, may influence selection decisions. But such factors were not sufficient for understanding the decisions. Rejections based on poor credit ratings or on refusals to contribute skills to the co-op raise issues of interpretation and conflicting use values. Those that involved the rejection of people in serious housing need who were viewed as unlikely to participate in the co-op raise these issues even more strongly. They emphasize the extent to which the creation of co-ops reflects conflicts over use values, that is, the varied meanings and satisfactions of housing.

In later member selection decisions, the tension between choosing the right kind of neighbours and keeping access to the co-op open, especially for those most in need of affordable (and at Windward, accessible) housing, remained. But once subsidies were fully allocated, there could be little movement on waiting-lists for those needing housing-charge assistance.

Deciding among those who could afford the rent became easier, or at least more mechanical, as the member selection committees gained experience. But the committees had to be willing to process applications. At Windward, this was a problem. Furthermore, experienced interviewers could make strong cases for applicants they favoured and minimize the likelihood of acceptance for others. Questions of personal bias arose at Windward. These contributed to an explosive period in relations between the board of directors and the committee.

Member selection is one basic way in which people can exert control over a co-op community. This is much more than a question of exerting control by choosing one's neighbours. The consequences of choosing and being chosen also are important. Those who have passed through the screening process and joined the co-op feel they have qualified for membership in a way that is different from just renting an apartment. Those doing the selecting feel a sense of responsibility for the people they have accepted. They encourage new members to participate, and worry about low levels of involvement. In both co-ops, the member selection committees recognized how fundamental their role was, not only to choosing initial members who would be good neighbours at Harbourside and Windward, but to maintaining those co-op communities over the years.

CHAPTER SIX

Beyond Barriers

Bringing Laurie Home

'The Quad with the Bod' read Carl Dowling's yellow T-shirt the day we first interviewed him in July 1987. Carl had been a quadriplegic since March 1980 when, as a twenty-eight-year old former policeman in Thunder Bay, Ontario, he went out one winter night for some fun. He raced down a ski hill in an inner tube, hit a mogul, spun fifteen feet in the air, crashed to the ground, and broke his neck in two places. For the next seven years, he lived in hospitals and chronic care institutions in Thunder Bay and Toronto.

The lack of housing for people with disabilities in Toronto frustrated Carl. He waited in a chronic care hospital for several years for an apartment to become available that offered the high level of attendant care he needed. When there were no openings, he became an active volunteer. He began to organize his own project to provide housing with attendant care.[1] Through this work he met people on the founding board of directors at Windward. Carl was attracted to Windward because it offered accessible, subsidized housing with attendant care. When his own project ran into insurmountable difficulties, he applied to Windward. He knew little about housing cooperatives when he applied, but had an image of them as housing for poor people, overcrowded, and dirty. He has been pleasantly surprised.

By the time of our first interview, Carl had lived in Windward only five months, but he was already a keen supporter of the co-op. He enjoyed furnishing his sixth-floor apartment. After so many years living in a hospital room, virtually all the furniture was new: a large, white sectional sofa, stereo, and bookshelves with family pictures. The big windows in his living-room looked out over sailboats moored at a yacht club.[2] As we talked, Carl's daughter Laurie, a sandy-haired ten-year-old, played poker on his Apple computer. A grey kitten bounced from her lap to Carl's, then launched an attack on the tape recorder used for the interview. The scene was deceptively ordinary – a Dad, his daughter, a kitten, a hot summer day in the city.

For Carl, the ordinariness was wonderful. 'First of all the mix of people, the disabled integrated among the able-bodied was a great concept ... The non-disabled members have just accepted the disabled people so well and they're learning more about different disabilities by being surrounded by them. It's just super.'

'Let me give you an idea of what the co-op spirit is like,' said Carl, and he began to talk about Laurie. She was visiting from Alberta where she lived with her mother. This was the first time Carl had seen her in more than six years. For the first time he had a place for her to stay. As soon as he moved into his apartment in Windward, Carl phoned his daughter and invited her to visit for a couple of weeks in the summer. Then he realized he did not have enough money to pay for her air ticket:

I'm on Canada disability pension and it would take me two years to save up that kind of money. So I had to phone Laurie back and tell her that I was sorry, that I just couldn't raise the money to bring her down.

Well, later that night some neighbours on the third floor, friends of mine, came over for a cup of tea. They asked when Laurie was coming and I told the story. I pulled out some albums and I was showing some pictures of Laurie taken when I was first injured and Laurie was two. I had to call one of the staff members to drain my urine bag, and while I was out of the room, these friends stole two pictures out of my album.

They went around the building showing people the pictures and raised enough money to bring Laurie home. They raised $576 in one night. When they left my place they had said, 'Don't worry, you'll get to see your kid!' And I said, 'Yeah, I'll save up. I'll get her here.' [Later] they came up and said, 'Get on the phone. Your kid's coming home. We've got the money for you.' I was just flying. I was just so flabbergasted. I mean I've only *known these people four or five months. They and the rest of the people in the co-op are just incredible.*

Co-ops and People with Disabilities

In this chapter we present some background on the people, like Carl Dowling, with varying degrees of mobility impairment who lived at Windward during our study. The co-op provided alternative housing and independent living for some people who would otherwise have had to find the care they needed in institutions. For others, such as couples in which one partner had a physical disability, the co-op was especially attractive as an integrated housing environment in which the mix of people with and without disabilities went without notice.

The rest of this chapter addresses three questions. First, is there something peculiar to cooperatives as forms of social organization that encourages independent living, integrated housing, and social interaction among people with different levels of physical abilities? We suggest that member control, security of tenure, and residents' involvement are important positive factors.

Second, we explore the causes and extent of satisfaction with life in the co-op among Windward members with disabilities. An extended case of dissatisfaction tempers the enthusiastic views of most such residents. The final question is: How much social interaction took place between non-disabled residents and those with disabilities? Committee meetings, neighbourliness, and social events within the co-op encouraged social interaction. Yet the focus for most Windward residents' lives continued to be outside the co-op in friends, family, work, school, or other social activities.

The real success of the co-op as integrated housing, we suggest, is that social interaction within the co-op was not especially intense. It was just 'normal.' As among able-bodied residents, some people with disabilities enjoyed socializing within the co-op, and others did not. We conclude that there were two keys to the strong satisfaction that many people with disabilities expressed. These were, first, realistic expectations about what living at Windward would be like and, second, willingness to become involved and play active roles in co-op life.

Co-op Members with Disabilities

People with physical disabilities were as diverse in their backgrounds and lifestyles as other Windward residents. Of the 158 members of the co-op in 1989, twenty-seven had disabilities. That is, there was at least one person with a disability in twenty-six of the one hundred units. A few of those with disabilities could walk with assistance; the others relied on manual or electric wheelchairs. Members' disabilities included those resulting from multiple sclerosis, muscular dystrophy, cerebral palsy, rheumatoid arthritis, and, more commonly, accidents. Ten were quadriplegics; the others were paraplegic or used wheelchairs for other reasons. The extent of people's mobility varied considerably within and between these categories. As well as those whose mobility was severely restricted, there also were wheelchair athletes.

Along with the variety of disabilities came a wide range of incomes, educations, and housing backgrounds. Not surprisingly, incomes tended to be lower for those households in which one member had a disability. Fully 65 per cent reported annual gross incomes of less than $30,000 whereas only 29 per cent of the other households had incomes in this range (see Table 6.1). Among the other households, 45 per cent reported incomes of $50,000 or more a year. Only 15 per cent of households with a mobility-impaired member earned such large incomes.

Educational levels among people with disabilities overall were lower than among the able-bodied members' which possibly reflected more difficult access to educational opportunities. Only 45 per cent of mobility-impaired members had more than a high school diploma, compared with 79 per cent of the other members of Windward (see Table 6.2).[3]

Some accident victims, like Carl Dowling, spent years living in institutions before moving to Windward. Others with limited

TABLE 6.1
Relationship of mobility status and annual gross income per
household (Windward co-op 1989)

Mobility status of household members	Less than $30,000 (%)	$30,000 or more (%)
No disability	29	71
Some disability	65	35

TABLE 6.2
Relationship of mobility status and educational level
(Windward co-op 1989)

Mobility status	High school or less (%)	More than high school (%)
No disability	21	79
Some disability	55	45

mobility from birth had always lived at home with a parent or other caregiver. Still others shared their home with a non-disabled spouse. There were eleven couples in the co-op in which one partner had limited mobility. In one married couple at Windward both partners had disabilities.

Co-op members with disabilities who were living away from home for the first time and those moving out of institutions faced a particular sort of adjustment. They had to actively take control of their own care needs, whether this meant doing things for themselves or directing their own attendant care. In other words they had to develop the necessary skills for 'independent living.'

Independent Living and Integrated Housing for People with Disabilities

Efforts, often of people with disabilities themselves, to make university campuses more accessible for students with physical disabilities led to the development of the independent-living movement in the United States. Over the years its focus has broadened, backed by legislation beginning with the Rehabilitation Act of 1973. Advocates contrast the paradigms of rehabilitation and independent living. In the older rehabilitation paradigm the problem was assumed to be with the person. He or she was led to take on the dependent role of patient and to believe that success depended on following doctors' instructions. For the independent-living movement, the patient-doctor relationship is an obstacle rather than the key to success. In this paradigm 'the problem resides in an environment that includes the rehabilitation process, the physical environment, and the social control mechanisms of society-at-large. To cope with these environmental barriers, the disabled person must shed the patient or client role for the consumer role' (Crewe and Zola 1983: 22).

Attendant care is an important part of the independent-living approach. In the rehabilitation paradigm the emphasis was on self-care. No matter how long a task required, 'I can do it myself' was the goal. But in the independent-living approach 'a person who can get dressed in fifteen minutes with human assistance and then be off for a day of work is more independent than the person who takes two hours to dress and then remains homebound' (ibid.: 24). The disabled person becomes a consumer who directs the provision of the attendant care he or she needs.

A requirement for acceptance at Windward was that disabled members had to be able to direct their own attendant care. Participation Apartments, which provided the attendant care in Windward, operated out of an office in the co-op. As its name implies, the attendant care service was based on consumer participation in its management. Participation Apartments provided assistance to twelve co-op members whose care needs ranged from 'low' to 'high.' The provision of attendant care made it possible for people who need assistance to live independently outside of an institution in housing that was integrated into the community.

The social integration of co-op members with and without disabilities is linked to the more general trend toward 'normalization' or deinstitutionalization, with the related political, economic, and attitudinal changes it represents. 'These concepts [of normalization or deinstitutionalization], when applied to the disabled would suggest that the physically and mentally disabled should be assisted in achieving their *maximum potential* for independent living. Thus, the disabled person (and his family) would approach as *closely as possible* the normative housing arrangements of society as a whole' (Medicus Canada 1982: 65; emphasis in original).

The related concept of integrated housing assumes that people with disabilities should have the right to live under the same conditions as the able-bodied.4 They should have housing that is accessible, has good support services, is mixed in among the able-bodied, and that allows them to live in the residential arrangements they choose (that is, as a single person, a family, etc.). As Konecny (cited in Medicus Canada 1982: 66) points out, 'Integrated housing is more an environmental concept than a physical entity.'

One of the goals of integrated housing is to reduce dependency and institutionalization (Canadian Paraplegic Association 1974: 8). The contrast between chronic care institutions and integrated housing was strikingly apparent to Carl Dowling, whose daughter's visit to the co-op began this chapter. How well did Windward satisfy his housing needs? 'It's like heaven,' he said,

I can't think of any other way of describing it. When you've been in a hospital or an institution for seven years, you know, this is just like heaven.

I feel so much more relaxed. I have my privacy now. I have my independence. I come and go as I please. I have people over as late as I want. I can play my stereo past ten or eleven o'clock. And the whole transition from institution to this apartment took about two hours! There's a saying that institutionalization is addictive, the longer someone's in one the more addicted they become to it. They become so dependent on the institution and they're almost afraid to leave it, because every day they know they're going to get up and have breakfast with the same group of people. They can have lunch with that same group of people, and they're going to watch TV after supper with the same group of people. They go through this day after day after day. I'm just thankful that I never got addicted to that institution. I couldn't get out of there quick enough.

Institutions such as Carl Dowling described have been viewed as 'the most visible obstacles to normal functioning' for they 'isolate people with disabilities from normal integration with the mainstream of life' (Nelson-Walker 1981: 95). In contrast, the housing environment at Windward obliged able-bodied members and those with disabilities alike to participate in the operation of the co-op. What is it about a housing cooperative, as a social form, that *should* encourage integration of nondisabled people and those with disabilities? How well has this particular co-op satisfied its members with disabilities? How well has it worked out in terms of social interaction between people with different levels of physical ability?

Housing Cooperatives as a Form of Integrated Housing

As a social form, housing cooperatives are consistent with the goals of integrated housing and seem likely to encourage social interaction between able-bodied members and those with disabilities. One comparative study of four projects in western Canada concluded that a housing cooperative developed by a combination of people with disabilities and others provided the 'most suitable habitat.' The authors (Communitas Inc. 1981: 67) observed that the cooperative model 'comes closest to ensuring direct control of the corporation by the disabled, accountability, responsiveness to changing needs of members, security of tenure, integration with non-disabled members, and appropriate other services.'

The involvement of potential residents is an important aspect of the development of housing cooperatives and people with disabilities can easily be incorporated into this process. A number of studies have found that the more active a role people with disabilities play in the development of their own housing, the more likely the project is to be successful (ibid.: 67; Medicus Canada 1982: 112).

Member control is a fundamental principle of cooperatives in general. For people with disabilities operating within an independent-living framework this is especially important. Establishing a sense of control over their housing is part of trying to take charge of other aspects of their own lives.

Security of tenure obviously is important, especially for residents who may want to make additional modifications to their units at their own expense. Cooperatives like Windward reinforced security of tenure with the availability of subsidies so that a household's rent could be geared to its income. Limiting housing charges to no more than 30 per cent of a household's gross income was beneficial to those people whose limited mobility might also limit their incomes.

Finally, the obligation to participate in committee work encourages social interaction among all members. In theory at least, 'co-operatives can allow for integration to occur between persons with a disability and those who have none. Since they are self-initiated and managed, ... there is more control and responsibility placed in the hands of the members' (Besruky 1984: 10).

How Satisfied Are Residents with Disabilities?

One aim of our research at Windward was to learn from members with disabilities themselves how satisfied they were with living in the co-op both as a physical and a social environment. The social dimensions of Canadian cooperatives and non-profit housing projects that include residents with disabilities have received less attention than their physical features. For example, an evaluation of Auberge co-op in Ottawa, the first housing co-op in Canada for people with disabilities, mainly addressed the accessibility features of the ten houses in the project, concluding that its social and attitudinal success was too difficult to assess without baseline data (Johnson 1982).[5] In part because we followed households from the time Windward opened, we were able to assess residents' satisfaction with both the physical and social features of the co-op.

In each of the three years of the study, we interviewed members with disabilities from eight households. Because of turnover we had to replace two participants each year but we were able to work with six of the households for the entire period. We supplemented interview data with a survey of the entire membership in September 1989 (see note 3). Our findings fall into two categories: the physical form, or Windward as accessible housing, and the social form, or Windward as a cooperative.

Satisfaction with Windward's Accessibility

People's expectations make a great deal of difference to their levels of residential satisfaction. Kathryn Boschen (1984) has argued that this may be especially true for traumatically injured people with disabilities. She uses a model based on the notion of 'person-environment fit' to predict such people's happiness, adjustment, and well-being 'by the congruence between an individual's desires and the resources or attributes of the environment.' While our study is not a test of her model and the disabilities of many Windward residents did not result from accidents, the concept of person-environment fit provides a way of thinking about the different degrees of satisfaction – and dissatisfaction – with Windward as accessible housing.

According to our survey, for 45 per cent of the members with disabilities accessible housing was the main reason they joined the co-op. Anticipated affordability, which (at 34 per cent) was the leading reason non-disabled members gave for joining, ranked first for 25 per cent of those with disabilities. While 40 per cent of the able-bodied members said that the principal reason they continued to live at Windward is *affordability*, 40 per cent of those with disabilities chose *accessibility*.

By and large, members with disabilities were satisfied, but not as satisfied as the others. Only 60 per cent of the respondents with disabilities reported that they were fairly or very satisfied with living in the co-op, compared with 75 per cent of the non-disabled residents. One-quarter of those with disabilities and 13 per cent of the other respondents said they were dissatisfied. This overall assessment involved satisfaction with the co-op in general, not just as accessible housing.

For members with disabilities ratings of the accessibility of their units were higher than their overall satisfaction levels. Units were rated as good or excellent by 70 per cent of disabled respondents; only 15 per cent rated them as poor. This suggests, as we will explore shortly, that dissatisfied members with disabilities were bothered more by some of the social aspects of co-op living than by the housing itself.

Some were dissatisfied with the lack of amenities in the neighbourhood, as were able-bodied residents. Shopping was a problem for members without cars, for there was nowhere to buy even a carton of milk within about a mile of the co-op. As among the able-bodied members, some people with disabilities complained about the location, with its noisy fireworks displays and summer crowds. Yet others enjoyed the vibrant activity of the waterfront and easy access to events at Harbourfront, the Skydome stadium, and the Canadian National Exhibition.

When the co-op first opened many people with disabilities had complaints. There were numerous accessibility problems. Elevator button panels were the wrong height. The front door was too steeply ramped. The garage entrance was too low to admit vans modified for people with disabilities. But most defects were corrected within the first few years. By the end of our study the only area of the co-op that continued to be the subject of complaints was access to the courtyard, a problem that the installation of an automatic door opener later solved.

Some units needed further modification to better suit their residents' needs. In 1989, a grant was obtained to provide up to $5,000 per unit for additional modifications although there were income limitations on recipients. Some members who could not qualify for a grant were reluctant to pay for modifications to a unit they did not own. For them, lack of equity was a problem. If they could have sold their unit upon leaving the co-op, the modifications might have seemed worthwhile. But, as the survey results indicate, residents with disabilities by and large were satisfied with the accessibility of their housing. Moreover, all but one of the people with disabilities we interviewed spoke positively about most aspects of the building's accessibility. Windward's resources exceeded the expectations of members like Carl Dowling who had spent years in chronic care hospitals. In terms of person-environment fit, for such people it was 'like heaven.'

But one woman we spoke with was deeply disappointed with Windward. Maria Etzioni liked to speak her mind. When Windward won an award for accessible design in 1987, she was featured in a Toronto newspaper article complaining that the award was undeserved. Each of the three years that we met, Maria spoke articulately of her dissatisfaction with the co-op. She even wrote a cheerful note on the anonymous survey form with which we ended the research and signed it, 'Still Unhappy.'

Maria was a vivacious, dark-haired young woman who worked full-time as a civil servant, spoke at least three languages, and used a wheelchair. In 1986, she married Howard Unger, also a civil servant. He was a quadriplegic requiring medium to high attendant care. They married in anticipation of moving into Windward, which they thought 'sounded like Utopia.' Howard lived in Oak Street co-op in Toronto where he had attendant care, but his unit was a small one-bedroom. Maria lived in a two-bedroom apartment in a high-rise where some units on each floor were accessible but there was no attendant care. Windward offered attendant care and the couple could have a two-bedroom apartment.

Maria and Howard chose a unit on the ground floor. She had lived in high rises and was tired of waiting for elevators. 'What the heck,' she thought, 'Let's get the first floor. Then we can just zip out the door.'

Maria's expectations were high partly because she had lived in comfortable accessible housing elsewhere in the city. But also she thought that the people developing Windward would be very responsive to the housing needs of those with disabilities. Mobility-impaired people were active members of the founding board of directors. Maria was pleased with the people who handled her application. 'They were listening. They were willing. They answered all my questions.' When members met with the architect just before moving in, Maria said, 'There I was with my hand up asking all my questions and everything was yes this and yes that. Are you going to have this? No problem. And are you going to have that? No problem. Are the cupboards going to be low? Yes, definitely, absolutely.'

Maria was disappointed as soon as they moved in. The cupboards were too high. The threshold leading to the patio was too big a bump for a wheelchair to cross. The rooms seemed too cramped. Turning radiuses were too small. There were holes in the walls, bits of parquet flooring that kept lifting, leaks, poor paint jobs, and so on. She was annoyed that in order for the cupboards to have been lowered she needed to have filed a requisition. This was the downside of customizing each unit to the resident's needs. At her previous apartment such modifications had been standard: 'I never had to request lower cupboards or lower sinks or lower shelves or lower anything. That's what comes, it's understood.'

Some of Maria's dissatisfaction with Windward's accessibility stemmed from her housing experience. She had come from an accessible, roomy apartment where most of the modifications she needed were standard. Also important were her high expectations of Windward as a 'utopia' which promised more responsiveness to people's needs than it could deliver. Yet part of her dissatisfaction rested with societal expectations of people with disabilities. She felt that society expects mobility-impaired people to live alone or to marry able-bodied partners.[6] Wedding china, she pointed out, can be stored in a high cupboard if there is an able-bodied person to reach it. 'It seems to me that society is saying "Oh, you good little people, we're going to let you live on your own. But we won't give you total independence and we won't let you make your own choices." I say, okay I want to marry someone in a chair, give me the space. But I have no choices.'

Larger units are more expensive to build, but she felt it was unfair to assume that people with disabilities would not marry each other. Designing units large enough for two wheelchair-bound people to use would be worthwhile, both for couples in wheelchairs and for everyone who socialized with people in wheelchairs. Windward went only halfway toward achieving this goal, in her view. She concluded: 'It's nice to think, that, yes, the federal government is providing housing for the disabled. And for some people who have never been on their own, who have lived in institutions or at home in their own little room, coming to a place like Windward must be heaven. But for someone who has seen something better this is atrocious. It really is.' Her husband agreed. 'We were led to believe that this was going to be ideal, the model place of the decade when it was finished. And in so many ways it wasn't. If we could have seen what we were getting we would have cancelled out.' But he was less impassioned in his objections to Windward than Maria. In part, this probably reflected differences in temperament. Furthermore, Howard moved to Windward from a one-bedroom unit, had previous experience in a co-op, and required attendant care, which limited his housing choice. So, all in all, his expectations were somewhat different and his dissatisfaction less intense than his wife's.

Maria used the image of a rat trapped in the bottom of a box to describe how she felt. The box was the little apartment and the trap was that they could not move unless they could find a place with attendant care for Howard. Such places, they know, are extremely hard to find. 'Everything is so tiny compared to what I'm used to, and also I feel like a rat because I can't get out of this little hole. And also if you're not happy at home your whole outlook on social life changes and you don't want to go out and meet the next door neighbour.'

Satisfaction with Windward as a Cooperative

Maria said that she had too much resentment against the co-op as a building to even bother to participate in the co-op as a community. Like Maria and Howard, some other households of members with disabilities lived at Windward because of its accessibility and attendant care. Some simply wanted to be independent. Paraplegics who work full-time, cook for themselves, and do their own laundry and housekeeping understandably may feel they have little time to give to co-op participation. Others just were not interested in the cooperative side of living at Windward. They were not attracted to the place because it was a cooperative; some wished it were an ordinary rental apartment building.

How did these people get into the co-op? The criteria for member selection were the same for able-bodied applicants and people with disabilities, including those who needed attendant care. Some co-op members felt that mistakes had been made. As we have discussed in the chapter on member selection, what applicants will *say* in an interview may have little relationship to what they *do* once accepted. It is easy to promise to participate. But the 'mistakes' made in accepting members who need attendant care sometimes had other consequences. As one person put it: 'One of the difficulties is that if you have people with spinal cord injuries and they're coming through quite often painful experiences and have drug treatment, then you get people who are susceptible to drug use.' This was a concern in the co-op from time to time, as were rumours of drug dealing.

Yet even among those using the attendant care service there was some appreciation of Windward as a cooperative. When asked on our survey, 'Compared to other accessible housing how does the fact that Windward is a *co-op* affect your satisfaction with living here?' nearly two-thirds of those respondents using attendant care (five out of eight) viewed the co-op favourably. Among respondents with disabilities who did not require attendant care 80 per cent gave positive responses.

While there was a perception in the co-op that members with disabilities participated less than others, this was probably not true. Both members with disabilities and others expressed concerns that the rate of participation by the former in the co-op was quite low. As one mobility-impaired person commented, 'Some members are pretty active. Still I would say about half or less are not active at all.' However, our survey findings did not support this view: 80 per cent of the respondents with disabilities had served on a committee, compared with 86 per cent of the rest of the membership. Even assuming that the people with disabilities who failed to complete our survey were all non-participants, not a reasonable assumption, the participation rate for members with disabilities still would be around 60 per cent.

Members with disabilities served on and headed most major committees in the co-op. One was president of the co-op, others served on the board of directors. Another member led a movement of dissidents to inquire into alleged financial mismanagement within the co-op. Some mobility-impaired members participated little, others were moderately involved, and a few were deeply involved in shaping Windward. Some were critics of the co-op, some were its strongest supporters. It is impossible for us to separate the contributions to the cooperative and attitudes of people with disabilities from those of other members. The members with disabilities did not act as a bloc or faction in the co-op.

Yet, disturbingly, our survey revealed a common feeling among the respondents with disabilities that people generally had less influence in the co-op than they should and that they in particular had less influence than they would like. There were marked differences between the views of able-bodied respondents and those with disabilities on whether members in general had sufficient say in making decisions at general meetings. Of the disabled respondents, 36 per cent felt members had 'too little' or 'far too little' say, while only 23 per cent of able-bodied respondents felt this way. Furthermore, 50 per cent of respondents with disabilities felt that, as a group, they had too little influence in running the co-op, a view that only 13 per cent of the able-bodied respondents shared. Most of the able-bodied (82 per cent) felt the influence of members with disabilities was about the right amount. Yet only 44 per cent of those with disabilities agreed.

Another question we posed asking about feelings of personal, rather than group, influence was: 'To what degree do you feel you can really influence what happens in the co-op?' Among respondents with disabilities, 60 per cent felt they had little or no influence over what happened in the co-op, whereas only 28 per cent of the able-bodied respondents shared this view (see Table 6.3). But about the same percentages of those with disabilities (25

TABLE 6.3
Relationship of mobility status and sense of influence over co-op
(Windward co-op 1989). Responses to the question: 'To what
degree do you feel you can really influence what happens in the
co-op?'

Mobility status	'Not at all' or 'Slightly' (%)	'Moderately' (%)	'Considerably' or 'A great deal' (%)
No disability	28	50	22
Some disability	60	15	25

per cent) and ablebodied (22 per cent) said they could influence
what went on in the co-op 'considerably' or 'a great deal.'

The response to this question suggests that the disabled respondents fell into two categories, those with a fairly strong sense
of their own ability to influence what went on and those who felt
rather powerless. But why? This split does not correlate with the
extent of their participation in the co-op, at least as measured by
serving on committees, or with whether their previous housing
was institutional. Nor is their sense of a lack of influence related
to satisfaction levels. Two-thirds of those who said they had little
or no influence nevertheless expressed satisfaction with living in
the co-op. Attendant care did not seem to be a factor. The kind
of disability, however, seemed to make a difference. None of the
quadriplegic respondents expressed feelings of a lack of influence. All of those who felt they could influence the co-op considerably or a great deal were paraplegic or quadriplegic. We did
not collect data on whether the disability resulted from an accident, which may play a role here. Furthermore, the number of
respondents in each category was very small and the results should
not be over interpreted.[7] Nevertheless, a comment that a mobility-impaired Windward resident with a strong sense of personal
influence made to us in an interview during the second year of
our study is worth noting. Did the people with disabilities act as
a bloc? 'I don't know,' she replied.

I think I'm maybe more concerned about it or more opinionated
than a lot of people with disabilities that I've come across.

I don't know the reason why ... Maybe, well, I'll just guess at a reason. Quite a few of them have been disabled from birth. So the way the disabled are treated in society today is a big bonus for them, you know, because things were so bad back when they were growing up. But for me it's different. I just recently had an accident and became disabled, so all the rights I had as an able-bodied person I still expect as a disabled person. So I speak up more than a lot of other people in the building.

In the end, individual differences in personality and life experience may best account for the differences in feelings of influence in the co-op among members with disabilities. Our interviews over the years with mobility-impaired members indicate that those who did get involved in the life of the co-op, like their able-bodied peers, had a strong sense of their ability to influence things. Their involvement was not simply a matter of serving on committees. It took the form of informal socializing, speaking at general meetings, and, as one member with a disability said, 'being a watchdog' defending those interests of personal concern. The people with disabilities who felt most able to influence what happened in the co-op were active participants who got out of the co-op what they put into it.

This is not to say that all who took an active part were satisfied – some were not – nor that all felt their attempts to influence the co-op had been effective. One dissident activist, for example, felt strongly that the co-op had been 'dominated by a few autocrats who run it as if it was their private fiefdom.' Another expressed a closely related sentiment that some able-bodied members also shared and that we will consider in more depth later in the book: 'A very small group of people run the co-op. They say what's happening. As long as they run it all right and it doesn't bother me, that's fine. Just don't ask me to do anything, because I don't want to.'

A more common approach was to try to strike a balance. As another member with a disability commented, 'On the one hand you don't want to make it such an issue that you sort of see yourself as a special interest group within the co-op. But on the other hand you want to be sure that your interests are represented.' This person, while not especially active in a formal sense, was vigilant, concerned, and, although by 1989 she was not very satisfied with living in the co-op, continued to feel that she had considerable influence over what was happening.

Social Interaction between Able-Bodied Members and Those with Disabilities

Living in a fully accessible building in which one-quarter of the households included at least one person with a disability was a new experience for all residents (see Fig. 6.1). The lack of physical barriers did encourage social interaction between people with different disabilities and others, but it was a gradual process. With few exceptions, the people who moved into Windward in the winter of 1986–87 were not only new neighbours, they were strangers.

As well, they came from diverse housing backgrounds. According to the results of our 1989 survey, only 10 per cent had lived in another housing co-op; 12 per cent had owned their own homes; about the same percentage (13 per cent) had lived in non-profit housing. Most (60 per cent) moved into Windward from private rental accommodation. Among the able-bodied members, we know of only three households whose members had been friends before moving into the co-op. A few others got to know each other through involvement in the creation of Windward.

More of the people with disabilities knew each other before they moved into Windward and initially they tended to socialize mainly among themselves. Attendant care played a role here, as one member explained: 'You have to remember that the population that Participation Apartments brings in has among it people who have known each other for a very long time. They may not have lived in close proximity for a long period of time but, say, we were in Bloorview Children's Hospital together. We grew up in that kind of environment together. Or we were involved in wheelchair sports, that kind of thing.' In this man's view, such friendships had an impact on social interaction at Windward.

Figure 6.1
A Windward resident waits for transportation at the co-op entrance. Living in a fully accessible building in which one-quarter of the households included at least one person with a disability was a new experience for all residents.

'That's not to say [this impact] is negative but to say that if there has been a sort of segregation this could be part of the reason.'

There seems to have been a third reason for an initial lack of interaction between able-bodied members and those with disabilities. As we have seen, most residents of the new co-op were strangers and those who did know each other were mainly people with disabilities with shared backgrounds. In addition, there was the uneasiness of able-bodied people, who were uncertain how to respond to their neighbours' disabilities, which further distanced the two types of members in the early days of the co-op.

In the same interview in which Carl Dowling told us about Laurie's visit (only a few months after the first members moved into Windward), he suggested that the able-bodied people wanted to interact more with those with disabilities but did not really know how. He tried to help them along. His comments reveal how the slow process of social interaction between able-bodied people and those with disabilities began to develop at Windward in 1987:

> The people here, they're genuinely interested in the disabled in Canada and they want to learn as much about them as they can. But a lot of them are afraid. They're afraid to ask questions. Or they're inquisitive but they're afraid to ask. And then when one sees that, it's up to the disabled person to make these people talk. You know I do that all the time. If I see somebody who's feeling a little bit uncomfortable because of my disability, then I'll try to force them to talk either by cracking a joke about my disability or just trying to make them feel the need [to talk]. Then they understand a little better. Once they get to know you and talk to you, talk to you about the disability and how it affects your life socially, sexually, and physically, about architectural barriers, you know, and stuff like that, they feel more comfortable. They feel a hell of a lot more comfortable.

The education of able-bodied people so that the wheelchairs disappeared from view and they saw people, not disabilities, gradually but effectively broke down the social segregation apparent in 1987. By 1988, the able-bodied spouse of a member with a disability said: 'All the walkies are very much adjusted to the wheelies now and to handling them and helping them. You see it even at social functions. You know, people aren't ill at ease with them any more. I think there's always that tiny little line where people are a little intimidated. It's a natural thing. But on the whole I feel that they're completely integrated here.'

A year later things had progressed so much that an able-bodied member could dismiss our question, saying, 'The disabled issue isn't even an issue here.' In some ways she was right, not because people with disabilities and others all interacted socially, either among themselves or with each other, but because by 1989 non-disabled members and those with disabilities felt comfortable just being themselves.

The Cooperative Form and Social Interaction

To a large extent the passage of time accounts for more comfortable social interaction among people, with or without disabilities, in the co-op. By 1989, there had been a birth and a death in the building and a marriage between co-op members in the courtyard. Casual encounters in the laundry room or elevator, as in any apartment building, contributed at least minimally to knowing your neighbours. But, as a social form, cooperatives place a greater emphasis on social interaction than do other kinds of housing. At Windward this included contact between mobility-impaired and non-disabled members. Three aspects of Windward as a cooperative seem to have contributed to increased social interaction: committee meetings, neighbourliness, and social events.

A basic assumption of the co-op housing movement is that committee meetings provide a way for members to get to know each other, deepen their involvement in the co-op, and thereby increase their own sense of control over their housing. At Windward, participation in committees and attendance at general meetings encouraged interaction between able-bodied members and people with disabilities as well as stimulating social interaction more generally. The observations of one person with a disability outline a common scenario: 'It's the fact that it's a co-op setting [that encourages interaction]. At each general meeting we get to meet more people. I just met a couple last week that I'd seen many times to say hello to but never really met. Since then they've been up here, not really to a party but to a get-together Victoria Day weekend to watch the fireworks. "Come on up," I said. We had a drink. I had the stereo going. Since then I've seen them about umpteen dozen times, and we've chatted out in the courtyard. It's been great.'

Co-ops have no monopoly on neighbourliness, but the chance to choose one's neighbours through the member selection process and the opportunity to get to know them through meetings can nurture neighbourly interaction. In interviews, people frequently told us that one big difference between the co-op and their previous housing was that in the co-op they knew their neighbours. Their examples of neighbourly concern included social interaction between able-bodied members and those with disabilities: 'There are, for instance, people in this co-op who are disabled and there are many other people who are helping them to make their independent living, well, independent. You know, shopping for them, picking up things for them, caring for them when they're ill, checking in on them. Maybe that sort of thing happens in any good neighbourhood. But I think because it's a co-op and people meet each other through committee work that they know each other and therefore are able to help each other and, well, care about each other. And that to me is a very important part of the co-op.'

A higher percentage of people with disabilities than others attended social events organized by the co-op, perhaps because these parties were easily accessible. Half of those responding to our survey who had disabilities said they attend most or all social events in the co-op whereas only 25 per cent of the able-bodied gave this response. The social committee tried to encourage their attendance by choosing and arranging furniture for the common rooms so as to make it easy for people in wheelchairs to socialize with each other and with non-disabled members. They also tried to make everyone feel comfortable in other ways: 'Some of us came up with the idea that we'd serve people coming up to the buffet instead of letting everybody help themselves. That worked out well, so that the people in wheelchairs felt part of it.'

Some of the best co-op parties were not organized but simply grew out of meetings. One member with a disability reminisced: 'One of the best parties anybody'd ever been to started with work on the budget. We had to call a guy over to get information from his committee. He came over with a drink in his hand. We got information from him and we started talking and we had a drink. Then the work stopped and we decided to cook spaghetti. So the three of us are eating spaghetti on the balcony and we look down and see [some friends] eating in the courtyard. "So come on up!" we say. It started that way and people just kept strolling up. It turned into a party that lasted until 7 o'clock the next morning. We had eggs benedict at 7 o'clock in the morning.'

The building itself made social interaction between people in wheelchairs and others possible. People in any unit could say "Come on up!" to someone in a wheelchair. Visiting each other's apartments, everyone recognized that their units were the same (see Figs. 6.2 and 6.3). The design and accessibility features were common to all units, except for such modifications as counter heights or shower style. The needs of those with disabilities became the norm for Windward. So, in a sense, the able-bodied became integrated into the world of those with disabilities rather than the other way around.

Resistance to Social Integration

Very occasionally we heard comments suggesting a reluctance on the part of a few able-bodied people to interact with those with disabilities. Someone in a wheelchair observed: 'I'm sure there are people in the co-op who don't have any interest in becoming integrated with people with disabilities. They don't want to know what's going on with us guys.' An able-bodied person explained this as a response to people with disabilities with a chip on their shoulder: 'A lot depends on personality. It's like anything else. If you enjoy somebody's company the wheelchair disappears. But if you're looking out at life through a sour grapes attitude people are going to get depressed when they're around you and tend not to [want to be with you].'

Among the able-bodied members of the co-op there were some who were not interested in socializing with their neighbours, regardless of what they were like. This also was the case for some members with disabilities. As with the able-bodied, there were many personal, idiosyncratic reasons for their antipathy to social interaction within the co-op. One factor to consider, however, is the provision of attendant care. Ironically, attendant care both encourages and discourages the mixing of people with disabilities and others. It encourages integrated housing, because it makes

Figure 6.2
Visiting each other's apartments, everyone at Windward recognized that their units were the same. An apartment occupied by a person who uses a wheelchair shows how floor-to-ceiling windows improve the view for everyone and how 'ordinary' a fully accessible apartment looks.

independent living possible for some people with severe disabilities. But at Windward it discouraged social interaction to some extent.

Initially, only 15 per cent of the households at Windward were to include a person with disabilities. With the decision to provide attendant care came an increase in that number to 25 per cent. This made some economic sense in that the building was already planned to be fully accessible, but it increased the costs associated with special modifications for those with severe disabilities. Some felt that the higher proportion of residents with disabilities and the connection that about half of them shared through attendant

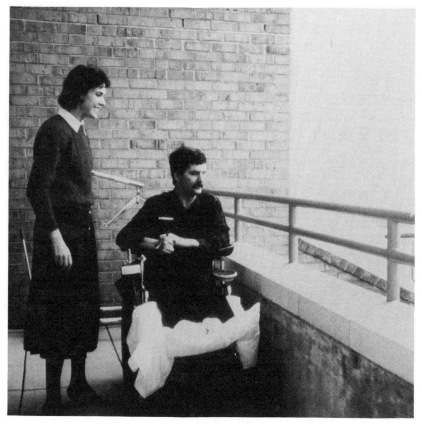

Figure 6.3
Anthropologist and Windward resident admire view from latter's balcony.
Photo courtesy of Harriet Critchlow.

care encouraged a ghetto-like situation. Bringing people with
disabilities into the co-op who already tended to socialize largely
with other people like themselves may have discouraged them
from extending their social networks.

Participation Apartments, on the one hand, provided a comfortable atmosphere in which people with disabilities who had
known each other a long time 'can hang out with other disabled
people – fewer questions, more things in common, just as any
group that has something in common tends to form friendships.'

On the other hand, as this person went on to observe, attendant care can be 'a trap' that people with disabilities fall into, socializing only with people like themselves. With attendant care in the building, he concluded: 'Whether the co-op is facilitating more integration or not I say is still pretty much of a question mark.'

Should the co-op have done more to encourage people with disabilities to interact with able-bodied members? In the view of this person with disabilities, probably not: 'It's such a difficult area for the board, for the committees, for the non-disabled people to try and come to terms with, because I think there's this feeling that you don't want to lump [those with disabilities] all together and you don't want to make them special. Is there something more that could be done? Probably not. From what I can tell from many years of seeing what happens, the fact that people are disabled probably doesn't make much of a difference generally as to whether they would integrate or not into society.' For people with disabilities who had no interest in socializing beyond their existing circle of friends, in other words, the mix of able-bodied members and those with disabilities at Windward made little if any difference.

Mixed Couples and Social Interaction

Couples in which one partner is able-bodied were one category of residents for whom the unusual environment at Windward *did* make a big difference. We interviewed seven of the eleven such couples in the co-op and all expressed very positive feelings about Windward as an integrated environment. These people ranged in age from their twenties to their sixties. Their disabilities ranged from among the most severe in the co-op to others that were relatively minor. Some were on deep subsidies, while others paid some of the highest housing charges in the co-op. Some were not very satisfied with the co-op as a co-op, others were among its biggest boosters.

All that these couples had in common was an appreciation of Windward as integrated housing that allowed them to live normal lives. In a sense, they could live as if both partners were able-bodied in that the building gave the partner with disabilities freedom of movement. In another sense, though, they lived in a world in which the distinction between people with disabilities and the able-bodied had almost disappeared. Of course, the distinction had not disappeared. Several people with disabilities commented to us that the important thing was for non-disabled people to accept them as they were, not to pretend that there were no differences.

The sight of other people in wheelchairs was hardly less common than the sight of people walking through the corridors. The mix of mobility-impaired and non-disabled became taken for granted. Those who wanted to could socialize with other mixed couples like themselves. Three of the seven couples we interviewed became good friends over time and got together frequently for a meal or a cup of tea. Both those with disabilities and the non-disabled members of these couples found support in these friendships based on shared experiences.

For couples in which one person had disabilities, the provision of attendant care had very positive aspects. First, it separated some of the functions of caregiver from those of spouse. Marital relationships can easily become nurse-patient relationships when one partner has a disability. This can strain the relationship severely, especially if the onset of the disability is traumatic. As one man whose marriage broke up after his accident explained:

I put so much pressure on my wife. I expected her to do everything, not an attendant. It just got to the point where she burned right out because she was not only looking after my physical care needs, she also had to look after [our child], and the housework and the shopping and make sure the cars were all right ... A unique thing about this project is that Participation Apartments caters not only to a disabled person but to a couple as well, where there's only one disabled member in the family. They will come in and do all the physical care needs of that person, which could mean bowel routines, showering, dressing, transferring, lifting, stuff like that. Then

the other family members are responsible for the cooking and keeping the apartment clean and stuff like that.

Another positive aspect of the availability of attendant care is
that it gives both partners independence. Either person can come
and go according to a daily schedule in which nursing care is not
a consideration. And partners can come together or break up in
a 'normal' way. Attendant care allows a person with disabilities
to choose to stay with, or separate from, a partner without making
his or her needs for physical assistance a factor in the decision.[8]

Interaction among People with Different Degrees of Disability

Living in Windward taught able-bodied people more about those
who had disabilities. Yet it also taught people in wheelchairs about
interacting with others whose disabilities were different from their
own. The relatively large number of residents with disabilities
and the range of impairment contributed to everyone's learning
experience. Residents, as a woman in a wheelchair said, 'have
seen people [in the co-op] who are in the Olympics, people with
disabilities who are very muscular and strong. And they've seen
people like myself who can't lift more than two pounds. And
they've seen some who are more, well, more or less deformed.
They've run into all kinds, and it's great.'

One thing that struck us in analysing our interviews was the
way in which people who were themselves in wheelchairs spoke
about learning to interact with other people with disabilities. A
co-op couple, one of whom is in a wheelchair, described how they
met one quadriplegic man before the building was completed.
The person in a wheelchair explained that they got to know each
other through committee work: 'Gradually our conversation
turned to other than [committee] matters. We moved into the
building and our friendship continued. We'd run into each other
in the hallway and speak and pass the time of day. Now, at this
stage of the game we will maybe take up his supper on occasion.
We know his likes and dislikes. We've reached the point where
we don't feel uncomfortable holding a glass up to his lips and

letting him sip. Now that I mention this it seems like a small thing. But many able-bodied people they don't ... you'd feel uncomfortable feeding an adult ... another adult. You've got to break down some barriers.'

Other people with disabilities in the co-op spoke of learning to deal with those in wheelchairs who had difficulty communicating. One young woman told of trying without success to persuade another who found communication very difficult to volunteer for a committee. Another woman whose disability restricted her mobility only slightly spoke of spending a day in a wheelchair to learn more about the life of her friend with cerebral palsy. Eventually, she felt comfortable helping her friend with toileting. 'I think it strengthens friendships,' she said, 'when all the barriers are down.'

Are the Barriers Down?

Are the barriers down at Windward? Our conclusion was that the co-op worked very well as integrated housing. One measure of its success as integrated housing was that social interaction between able-bodied people and members with disabilities was only partial.

Social *interaction* is not the same as *integration*. Integrated housing aims to provide equality of opportunity for people with disabilities to lead 'normal' lives. To some extent Windward ensured that the results, as well as the opportunities, would be equal because the building was designed so that able-bodied people lived in facilities designed to the standards of a person in a wheelchair, not the other way around. But social interaction varied from person to person, regardless of whether one was in a wheelchair.

For some people with disabilities, leading a normal life meant emphasizing the right to privacy. For others it meant being able to party all night. Windward required participation on committees and attendance at general meetings. Some members, whether able-bodied or with disabilities, resented this requirement. Others enjoyed it and found committee work a good way to make friends.

Except for the obligation to participate in the co-op, Windward allowed its members the freedom to interact socially as much or as little as they wanted. The members with disabilities, like their able-bodied neighbours, responded to this freedom in many ways, some of which we have described in this chapter.

We found that satisfaction with co-op living was highest for those people with disabilities whose previous housing experience (for example, in institutions) made Windward look like 'heaven' by comparison. It was lowest for those, like the couple whose dissatisfaction we described earlier, whose expectations about the building's accessibility were not met.

We found that minimum participation rates, measured by whether a member had ever served on a committee, were about the same for people with or without disabilities. However, respondents to our survey who had disabilities felt less able to influence what happens in the co-op. This may well be related to differences in the life experiences of people with disabilities compared with the able-bodied. But a sense of involvement in the co-op also seemed important. The people with disabilities who took an active role in the life of the co-op, as critics as well as promoters, felt able to influence what happened there. They felt that any member could make a difference. Similarly, the extent to which people with disabilities were integrated into the co-op was more than a matter of individual uniqueness. It related, as well, to involvement with the co-op as an association rather than just living in it as an accessible building. The co-op was a place to live for those who wanted integrated housing; it was a way of life for those who wanted social interaction. As part of this way of life, those who chose to be involved in the co-op could improve their understanding of others whose physical abilities were different from their own.

Housing integration, we have suggested, flows from accessibility, but social interaction among people with different physical abilities is less easily built in. The people with disabilities at Windward felt free to socialize or not. They relished their independence, and that freedom included the option to make friends with

Figure 6.4
A Windward member cooking supper for friends from her wheelchair. The photo shows kitchen modifications. The modified range is still too high for her to handle pots safely.

able-bodied people or those with disabilities, sustain old friendships, or keep to themselves (see Fig. 6.4). A young woman in a wheelchair summed it up: 'It's nice to live in a place where you're not really told where you're going to live, how you're going to live, and what you're going to do!'

CHAPTER SEVEN

For Richer and Poorer

Not Just a Place to Live

Trying to shatter stereotypes of cooperatives as low-income housing, the Cooperative Housing Federation developed a promotional film called Not Just a Place to Live. *It tries to educate prospective co-op applicants about the mixture of people co-ops bring together and underscores the importance of local control. The film presents cooperatives as mixed environments that house families from a wide range of backgrounds. Members' choices help determine how they want to live, the film points out, and people working cooperatively can do together what they could not accomplish on their own.*

The film made a lasting impression on Judy Jameson, a Harbourside member. In 1984 she was living with her three-year-old son in Metro Toronto Housing. The apartment depressed her. The project was filthy, overrun with cockroaches, and no one seemed to care how the building looked. She felt surrounded by people with whom she had nothing in common except their shared predicament as single mothers in need of assisted housing. She wanted to find a place to live where her child could relate to families other than those composed of poor single mothers and their children. Through friends, she heard that co-ops offered attractive, affordable housing. She applied to Harbourside after seeing Not Just a Place to Live. *'One of the things I remember from that film was that they said a co-op is where you expect to see people going to work in the morning in their Cadillacs, on their bikes, and on public transit. I thought that was kind of neat. I think we do have a Cadillac that lives here somewhere. And to me that's how it should be.'*

She liked the mixing of income levels as well as family types. And she liked not knowing or caring who was on subsidy: 'I mean if somebody's a lawyer and his wife's an architect then you know that they're not on subsidy. But to me it doesn't make a difference. Maybe it's because I'm on subsidy. I don't know. But I never think of myself as different to anybody else just because I'm subsidized. To me that's one of the reasons we [single mothers] are here. Because we want a decent place to live and we want somewhere to bring our children up. We could all be living in Metro housing and know we were all subsidized and be suicidal!'

Yuppies or People on Welfare?

Before Windward opened it was criticized as a co-op for yuppies who wanted to be able to moor their yachts near their lakefront homes. Others feared that the co-ops and public housing on Bathurst Quay would become Harbourfront's ghetto filled with people on rent subsidies. Surely, it seemed, social housing would drag down the image of Harbourfront as a centre for the arts and as a prestigious place to live. Or the opposite would happen. Those without much money would find they had no place to live on the waterfront after all.

In fact, neither scenario happened. The co-ops started out as and remained a mixture of richer and poorer people. For reasons we will explore in this chapter, neither drove out the other.

In part, the coexistence of people with different income levels was built into and protected by the co-ops to try to avoid some of the problems associated with public housing. Furthermore, both the relatively affluent and those in need of assisted housing benefited financially from living in the co-ops. Finally, the mixture of richer and poorer residents brought with it a variety of family types, ethnic affiliations, interests, and views that many residents found stimulating and enlivening. This mixture is part of what makes co-ops attractive to both richer and poorer residents. It also contributes to certain tensions.

In this chapter we consider what mixing incomes meant to

people living in the two co-ops. Reflecting society at large through the creation of mixed-income communities has been a fundamental goal of the cooperative sector. Yet government support for mixing incomes has been tentative at best. While this largely reflected a political and economic climate of restraint and conservatism, it also was a product of uncertainty about what benefits actually accrued to residents from living in mixed-income projects. It is clear that ghettos of low-income households do not work. But the benefits of mixed low- and middle-income housing are not yet well documented. So little study has been done on this topic that the Co-operative Housing Federation of Canada included it on its 'shopping list' of priority research topics.

We cannot judge what the 'best' mix of incomes may be, but we can offer an assessment of how well the mix in these two co-ops worked for residents in the projects' first few years. Here we consider economic advantages to residents and the costs to government of mixed-income co-ops. We evaluate the impact of subsidy status on participation rates and members' satisfaction with living cooperatively.

We also explore the views co-op members held initially about living with neighbours who were considerably richer or poorer than themselves. We consider how and why those views changed during the three years of our study. Some learned greater tolerance and developed deeper understanding of people different from themselves. Others found their attitudes moved increasingly, as one disgruntled member put it, 'to the right of Genghis Khan.' We assess differences between the two co-ops on issues related to income mixing. And we consider the future of income mixing in the two co-ops as more subsidy funds become available internally.

On balance we conclude that income mixing provided much of the vitality of these two co-ops. One sign of the success of this mix is that there was no simple division between market rent and subsidized people in either co-op. Instead we found a continuum of people with a variety of income levels whose housing was subsidized to different degrees. Members did not always line up on co-op issues according to subsidy status. Rather our survey and interviews revealed people trying to work out what it meant to live among neighbours who were a few or many degrees different from themselves. These differences were not only in income, but often in cultural background, occupation, and family structure. Local control backed by a mandate to include low-income households, we conclude, is the key to understanding how and why mixing income levels worked in these co-ops.

Single parents like Judy Jameson are not the only ones for whom mixed-income cooperatives are attractive. Other kinds of families and single people in need of rental assistance also may welcome the mix of income levels in the co-ops. So may people with special needs. Cooperatives can provide a 'normal' independent-living environment for people with physical disabilities as we saw in the last chapter. Many of these people need assistance to meet their housing charges while some can afford to pay full rent, so a mixed-income building that is completely accessible, such as Windward, is especially appropriate.

There are benefits that the co-op sector sees mixed-income co-ops as providing to such members. Security of tenure in the co-op combined with the availability of subsidies creates a stable housing environment for members, whatever their income. This security allow a low-income single mother, for example, to go to school or train for a job that will enable her to get off the housing charge subsidy eventually. It allows her independence, for example, from boyfriend, ex-husband, or parent on whom she might otherwise be dependent for help in paying the rent. As well, the housing environment is a continuing presence in the members' lives that is thought to instruct by example. A middle-class pride of place may be something all members come to share, or so members from that background hope. Co-ops provide a place for people to learn new skills from each other, especially through committee work, and to develop self-confidence. Finally, mixed-income co-ops offer the possibility of a sense of community in that they integrate a 'slice of life' rather than housing only those in financial straits. A member of one of the co-ops we studied who had experience with other co-ops gave an example that sums up these benefits:

A subsidized rent is a really important thing to people. You know it gives them not only security of tenure but security of mind. A friend of mine went into a co-op at a fairly late stage in her life. She was separated with two kids and was on subsidy. I remember how proud she was when she called me up one day. She said, 'I'm not subsidized any more!' I mean she'd made it. It was one of the marks of making it. For that reason she felt really good, and she also felt good that there was now another subsidy available for someone who needed it.

The subsidy had really made a difference ... It gave her at least the breathing space financially. It also gave her a lot of informal support in terms of community. There were babysitters available and there were people to yell at when life became too much. And there was dignity and respect, you know. The potential to take on real leadership and learn. She got really good training in leadership skills.

Mixed-Income Co-ops and Middle-Income People

It is easy to see why low-income single mothers and people with disabilities might be enthusiastic about mixed-income cooperatives. But what about two-parent families who earned too much to receive housing charge assistance? What attracted them to the mixed-income aspect of these projects?

More than half the households in both co-ops paid full rent. Median household incomes in both co-ops were $40,000–49,000 before taxes, according to our survey. Why were people who earned such incomes living in places that also included 40–45 per cent low-income, subsidized households? One answer which we will consider in some depth in the next section of this chapter is that every household, whether directly subsidized or not, derived economic benefits from the way co-op financing is structured. Affordable housing was the main reason people joined both Harbourside and Windward. This is a concern that those earning just enough to pay the rent shared with those who were not earning quite enough to pay it without assistance.

Incomes in the $40,000–50,000 range do not allow a family

to live particularly well in Toronto. By the time we completed our three-year study, Harbourside co-op had raised the income ceiling for housing assistance to $44,700. In other words, a family could earn that much and still be eligible for housing charge assistance because it might otherwise pay more than 30 per cent of its income in rent. In this housing climate, the availability of emergency subsidies benefited professionals as well as lower-income people. For example, one professional couple told us how much they appreciated receiving an emergency subsidy when they both suddenly lost their jobs.

Another reason is that many wealthier people joined the co-ops for reasons that had nothing to do with the mixed-income nature of the projects. The opportunity to live with people poorer than themselves was not nearly so attractive as the chance, from the single mother's perspective, to live among more-affluent two-parent families. Rather, as we have pointed out elsewhere, the co-ops seemed attractive because of the shortage of rental housing in Toronto, and especially the shortage of housing affordable for middle-income households. The co-ops' waterfront location drew higher-income people as did Windward's appearance. Sharing this location with less-well-off co-op members was often a secondary consideration, but one that had consequences for all concerned.

Some co-op members talked about a third, non-economic dimension of the income mix, one that attracted them to cooperative living. They tried to express to us the hopes they had for the co-ops as places that, partly through mixing income levels, would become communities of like-minded people. Some wealthier professional residents lived at Harbourside or Windward as part of a commitment to bring about social change. Others just liked the diversity. One anonymous comment written at the end of our survey observed, 'Harbourside is a great place to live. It is an excellent location. There is an excellent mix of people and always something going on on weekends. I have owned a couple of homes and can afford to buy another one, but I prefer to live at Harbourside due to the mix of personalities, ethnic, and social groups. This is truly a small community in the middle of a big city.' For this person, mixed uses, mixed incomes, and mixtures of people were stirred into community in the co-op.[1]

How and Why Incomes Are Mixed in Housing Co-ops

Too often, in North America 'public housing is really a graveyard of good intentions' (Sayegh 1987: 340). Low-rental projects have created serious 'sociological problems, inflation and resentment on behalf of subsidized tenants, neighbourhoods and taxpayers' (ibid.: 345). One of the failures of public housing that cooperatives seek to overcome is the challenge of working housing for low-income people into ordinary neighbourhoods.[2] Mixed-income co-ops, in other words, are a way of responding to NIMBY (not in my back yard) protests and encouraging community acceptance.

Income integration was one goal of the 1978 cooperative housing program, under section 56.1 of the National Housing Act, which financed Windward and Harbourside. This was 'in part a reaction to the social and community acceptance problems which faced large-scale public housing projects in the 1970s' (CMHC 1983: 5). Community acceptance, it was hoped, would be greater for mixed-income cooperatives in which members shared responsibility for maintenance of the housing.

Income mixing was built into the section 56.1 program for two additional reasons (ibid.: 162): 'First, a mix of assisted tenants with tenants paying market rents would contribute to the financial viability of the projects. Second, social problems associated with projects which contained high concentrations of low-income households would be reduced.'

The contract between CMHC and the co-ops that were created under section 56.1 required that at least 25 per cent of the households must be in need of housing charge assistance.[3] Federal subsidies provided assistance to households which would otherwise have had to pay more than 30 per cent of their gross income in rent. The percentage of income payable in rent was determined on a sliding scale. For example, at Harbourside initially households earning less than $16,000 were expected to pay no more than 25 per cent of their gross income in rent, whereas it was acceptable for those earning up to $35,000 to pay as much as 30 per cent of their income in rent before receiving assistance.

Subsidies funded by the federal government were administered by each co-op. The size of the pool of subsidy money available to a particular co-op was determined by a formula that also reduced everyone's rent to the low end of the market for the area.[4] This formula began by calculating the mortgage payments that would be required to amortize a 35-year mortgage for 100 per cent of the capital costs at current interest rates. Next, the payments needed if the interest rate were only 2 per cent were calculated. The difference between these two figures was the amount of monthly assistance for which the project was eligible. At Harbourside, for example, the difference on capital costs of $3.9 million between payments at the prevailing rate of 11.625 per cent and 2 per cent amounted to $298,185 in 56.1 assistance annually, or $24,849 per month.[5]

The monthly assistance money from CMHC was used, first, to reduce all housing charges in the co-op to the low end of market rents charged for similar housing in the neighbourhood. This calculation is made only once, at the time the co-op opens. This amount was called a Mortgage Interest Reduction Grant (MIRG) under section 56.1. At Harbourside the MIRG was $136,187 per year. Initial reduction in each household's rent averaged $198 per month ($2,376 annually). This subsidy benefited all residents financially. But because it was invisible members sometimes needed reminding that everyone in the co-op, not just households that paid rent geared to their income, was on subsidy.

The subsidy pool available for further housing charge assistance then was the difference between the total monthly assistance for which the co-op was eligible and the MIRG. Harbourside's section 56.1 annual assistance total of $298,195 less a MIRG of $136,187 left an initial subsidy pool of $161,998, or $13,500 per month.

The total amount of assistance the co-op receives from CMHC is constant for the term of the mortgage, but the relative amounts of MIRG and subsidy pool change after the first three years.[6] In the fourth year the 'step-out' period begins. The mortgage payment increases by 5 per cent compounded annually until the co-op finally bears the full load of mortgage payments at the conventional interest rate out of its housing charges. Since the total amount of assistance remains unchanged, the decreasing MIRG frees up more money for the subsidy pool. So as rents rise under pressure to pay more of the mortgage, more households may qualify for rent geared to income subsidies. The money will be there to help them because the subsidy pool increases as the amount of MIRG goes down.

A co-op has considerable latitude in deciding how to allocate its subsidy pool so long as it meets the section 56.1 requirement that at least 25 per cent of households receive housing charge assistance. It is usual to leave some funds for emergency subsidies in case, for example, members lose their jobs or become ill and are unable to work temporarily. The remaining funds are spread, thick or thin, among households requiring reductions in rent on a more permanent basis.

We should emphasize that the range of actual rents paid in these co-ops was great. At Harbourside, housing charges at the time of our survey ranged from $1,045 per month for a four-bedroom townhouse at full rent to $136 for a heavily subsidized two-bedroom unit. Approximately 45 per cent of the co-op households received housing charge assistance. At Windward, rents for the same period ranged from $1,367 for the most expensive four bedroom unit down to $32 for the most deeply subsidized one-bedroom apartment; see Table 7.1 for the range of housing charges in 1988–9). In 1989, between 41 per cent and 46 per cent of Windward households were on subsidy.

The distribution of the subsidy pool at Windward in January 1988 illustrates how the co-ops tried to maintain a mixture of deep and shallow subsidies. As Table 7.2 shows, an average of $301 per month subsidized housing charges for eleven households able to pay more than half of the rent themselves. A further nineteen households which could pay at least 20 per cent of the rent themselves received an average of $533 monthly in housing

TABLE 7.1
Housing charges, Windward co-op,
1988–9

| Less than | Percentage of households | |
	1988	1989
$ 200	18	14
400	14	15
600	13	10
800	15	17
1,000	26	30
1,200	12	12
1,400	1	1

TABLE 7.2
Proportion of housing charges paid by subsidies,
Windward co-op, 1 January 1988

Percentage of housing charge paid by household	Households (with disability + able-bodied)	Total subsidy (monthly)	Average subsidy per household
>50	11 (3 + 8)	$ 3,307	$301
20–49	19 (7 + 12)	$10,120	$533
<19	43	$21,548	$501

charge assistance. For the thirteen households unable to afford even 20 per cent of the rent, subsidies amounted to $625 per unit. The total subsidy pool at that time was $21,548 each month. Nineteen of Windward's twenty-seven members with disabilities needed some degree of assistance to pay their housing charges. They accounted for almost half of Windward's subsidy pool.

The section 56.1 non-profit and cooperative programs were evaluated unfavourably in 1983 and phased out in 1985. The evaluation (CMHC 1983: 8) concluded that the 'programs are ineffectively targeted to those most in need. Depending on the criterion used, between 47 and 69 percent of the households served by the programs would be considered to be low and moderate income. Only 21 percent of the programs' client group are low-income households using the Statistics Canada low-income cut-offs, although the incidence of need for housing assistance is overwhelmingly concentrated among this income group.'

Subsequent programs have emphasized better targeting of housing for people in the greatest need. For example, under the 1986 non-profit program 40 per cent of units are designated as deep subsidy, 40 per cent receive shallow subsidies, and only 20 per cent pay market rents. Housing entirely for low-income households also is making a comeback.[7]

Perhaps because they came into existence in this climate, both Windward and Harbourside included far more households on subsidy than they were required to under the section 56.1 program. As the mortgage step-out proceeds and their subsidy pools increase, it seems reasonable to expect that the percentage of households receiving housing assistance also will rise.

Different Incomes, Like-Minded People

There is much more to mixing incomes in housing cooperatives than the economics of MIRGs and subsidies. Some moderate-income people, like their richer and poorer neighbours, joined the co-op partly in hopes of finding more than an affordable place to live. In one of our 1987 interviews, a couple discussed the kind of community they sought in joining Harbourside. Their comments point to some of the perceived benefits that flow, at least indirectly, from mixing incomes. They spoke of joining the co-op to escape a ghetto of working-class people more or less like themselves in income level, but worlds apart in their attitudes and interests.

Ted and Kathy lived in the Toronto suburb of Scarborough before applying to Harbourside. As Ted said, they lived 'way out there. And it doesn't matter where you go, beyond a certain point in Scarborough everything is a six-lane highway. You've got little shopping plazas here and monstrous apartment buildings there. And it doesn't matter what street you're living on [it's all the same.] We were living in an apartment, and just living in that apartment would have been enough incentive to move anywhere else. The neighbourhood was terrible. You knew that it was spring not by the first robin but by the first smashed beer bottle!'

More than the neighbourhood bothered them. Ted stayed home with their baby and worked as a freelance writer while Kathy returned to her job as a secretary:

I used to take [the baby] out every day. One day I had this over-whelming feeling that the people who were living in that apartment building were just waiting for something to happen. I never quite understood what it was they were waiting for. It was not necessarily horrible. But there they were. They were spending their lives in this place and there was no change.

As far as they were concerned, the seasons passed but it really didn't matter. It really didn't matter if their rent was hiked. It really didn't matter if they lost their jobs. It didn't matter if they found new ones. It didn't matter if their kid failed grade two. It didn't matter. It wasn't as high minded as this, but it was almost as though there was this transcendent feeling of, 'Oh, well, this too shall pass.' But of course it was nothing like that. It was just that they had given up.

It was a working-class, petty-criminal kind of place. I had the feeling that these people had been kicked once too often. Louis Brandeis, the Supreme Court Justice in the United States, said that even a dog knows the difference between being kicked and being tripped over. Well, I don't think they knew the difference. I really couldn't put my finger on it until one day I walked outside and I'd just seen too much dogshit and broken beer bottles in the parking lot. Then I realized I'd been there for six years and I was in the same position [as the rest of them]. The atmosphere, it seemed, was slowly pressing in on me.

Ted pointed out that the basis for their negative feelings was not a matter of class differences: 'It really has nothing to do with educational background or anything like that. I mean for a long time I worked at construction, road construction. And most of the people over there were constantly trying to improve them-selves. So it wasn't that there was a different class of people in the broad sense, but I found great difficulty in conducting a conversation with anybody over there.'

At Harbourside, Ted and Kathy found people who were richer and poorer, but who were like themselves in other ways. As Ted commented: 'One great advantage of moving into this co-op is that I found more people in the space of two weeks with whom I could hold a decent conversation than I had in the whole seven years I lived in the other place.'

This sense of having something in common with people in the co-op cut across subsidy and income lines. Ted's view was one we heard Harbourside residents express often. We heard it from people who earned high incomes and from those on deep subsidy, from those with masters' degrees and those who left school at the age of fifteen. This sense of shared values, however, was less evident at Windward.

The size and design of the two co-ops made a difference here. Harbourside is about half the size of Windward and a large proportion of the units (29/54) are townhouses. Townhouses opening onto a courtyard encourage casual socializing with the neighbours. Kathy explained: 'We don't invite a lot of people over here. And they don't come to our door. Occasionally, yes, but not on a regular basis. We do our socializing outside in the common areas, in the front shovelling snow, in the back when the kids are playing.'

Harbourside's neighbourliness had a price. Kathy said, 'You see one of the advantages of being in a co-op is that you have all these neighbours and all these friends, but that's also the major disadvantage.' She recounted an argument with a neighbour in the co-op. If the neighbour had been from another building Kathy could have openly ignored her, been rude to her. 'I'd have said something verbally abusive and walked away! I wouldn't have thought twice about it. But, see, in this case I *do* have to think about her. She's my neighbour and I have to worry about [what happens] when I see her the next time. Because she'll be here, our children will grow up together, she will be my neighbour. That is the problem.'

Windward's size offered residents somewhat greater anonymity. But even there we found residents keenly aware of the need to try to get along with people who could be neighbours for a long time.

'You Can't Tell Who's on Subsidy'

One aspect of getting along with neighbours in the co-ops was tolerating their differences. And one of these differences was in income. A stock phrase that members used over and over again in our interviews was, 'You can't tell who's on subsidy.' In part, we feel, this was a way of saying that they realized subsidy information was confidential. It could not be told. But there was also a concern to reassure us, and perhaps themselves, that people on subsidy were just like everyone else. Ultimately, the message was that income differences made no difference in co-op living.

The results of the survey we conducted in September 1989 only partly supported this message. We found that neither income level nor subsidy status made a significant difference in members' satisfaction with living at Windward. It is harder to evaluate the Harbourside results. On the one hand, we had a higher response rate among non-subsidized members.[8] On the other, the subsidized respondents who did respond expressed somewhat more satisfaction with the co-op than non-subsidized respondents; 88 per cent of subsidized and 81 per cent of non-subsidized members were fairly or very satisfied. There was a similar degree of agreement between subsidized and non-subsidized Harbourside members concerning the extent of 'like-mindedness' in the co-op and the effectiveness of the selection process in choosing the 'right kind' of members, with subsidized people feeling marginally more positive than non-subsidized. But there was some evidence in our survey results that subsidized members had more of a sense of powerlessness in the co-op than those paying full rent. At Harbourside, 41 per cent of subsidized respondents said they felt they could influence what went on in the co-op only 'slightly,' or 'not at all'; only 25 per cent of the nonsubsidized respondents felt this way. Similarly, 44 per cent of people paying full rent felt they had 'considerable' or 'a great deal' of influence whereas only 24 per cent of people on subsidy gave this answer. At Windward, perhaps because of the co-op's size, members overall had less sense of personal influence on the co-op. Only 23 per cent of all respondents felt they could influence the co-op considerably or a great deal. Of those on subsidy, only 9 per cent felt this way while 29 per cent of the nonsubsidized did.

While these responses indicate income-based differences in members' experience, two points deserve mention. First, differences at Windward between the responses of males and females to the 'influence' question were much greater than subsidy differences. Only 12 per cent of the women respondents felt they had 'considerable' or 'a great deal' of influence, compared with 40 per cent of the men. Interestingly, there was no such gender difference at Harbourside. We cannot say for sure, but we suspect that both Harbourside's smaller size and its stronger sense of community contributed to women's greater sense of influence there.

A second point concerns differences in attitudes among people who were subsidized. We found that members, both subsidized and non-subsidized, identified two types of people on subsidy in the co-ops. These were lumped together in the subsidized category of the survey results, but their outlooks were very different. There were those who had what some called a 'welfare attitude.' They contributed little to the co-op and expected little in return, including little influence, except affordable housing. Then there were people on subsidy who sought to exert control over their housing and to gain control over their own lives with the support of the co-op. As one woman wrote on the back of our survey form, '[The co-op] provides a real sense of community and security when you're starting over.' A comparison of two women in Windward, presented to us in an interview with a third person on subsidy, illustrates this point:

There's two women here. Both on welfare. They hang around together. And one doesn't give a shit about the appearance of her apartment. Graffiti on the walls. Oh, the dirt! I don't know how

For Richer and Poorer 173

she can live in it. She doesn't look after her kids well at all. You walk in the house, you just wouldn't believe it.

Then there's this other girl. She's on welfare, too. And she hangs out with the crowd, you know, that is rough and tough. You know she's had a rough go of it. But she's a very thoughtful woman. She's very co-op minded and she's, like, very into helping. She organized a self-help committee to help people on welfare who need things. She'll help find social workers if people need them, things like that. She babysits for nothing. She's good.

Co-ops are carefully constructed to ensure that the message that attitude, not income, makes a difference is at least partly true. The selection process and an emphasis on confidentiality in subsidy administration help to ensure that attention is not drawn to income differences.

Confidentiality surrounded subsidy matters. Only the coordinator knew who was on subsidy or how much people paid in housing charges, unless the members themselves chose to make this known. Of course, members could and did guess about subsidies. But those whose speculations were the most negative, and those whom they criticized, were both extreme types of co-op members. Neither fit in very well. Both slipped through the net of a selection process designed to keep them out.

We have discussed the selection process in chapter 5, but one aspect of it needs elaboration here. The selection process appeared to favour applicants with middle-class values, although it was not biased towards middle-class incomes. Specifically, the selection process favoured people who held positive views of individuals' abilities to change themselves and control their housing. People so caught in poverty that, as Ted said, nothing 'really matters,' were seen as having little to contribute to the co-op and were passed over. Instead, the co-op chose other low-income households which seemed to have hope, energy, and a willingness to participate. Some higher-income applicants who assumed the poor deserved their poverty also were rejected. But others at both ends of the income range slipped through the selection process and into the co-ops.

Selection favoured richer and poorer applicants who seemed to share certain attitudes. We can extrapolate these attitudes from the interviews to some extent. These views relate in part to the idea of local control, which was central to the co-ops. The attitudes sought in applicants were those shared by 'good' – that is, satisfied and participatory – co-op members. They shared the conviction that personal action could improve their situations in life. They believed that individuals might need the support of others and society (as in housing assistance, for example) to take control of their lives. People who genuinely shared these attitudes, as opposed to those who expressed them merely in order to get in, formed the core of highly satisfied and committed co-op members. This core in both co-ops cut across income and subsidy status lines.

Some applicants shared these views only in part. Some of their applications were turned down; or if accepted often they did not feel they fit into the co-op. At one extreme were applicants on welfare who did not think they could improve themselves. They did not want to contribute to the co-op but felt social programs should support them anyway. A Windward member on subsidy herself told us how she would screen low-income applicants. 'I would look and see how they lived. How many kids they had. If they had any incentives to work. You know, if they were just on welfare for the fun of it and they figure it's a free ride. Let's just say I'd look for somebody that had drive and that wanted to make something of themselves and make something of where they lived.'

At the other extreme were professionals who were concerned to improve themselves but did not care about others or the co-op. These people, as one Windward resident commented, 'are bright and they can manipulate the co-op housing system better than people who go on the [assisted housing] waiting-lists because they have access to information and the skills to use it. These are people who would rather buy, who would rather buy anything! People who are not politically or ideologically drawn to the [co-op] concept are being driven into co-op housing because there's nothing else.'

Design and Mixed Incomes at Harbourside and Windward

Impressionistically, middle-income professionals were more common in Windward than at Harbourside, at least by 1989. For reasons of confidentiality, we could not collect detailed data linking incomes and subsidies to individuals in the co-ops; see Table 7.3 for summary statistics on income distributions. Our survey data from Harbourside overrepresent non-subsidized households, so incomes appear higher in Table 7.3 than they likely were for the co-op as a whole. Our observations and interviews indicated that higher-income people were attracted to both co-ops, but more so to Windward. A co-op sector activist speculated: 'I would bet that Windward stands a bit apart from the rest of the sector. It's a bit more middle class, and that has to do, frankly, with the funny appearance of the outside of the building. They made it look fancier than the typical co-op, you know. The typical co-op is a pile of bricks in Scarborough! So this one, I think, attracted higher-income people.' He went on to argue that housing higher-income people, as Windward does, was good for the co-op sector even if it meant housing fewer low-income people.

> Windward is good for the sector – except that the sector will never know it – in that you come closer here, probably, to having a slice of life than in a co-op where people predominantly want to live there for the principle of the thing. But the co-op sector will cut off their nose to spite themselves. They'll persist in being viewed as not a serious player in the housing market because they have a narrow view of who they want to serve. If they were more open to real people ... if they were prepared to believe that an executive working in an office downtown is a person too, trying to raise a family and so on, they might be given more opportunity to build housing here.

We suggested in the interview that governmental priorities on housing the poor, the difficulty of finding sites, and fiscal constraints also were considerations. He replied, 'Oh, yeah, I think the co-op sector is taking what it can get right now. There

TABLE 7.3
Distribution of household incomes at
Harbourside and Windward co-ops,
September 1989 survey

| Amount ($) | Percentage of respondents | |
	Windward (N = 100)	Harbourside (N = 54)
<10,000	6	9
10,000–19,999	12	7
20,000–29,999	18	15
30,000–39,999	8	15
40,000–49,999	17	11
>50,000	39	43

isn't much money, so they build whatever the government tells them they should be building.'

What the government was telling them to build was more housing in which housing charges were entirely geared to incomes. The 'co-op philosophy' of providing affordable housing for low- to middle-income people was being nudged in the late 1980s toward providing more housing for low-income people, not executives working downtown. This, not surprisingly, prompted NIMBY outbursts.[9] Such housing poses more than simply problems of community acceptance. It lacks the benefits mixed housing provides to lower-income people. And while it may more effectively target those in severe housing need, it eliminates those people with moderate incomes who also have a real need for affordable places to live in Toronto's housing crisis.

A comment made to us by a consultant who helped develop co-ops for a resource group points to the tension between building affordable housing and providing something more, partly through the inclusion of higher-income residents. We recorded this comment in a 1987 interview, when pressure for entirely low-income co-ops was less intense than at the end of our study. His observations point to the perceived importance of architectural design for attracting mixed-income residents whose presence, like the design itself, may improve the housing environment for low-income people.

I think ultimately our goal has to be to provide as much housing as possible. It would be foolish for us to suggest anything else. [But] I don't think we're willing to give up our social imperatives for the sake of just getting people in whatever housing we can. Not if that means putting them in communities that are disasters. Because if you create housing that just encourages and reinforces social problems you haven't helped anybody. You've just put them in a different prison.

So I think it's incumbent on us to create housing that serves as many people as possible but in a context that is socially useful. Co-ops, I think, make a lot of sense in that regard. They allow a variety of people with different incomes to live in one place. It seems to make much more sense than putting all the poor people in the same building.

Given that as a criterion, it immediately creates an architectural context that's different from [housing only poor people]. People with a middle- or upper-middle-income will not live in the same building that would have been provided for poor people. We have to always have in the back of our minds designing buildings that are going to serve a range of incomes. Which means we can't let it be just junk! We wouldn't be able to market it. We wouldn't get tenants. We have to keep all those things in mind if we're convinced that marketing to those middle and upper middle income people is as important as marketing to the poor people, and if we think it is important for those poor people that the [richer] others come in.

Unlike Windward's high architectural profile, Harbourside's conventional stacked townhouse design did not make it as much of a beacon for professionals seeking affordable housing. The location nevertheless attracted what one co-op sector person called 'a lot of yuppie types.' Several of these people moved out during the study period. A handful left at least partly because they were at odds with other co-op members. Yet, in our interviews at Harbourside, a stronger concern with community came through. The mixing of incomes there seemed to have been accompanied by more sharing of the attitudes toward individual and cooperative control that we outlined above.

Differences in Subsidy Issues at Harbourside and Windward

Harbourside

The importance members attributed to individual and collective control of their housing was crucial to Harbourside's fairly strong sense of community. Yet it also was the source of some of the most serious tensions in both co-ops. The administration of subsidy funds was part of the coordinator's job. Its day-to-day aspects were beyond members' immediate control. But setting subsidy policy *was* the members' job, and they debated hotly how this policy should affect the coordinator's administration of subsidies. A question central to the debate, and to the tensions it created, was: How can members prove they qualify for a subsidy' In other words, how could they demonstrate that without a subsidy they would have to pay more than 30 per cent of their gross household income in rent?

A simple answer, and the one to which Harbourside turned, was for households requesting subsidies to submit their personal income tax assessment notices to the coordinator. Each taxpayer receives one of these from Revenue Canada after his or her tax return has been processed and accepted. It confirms that the federal and provincial tax paid is the amount that really was owed. But this answer is not really so simple. The question of proof has many problematic dimensions. Whose income should be considered? What income should be counted? Is any request for proof an invasion of members' privacy? And is a tax statement enough proof to prevent abuses of the system? These questions were further complicated at Harbourside by the co-op's small size. It was hard to discuss subsidy policy issues in the abstract there. Each question was coloured by the personalities and experiences of the particular individuals involved. Subsidies, as one member told us, were 'confidential as far as the *office* part goes – in terms of how much people get and all of that. But our lifestyle here is so ... well, we do talk to each other so much. You're out in the courtyard – it really is like a little village – and you end up saying, "Oh, God, I haven't got my subsidy thing in yet!" For myself, I've never tried to keep it a secret because I think that fosters the separation [between subsidized and non-subsidized] even more – that sort of secret, shameful, you know, "who's on subsidy and who's not" kind of thing.'

Whose income should be considered in calculating need for housing charge assistance? This question became bound up with Harbourside's policy on guests. A guest's income, of course, was not considered in the calculation of a member's need for housing charge assistance. Guests who stayed longer than three months had to apply for membership in the co-op, at which point their income entered into such calculations. Some subsidized single women objected to this policy. They thought it encouraged their neighbours to pry. They also thought that this policy could make women feel pressured into more permanent relationships with male 'guests' at some cost to their own independence. A single mother on subsidy observed: 'Subsidized people are the ones who are vulnerable to problems of guests and privacy. They should be left alone. I don't think the intent of most people is to be cheating. I always mean to get off subsidy as soon as possible. It is not a nice situation. The father [of my baby] comes here all the time. But I don't want to be dependent on him. I don't think the money he gives me should be included [in my income].' She complained to us that when people in the co-op saw a woman like her with a male guest they said: ' "So, well look at her!" But they don't take into consideration that we women have pride and dignity too. There are things [like dependency] we just don't want! And that's why we came to a co-op. There is no other reason but that. And I think that's important to be reminded of.'

The question of what income should be counted was debated almost endlessly at Harbourside. Members complained about invasions of privacy, on the one hand, and made allegations about abuses of the system, on the other. Without simple, convincing proof of income, some members tended to use consumption as an index of income. They complained every time they saw that a person suspected of being on subsidy had made a big purchase. And people on subsidy complained every time they felt their privacy was being invaded. As one subsidized Harbourside member put it: 'I have heard people say "How come she can buy that car if she's paying such and such in rent?" Well, there are reasons. She got a loan from her brother-in-law. She cannot work without that car. She's paying for that car very harshly from whatever is left, right? And she's making a sacrifice. What's wrong with that?'

Ultimately, Harbourside decided to require Revenue Canada assessment notices as proof of income. The simplicity of this policy was seen as a strength that outweighed other drawbacks.[10] 'When we looked at how simple the verification process became if we used [the tax assessment], it outweighed the privacy concerns,' a member of the board of directors told us. By 1989, the board felt it had to change the tone of a 1988 draft subsidy policy that suggested they were trying to 'close all the loopholes and protect the co-op from all the cheaters.' Anyway, they recognized that 'we're never going to protect ourselves from the cheaters. So then we turned the policy around and looked at making it as equitable and as unobtrusive as we possibly could.'

Harbourside's wrangling over the administration of their subsidy policy probably is not finished. As one founding member of the co-op commented laughingly in 1989, 'Ever since I moved into the co-op there has been work being done by some group of people on revising subsidy policy. And it's not done yet!' The issues we have outlined here give an indication of the complexity and sensitivity of the problem of defining a clear policy while minimizing conflict between those who are subsidized and those who are not. It was a real challenge, as one member noted, 'to hand out money in as fair and unwelfare-like a way as possible. There is obviously a division in the co-op between who gets money and who doesn't. But [the co-op must] try to minimize that in terms of reporting income and baring your all.' The co-op, in short, had to maintain the image that income differences had no real consequences for how members were treated. Yet members had to have confidence that incomes, at least for those on subsidy, were accurately and honestly reported.

Whether Harbourside met this challenge or not, the lengthy subsidy policy debate did raise members' consciousness about subsidy issues. The Harbourside member quoted above continued: 'If we haven't succeeded in developing a more humane way, we certainly succeeded in making all of us think about how inhumane [the system] really is. That in itself is a step in the right direction. At least as a group we could acknowledge the strings attached to subsidies and to social welfare in general. I think it is important for people to think about that when they think about their neighbours on subsidy.' She was convinced that the prolonged discussion had led people to change their behaviour: 'I think there are less and less comments about new possessions that people on subsidy have – about people on subsidy who have cars. Those kind of things really irked some people at the beginning. They felt it just wasn't right that the co-op was sort of supporting them and "A furniture truck arrived the other day and there was this brand new couch and chair!" That sort of thing.' But everyone was more aware that all of them, whatever their income, were being subsidized through the mortgage interest reduction grant (MIRG): 'So people are beginning to see that we're all in this together. They see that people on subsidy who are making their way in the world on some level – you know, if they're getting new things and stuff – aren't actually taking it out of this person's pocket who is not on subsidy. That's the kind of thing that is *easing* here. There are a few people whose attitude isn't easing. And their attitude isn't as acceptable as it was maybe two years ago. People just don't put up with that from them.'

Most of the people whose attitudes had not eased had moved out of Harbourside by the time we concluded our study. There were no more than four or five in all. We interviewed three such households in three different years and three different locations. But the interviews were strikingly similar. These people shared the feeling that there was a strong sense of community in Harbourside, but that they had no place in it. They felt that people on subsidy exploited the system, took in boarders, boyfriends, and other 'illegal tenants' in violation of the guest policy, and lied about their income. All three made these allegations by innuendo: 'There's a woman who quit her job and went back to school but drives around in a red Mustang and wears a fur coat.' They represented themselves as disgruntled members of a middle class that was hard done by.

One who had struggled to earn a PhD and attained a professional position by working at menial jobs argued that the way the system operated was reverse psychology:

> Because in offering all this subsidy you're discouraging sacrifice. It's the same as if you're trying to train a puppy not to pee on your carpet. But every time he pees you give him a cookie. Because the way the system is set up you're better off not working! This is the side that I think the left wing people who try to *give* an opportunity to the poor are not seeing about the ones who work hard to get somewhere ...
>
> So it's not that I'm being selfish and saying I don't want to share my tax money with someone who needs it. I just don't want to give it to somebody who wants a bloody BMW when I don't have one myself! ... You see it's always the professionals, who work, who get attacked.

He had once campaigned for the social democratic New Democratic Party but now felt that he had been pushed far to the right by his experiences at Harbourside.

Windward

At Windward, the percentage of households on subsidy was a much bigger issue during our study than was the issue of how to administer and police subsidies. The central question was: How many households in the co-op should be on subsidy? Concern about this question surfaced in the fall of 1987 and debate continued, unresolved, through the end of our study in the summer of 1989.

The working out of this issue over time emphasizes how important a sense of local, democratic control was to the membership. As well, it points up how elusive real control could be because of the nature of subsidy financing and the role of the coordinator. It also shows how, even on an issue that could be expected to divide the co-op into subsidized and unsubsidized camps, positions cut across income levels and subsidy status.

Like other co-ops built under the section 56.1 program, Windward was required to make at least 25 per cent of its one hundred units available to households needing rental assistance. By 1989, the proportion had risen as high as 46 per cent. There were several reasons for this. First, the inclusion of about twenty-five people with disabilities, many of whom needed subsidies, meant that as soon as a few households of non-disabled people were admitted on subsidy the proportion exceeded 25 per cent.

Second, Windward's construction process was complicated and lengthy, as we have seen. The mortgage funds were drawn down several months before anyone actually moved into the building. Monthly subsidies were part of this money, under the formula described earlier in this chapter. So for almost four months subsidy funds accumulated at the rate of about $21,000 per month without any disbursement. CMHC allowed Windward to place $50,000 of this money in a reserve fund for emergency subsidies.

A final and crucial reason for the increasing percentage of Windward households on subsidy was the role the coordinator played in subsidy administration. Even after moving $50,000 of the excess subsidy money into a reserve fund, the coordinator had about $30,000 in extra subsidy funds to spend at the time the co-op opened. Rather than send this money back to CMHC unused, he allocated it as emergency subsidies. But, as he recognized in 1988, '[this] created a fair amount of expectation for emergency subsidies. We have [a few] households now that are just on perpetual emergency subsidies.' The coordinator kept allocating subsidies to any eligible household while the member selection committee and the board of directors continued to assume the percentage of households on subsidy was about 25 per cent. In the fall of 1988, the coordinator's report indicating that 41 per cent of member households were on subsidy seemed to come as a surprise to the member selection committee. Some felt that the coordinator had been acting too independently. They felt the board, and indirectly the members, should have more control over subsidy allocation. And some expressed the opinion that the percentage of households on subsidy ought to be capped, either at the original 25 per cent or at least at no higher than 40 per cent.

Support for the idea of capping subsidy levels came from people who held diverse positions. Some were confused about how subsidies worked. They felt incorrectly that a high percentage of households on subsidy would endanger the financial health of the co-op. Others seemed to have fears that could hardly be expressed in a socially acceptable way in the co-op. They were nervous about living with larger numbers of relatively poor people who might conspire to run the co-op. The subsidized people, they feared, might vote as a bloc to raise housing charges that would in effect be a burden only for the non-subsidized members. One member sardonically characterized people who shared this concern: 'They tend to lump everyone on subsidy together as this entity that's going to crawl out of the water one day and eat the co-op!'

Yet some of the people most in favour of capping the level of subsidies in the co-op were on subsidy themselves. As one member put it, 'People who I know are subsidized are sitting there saying "We don't want more of us."' For example, some felt, as one woman on subsidy told us, 'A lot of people on welfare to my way of thinking are undesirable. Certain types that can't help it ... I think they have to screen them carefully.'

A related concern was that some people were 'getting away with murder.' The appearance of the building seemed to be deteriorating as was the quality of life. Some laid the blame for this at the doors of the subsidized households. One man who had been an active socialist changed his views dramatically after living at Windward. He had once worked with guerrillas in the Third World, but by the end of our study he and his family had bought a house and left Windward. He came to feel that poorer members lowered the tone of the building by drinking, fighting, and letting their kids vandalize the co-op.

In fact, it was by no means clear that the problem households were the ones on subsidy. Others who were concerned about 'law and order' in the building were opposed to capping subsidies and recognized that both the source and the solution of the problem lay outside the subsidy question. They felt that the deteriorating appearance of the buildings resulted from the superintendent's health problems and inadequate temporary janitorial services. And they felt that vandalism occurred because both the richer and poorer kids had nothing better to do. Efforts were being made as we ended our research to create neighbourhood activities that would involve the young teenagers who were felt to be the main source of vandalism.

One founder of the co-op felt the issue should be seen not as a subsidy matter but as a question of people taking responsibility for their housing: 'It's stupid [to cap the level of subsidies]. It's the old misconception that people who need subsidy aren't as good as people who don't need subsidy. [The important thing is that] the standards of the building are the same for subsidized and non-subsidized people alike. Therefore, the problem does not revolve around whether a person is subsidized or not. It's whether they behave themselves reasonably in a co-op living environment.'

Partly, then, feelings that were expressed as anxiety about the number of people in the co-op on subsidy could be seen as a problem of enforcing standards through member control. 'One of the things that a co-op has,' the founding member noted, 'is an elected board. If the people say, "We have a problem; go solve it, board," then you go to work and solve it.' Furthermore, the subsidy capping issue raised once again the importance of member selection in fostering a similarity of attitudes that cuts across the differences in income in the co-op. One member's reflections in the summer of 1988 were particularly insightful:

> I don't know what the last figures were, but roughly 40 per cent, maybe as high as 45 per cent of the households are subsidized. My feeling is that I don't see a need for increasing nor do I see a need for capping them.
>
> I would say that I am quite happy with the present mix because

it seems to have given us a well-structured community. Just looking at the results [of that mix], I don't know who the subsidized people are in the co-op – other than a few people. I've sort of become accidentally aware that they are subsidized. As you meet people and work with them, it seems to be a good mix. I suppose my judgment of what is and is not a good mix to a large degree rests on their ideas or how they view those things that we're confronted with in everyday life.

I speak to people and I seem to hear the sort of views that are consistent with my outlook. I recognize myself as having somewhat of a bias toward conservatism in my day-to-day living. [Here] I hear liberal ideas and some radical ideas, but I like the mix. I think I would get fed up if they were all conservative views. And I suppose if they were all the other way and I were the only dissenting one, I might think that mix was no good. The results of this economic mix seem to have produced a community whose ideas and outlook on life don't seem too much at variance with my particular set of values, at least as yet.

The Future of Subsidies in the Co-ops

By 1989, the proportion of subsidized households had stabilized in both co-ops at 40–45 per cent, which made full use of the subsidy pool funds. Consequently, members paying market rent who moved out had to be replaced with other non-subsidized people. Subsidized households who left, of course, could be replaced by others needing assistance but such move-outs were rare, partly for financial and bureaucratic reasons.

While the income mix seemed to have stayed more or less the same, once it reached the 40 per cent level, family composition had changed somewhat. Judy Jameson, who had been so impressed by the film *Not Just a Place to Live*, observed in 1989 that the children of most of the single parents in Harbourside were of school age. There were no more single mothers with babies. She wondered: 'Why has this happened? Why aren't there any more babies?' Then she realized that there *were* new babies in the co-op but they all had two parents. With the subsidy pool fully used, there were no more places for young single mothers. Judy felt that in this way, 'we are not *making* a change [in the family composition of the co-op]; we are *preventing* a change. But not deliberately. It's just the way it happens.'

What will happen as the subsidy pool increases in these co-ops with the decline of the mortgage interest reduction grant? The additional funds no doubt will be used to increase the number of households on subsidy, but this money is unlikely to be used to include more new members on subsidy. As the MIRG declines and the co-op must pay a larger share of the mortgage payments, housing charges probably will rise.[11] More households which are already in the co-ops will then qualify for subsidies because they would otherwise have to pay over 30 per cent of their income in rent.

In 1989, the income ceiling was raised to $44,700 at Harbourside. At the general members' meeting at which the ceiling was raised, the possibility of using the larger subsidy pool to include needy outsiders was not even raised. One person who attended the meeting commented to us, 'It was clear that *nobody* was thinking in terms of that as a possible alternative, of opening up [the subsidy pool] to people outside.' She said that she decided not to raise the issue because of her own ambivalence about it. On the one hand, she was deeply committed to social housing and to giving needy people access to mixed-income housing co-ops. On the other hand, she was concerned about the middle-income people hit hard by increased housing charges who would pay more than 30 per cent of their income in rent if the ceiling were not raised. This was not the same as the view of those dissatisfied members who left the co-op feeling the poor benefit from a system that exploits the middle class. Rather, it was a viewpoint that favours protecting people in the co-op community and meeting their needs because they are members. Her view, obviously so widely shared as to need no discussion in the meeting, was that 'as members, they should get it before we give it to others.'

If subsidy assistance were not extended to these middle-income households, a problem would arise that is known as the 'gap' in social housing circles. A gap would appear between the highest-income subsidized households and the lowest-income full-rent members. In other words people with incomes in the $35,000–45,000 range simply could not afford to live at Windward or Harbourside. The co-ops would become housing that, ironically, was affordable only for the rich and the poor, not people in between. But redistribution of subsidy funds to include middle-income households probably will keep the 'gap' from opening up at Harbourside and Windward.

The future of income mixing in these co-ops, then, seems likely to be one in which the mix will remain more or less the same. The difference will be that, at least in the short run, more middle-income households will be on subsidy. The more households on subsidy there are, the lower the turnover rate in the co-ops is likely to be. This would seem to be especially true for households earning $35,000–45,000 a year who would be unlikely to qualify for subsidized housing elsewhere. The few new members probably would have to pay full rent, assuming the subsidy pool was fully allocated among established members. So, eventually, the income mix could be expected to include people earning higher incomes than the top end of current co-op members. There is also the possibility, remote though it seems, that along with changing government programs for affordable housing, new funds might be made available to increase the percentage of low-income members.

Conclusion

The program under which Harbourside and Windward were built required too few needy households (25 per cent) either to make full use of available subsidy funds or to ensure what at least some in the co-ops considered to be an appropriate mix of income levels. Both co-ops responded by increasing the *de facto* number of households on subsidy to 40 per cent or more by 1988. Yet both co-ops planned not to increase the percentage on subsidy further. They could do so as the size of the subsidy pool increases according to the section 56.1 program formula. But as of 1989 they had chosen to preserve the existing mix of income levels and provide more assistance to middle-income member households for whom increased housing charges otherwise would not be affordable.

Later government housing programs have targeted mostly those in greatest housing need. They have been less concerned than the section 56.1 program with subsidizing or providing affordable housing for moderate- to middle-income households. But our findings at Harbourside and Windward suggest that mixing income levels is an important element in so far as this contributes to the mix of attitudes, backgrounds, family composition, and so forth that makes a co-op into a community. Moreover, in Toronto's housing crisis, so-called middle-income households need affordable housing, too.

Some richer and poorer people want more than affordable housing. In co-ops they can have more. They can create for themselves a place to live that they control and to which they can feel a sense of belonging. Not everybody in the co-ops wanted or welcomed the kind of community that resulted. We have given examples of members who became progressively fed up with the mixed-income aspect of these projects. But for people with certain expectations and values, mixed-income co-ops work. As the comments we have included here testify, they worked for people who wanted not 'just a place to live' but a sense of community.

Co-op living shapes such communities out of members' diversity – in terms of income, for example – and out of the attitudes that those who fit best in co-ops share. These attitudes cross-cut income levels. They were at the heart of serious divisions within the co-ops on subsidy matters. Yet these divisions were not along simple subsidized–non-subsidized lines. The attitudes core co-op members seemed to share included an emphasis on the ability of people to gain control of and improve their housing and, to some extent, their lives. Some needed financial support from the state to achieve this, others did not. But for these co-op communities, attitudes matter. Income matters less.

CHAPTER EIGHT

Participating in Co-op Life

Two Views on Participation

A Positive One

In the spring of 1987, Enid Burton told us how she loved living at Harbourside co-op: 'I think it's wonderful. I've lived in a lot of different places and I've always felt that it was someone else's. I've never felt that I belonged there. In Metro housing I never unpacked my pictures. It was never home. But this is different. This is home. I mean, this will never be my house, I'll never own it. But to me this is my house [all the same].'

Having grown up in small farming villages in England, Enid had moved to Toronto five or six years before. Living in a large city and in apartments was new for her. And being a single mother with small children made her feel keenly the need for community. One thing about small villages she expected to find at the co-op was that other members would play a part in raising her children. Some people would see this as interference in their own affairs, she said, but she thought it would be positive. 'Things can't always be the way [people] want. But [the important thing is to be] doing something instead of always talking about [what you want to have done]. I'm a do-er.' She felt people should be expected to participate in the co-op. It is a cooperative venture where 'we should all work together, even if it's only picking up garbage.' The whole idea is to do things together. However, the co-op must be realistic about what people actually can do.

Enid joined the landscaping committee because of her love of gar-

dening. She dreaded having to serve on something like the finance committee because she felt she lacked the necessary skills and experience. The landscaping committee also suited her because she could take her children along to the meetings and work parties.

At first, Enid did not feel very confident about her abilities as a committee member. She was uneasy with collective decision making, such as she experienced at co-op general meetings. Gradually, though, she gained experience and confidence; soon she became chair of the committee. She felt she could actually affect the life of the co-op for the better. An example was park benches for the courtyard. Enid persuaded the co-op to buy eight of them, principally so that members who lived in the apartments upstairs would have some place to be. 'People need to have places where they can get together, not where they are made to go. I prefer places where people can meet because they want to. That's what happens now with the pathways. People come out and sit on the wooden planters and pathway walls ... [With] our park benches they can do the same thing, but it will be easier for people in the apartments to use the courtyard.'

Not everything was perfect for Enid in the co-op. General meetings often depressed her with their interminable discussions of building deficiencies. Participation could be frustrating. For example, that first fall everyone agreed to put down sod in the courtyard – until it became obvious the co-op had to choose between grass and laundry tubs. Then people said it was going to be winter soon, so laundry tubs were more important. For her, the others were being short-sighted. Yet by actively playing a part in running the co-op she came to feel she could make a difference. Enid hoped to stay at Harbourside for at least ten years, at least until her children were grown. Then she might move to another co-op, preferably in the country.

A Negative Experience

When we talked with Tom Norman in the summer of 1989, he was surrounded by packing-cases. With help from relatives, he and his wife were moving to a house they had bought in another city. There were several reasons for the move but one was that Tom had become disillusioned.

Tom had played a central role at Windward co-op. Years before the co-op actually opened, he had served on the founding board of directors. He had spent innumerable hours interviewing hundreds of prospective members over several years. Himself a paraplegic, Tom was concerned about the accessibility of the building and integrating people with disabilities and others. Above all, he felt strongly about the need for community at Windward.

There were a lot of promises, I guess, made last year ... in terms of improved cooperation, communication within the co-op. That hasn't substantially improved, as I see it ... I feel that the co-op is ... I don't know whether it's stagnating, whether it's failing to grow ... maybe it's growing, and I don't appreciate the direction in which it's growing. I'm not exactly sure.

There's been a lot of lip service paid to the community aspect of the co-op, and nothing really concrete done, in terms of trying to build it. And so, I'm not saying there should be sociable things every month, but I think there has to be a real *determination to get people on track, to educate, to encourage. I think there's a lot of that that hasn't been in place.*

The co-op's had serious problems in getting its business done at general meetings. An excellent example was that our annual general meeting couldn't be finished in one night because there were two ties in the balloting. By the time the second balloting was completed, there weren't enough people to continue the meeting. And that wasn't the first time. There was more than one occasion where the business of the co-op has failed because there was just nobody to do it.

At that same meeting, there was a discussion of the requirements for participation. Tom moved a deliberately controversial motion. The board of directors should consider requiring excuses for absences from general meetings and, if necessary, taking 'commensurate disciplinary action.'

The motion was put forward because, for essentially a year and a half, the board was unwilling to entertain any kind of position on participation. And my feeling was that, if nothing else, perhaps the motion at a general meeting would get enough people talking about it, that the co-op would go one direction or the other. Didn't matter to me which way they went.

However [laughing ironically], looking at what happened, there was no *direction, as far as I'm concerned. The co-op really didn't make any choice either way ... I didn't think there was any really serious discussion that went on. A motion that has significant impact, in terms of how the co-op is going to run – it's entrenched in the by-laws, it's entrenched in the occupancy agreement – and yet the end result was that there was really no result. By not really having discussed it, not really giving any alternate direction – by simply defeating the motion – I think it left a void.*

I'm not looking for any kind of a utopia. I don't think that that can exist. What I do think is that there are ways of making things significantly better than what they are.

Member Participation

Studies of urban citizen participation have shown that it tends to increase the satisfaction of users with communities, workplaces, parks, and housing. It often gives participants a sense of attachment and ownership. However, many kinds of citizen participation do not include actual power sharing on the part of urban authorities. Rather, they tend to involve the dissemination of information or consultation but not participation in actual decision making.[1]

What really differentiates co-ops from other kinds of housing is the quality and degree of member participation. Participation in the management of a co-op is more than a right, as it may be in a condominium.[2] In co-ops it is an obligation written into the occupancy agreement. Minimally, members must contribute a few hours a month to committee work and attend general meetings.

The rewards of participation are diffuse. They may include greater satisfaction with living in the co-op, the pleasure of personal and collective accomplishment, the feeling of doing one's duty, a deeper involvement with one's neighbours, a stronger sense of the co-op as a community, even the experience of empowerment. But there also are costs. 'There is a flip-side to the communal benefit of co-ops. Many people, myself included, aren't thrilled about getting involved in nursery detail, the budget committee, the garbage committee, the Co-op Day committee, etc.'[3]

In the city, especially, there are many competing demands on people's time, and serving on co-op committees may compare poorly with other ways to spend an evening.

Member participation tends to be greater in new co-ops. People are fresher and there is more work to be done than in established projects. Yet even in their first three years Windward and Harbourside fell far short of the 100 per cent member participation specified in the occupancy agreements that everyone living there had signed. Depending on the measures used, one-half to three-quarters of the members participated in any formal way.

In this chapter we suggest that levels of participation at Windward and Harbourside were no worse than one can realistically expect of urban co-ops. Going beyond formal participation on committees and attendance at meetings, we consider involvement in the co-op through less formal kinds of social interaction as well.[4] Members' experiences with formal participation and involvement in the co-op point to some of the rewards and costs of investing time and energy in co-op management.

Should universal participation remain a goal to which cooperative housing aspires but which it cannot expect to achieve? We discuss this question in the context of Toronto co-ops more generally. The Co-operative Housing Federation of Toronto had no simple answer to this much-debated issue, although it developed guidelines for motivating greater member involvement. Finally, we outline the steps Windward and Harbourside took to encourage participation among their members.

Our view is that given the impossibility of achieving anything close to 100 per cent participation, especially in urban co-ops, efforts would be better spent developing ways of involving smaller numbers of members in an ever-changing core of active residents. We conclude that participation might be organized with a view to frequent transfers of power and skills. Rather than trying to involve everyone at one time or relying always on the same small group of committed members, a shifting core of active co-op members could be encouraged to emerge and continually replenish itself. This requires organizational development. At least as important, the atmosphere on committees should be such that those who agree to participate once will be willing to do so again.

Involvement and Participation

For Enid Burton and Tom Norman, co-op involvement was both rewarding and frustrating. Both participated actively on co-op committees. However, involvement can go beyond formal participation on committees to take a variety of forms. Members' informal interaction and involvement in co-op social activities clearly are important for building community.

Not everyone enjoys or is good at committee work. Also, people's abilities to contribute time and energy vary considerably both over time with individuals and among members generally. It is important to bear in mind that co-op members did not spend most of their time in such pursuits. Some members did devote considerable time to co-op affairs. But their lives, like most people's, revolved mainly around work, family, and school. Too, there were many attractions in downtown Toronto competing with co-op social activities for members' interest. And most members had family and friends outside the co-ops.

A Few Statistics

Attendance at general meetings is a minimal measure of democratic participation. We calculated for Windward the percentage of meetings at which households had a member in attendance.[5] In 1988 (five meetings) and the first half of 1989 (three meetings), on average households had someone at about half the meetings. In 1988 and 1989, respectively, 12 per cent and 14 per cent of households attended no general meetings at all, while 26 per cent and 21 per cent attended more than three-quarters of them. We were not able to obtain such detailed data for Harbourside. However, we note that Harbourside co-op held general meetings almost once a month beginning in mid-1986. No meetings had to be cancelled because of a lack of a quorum.[6]

Our survey provided a snapshot of Windward and Harbourside in late 1989. Most members of both co-ops who responded found general members' meetings productive: 79 per cent at Harbourside; 67 per cent at Windward. But only 58 per cent at Harbourside and 52 per cent at Windward felt comfortable in attending them. Somewhat more women than men and people on subsidy felt uncomfortable at these meetings. When asked if they thought that members had a sufficient say in decision making at such meetings, 73 per cent at Harbourside and 67 per cent at Windward replied, 'about the right amount.' About 18 per cent and 25 per cent, respectively, thought members had too little say. At Harbourside, more women than men felt they had too little say, but whether members were receiving housing subsidies made no difference to their responses. At Windward the pattern was reversed: subsidy status affected the pattern of responses while gender did not.

At both co-ops, a large percentage of respondents (74 per cent at Harbourside, 86 per cent at Windward) reported that they had served on a committee at some time. Of those who had served, 65 per cent at Harbourside and 66 per cent at Windward found their experience generally positive while 15 per cent and 17 per cent, respectively, thought it negative. This committee service ranged from one to almost ten committees, with the average at about two. One should bear in mind, though, that 80 per cent of our Windward and 85 per cent of our Harbourside respondents had been members since 1987. Thus, committee participation at any particular time was somewhat lower.

Breaking down committee membership somewhat, we noted that at Windward gender, income level, educational level, and whether the member had a disability made no difference statistically in who joined. Respondents receiving subsidies tended to belong to committees somewhat more than did people paying market rents (94 per cent to 82 per cent).

At Harbourside income, educational level, subsidy status, and gender did not appear to make a difference in committee membership. Approximately three-quarters of both subsidized and market rent respondents had served on committees. The same was true for the other variables. However, these results may reflect the fact that people receiving subsidies and having low incomes were underrepresented among respondents. We know also that those who responded to the survey were more likely than non-respondents to be active participants in the co-op.

Other data on committee memberships we collected are more detailed for Windward than for Harbourside.[7] In both 1988 and 1989, roughly 67 per cent of households had someone serving on at least one committee or the board at some time during the year. Note that a smaller percentage of *members* served on committees. Only one member in most of these 'participating' households served on a committee (41 per cent in 1988, 48 per cent in 1989). Altogether, 50 per cent of households had members on one or two committees. A handful of households, however, were very active. In 1988 members of 6 per cent of the households belonged to from four to seven committees. In 1989, the maximum was five.

The overall picture for Windward, then, is of fairly broad (67 per cent of households) but rather shallow participation on committees. Most had only one household member on any committee. A small number of member households clearly participated much more heavily. But these figures are crude. They do not allow us to take into account that membership on some committees (or the board of directors) is much more demanding than on others. Being on the board or the finance committee may be much more of a commitment of time, for example, than serving on three committees simultaneously, e.g., the social, landscaping, and newsletter committees.

Participation rates seem objectively to have remained fairly constant over the first three years in both co-ops. But the extent to which members *felt* involved with the co-ops changed somewhat. At both co-ops, 30 per cent of survey respondents felt their involvement had increased. At Windward, about the same number (32 per cent) had the opposite response. Of Harbourside survey respondents, 43 per cent felt that their involvement with the co-op had decreased by 1989. In other words, more people at Harbourside thought they had weakened rather than strengthened their involvement with the co-op. A decline in involvement from the intense early days of establishing the co-op is understandable, even desirable. People we interviewed spoke in terms of 'mellowing' and 'acceptance' of the status quo. But decreases in members' sense of involvement at Harbourside left a core of 'pioneers' (both subsidized and non-subsidized) who continued to feel deeply committed but increasingly also overworked. They filled some of the most demanding committee positions and tended to the informal but continuous needs of the co-op, such as cleaning the oven in the community kitchen and pulling communal weeds.

Those whose reported involvement at Harbourside had diminished were more likely to be receiving housing charge assistance. Of the subsidized Harbourside respondents, 56 per cent reported that their involvement with the co-op had decreased, whereas only 11 per cent said their involvement had increased. The split was greater still among non-subsidized members: 40 per cent increased and 37 per cent decreased their involvement. These figures suggest that for people paying full rent, feelings of declining or increasing involvement were related to other factors. Except for a few subsidized households who were among the most strongly committed to the co-op, those receiving housing charge assistance tended fairly strongly toward decreasing involvement. As noted in the preceding chapter, subsidized Harbourside members had less of a sense that they could influence what happens in the co-op. This may reflect the declining involvement of many subsidized households with the co-op relative to the core of active pioneers, although some of them also were subsidized.

At Windward, 52 per cent of subsidized respondents reported a declining involvement with the co-op, while only 22 per cent of those paying full housing charges gave this response. Similarly, only 19 per cent of subsidized people said their involvement had increased, but 33 per cent of those paying full housing charges gave this response. People with disabilities were slightly more likely than able-bodied respondents to report increased feelings of involvement.[8] Among women, 34 per cent said their involvement had declined and 21 per cent said it had increased. Men at Windward reported the strongest increase in involvement (42 per cent), with 27 per cent claiming their involvement had decreased.

These data may reflect greater time constraints on lower-income households and on women generally. They may point also to growing frustrations these people experienced with co-op participation. We will return to these issues in the next chapter on member control over the co-ops.

Taken together, these data give us a general picture of participation, at least on committees. Committee memberships cut across some of the major social differences at Windward and Harbourside co-ops. While some members had not taken the opportunity to get involved in running their co-ops, at least one member of most households had. Income, education, gender, subsidy status, and whether a member had a disability (at Windward) do not seem to be related to who belonged to committees. There is some indication, however, that gender and subsidy status were related to feelings of declining involvement with the co-ops. In other words, while most households at least minimally met their obligation to participate, those receiving subsidies and, especially at Windward, women felt less involved in the co-ops than they had previously.

Members' Experience

Statistics tell the story of participation and involvement, but only in a general way. Broadly speaking, for many members, how much and how intensively they participated seemed to depend on how they assessed participation's rewards and costs. Social scientists have pointed out that the costs of participation in collective action often tend to be clearer and more definite than the benefits. Thus, writers like Mancur Olson (1965) have stressed the inhibiting effects of costs. Not everyone, however, seemed to weigh costs and benefits.

Why did people participate in these co-ops, other than to meet the terms of their occupancy agreements? We found a variety of reasons. Some co-op members clearly participated from a sense of duty or civic responsibility rather than some implicit utilitarian calculation. A few members of both Windward and Harbourside actively participated at least partly for ideological reasons. They believed strongly in the importance of community and sharing. For example, one Windward resident suggested that member selection procedures should be thought out more clearly so that there would be more socially and politically aware members. For this person, besides participation community should be fostered by 'a looser approach to property and boundaries. In concrete terms, this could mean we would all see a little of each other's interests/activities displayed on doors and in hallways.' This would involve giving up a certain amount of concern for tidiness and privacy. But it would result in greater knowledge and concern for others, a more 'homey' atmosphere. 'I think this approach to property functions on a metaphoric level, symbolizing our willingness to share of ourselves and accept others' sharings, thereby creating a greater sense of community.'

Another member argued that co-ops should try to become self-sufficient as an alternative to the 'speculative greed in the housing sector' and capitalism, more generally. He devoted his time and energy so that when co-op members had learned to run their organization well they could cut the ties that bound them to government. 'Eventually, the co-op's aims should be to teach people how to control their loosely united destinies, instead of being controlled.'

In the early days, one of Harbourside's most involved members thought that it should be a 'community of like-minded people.' Through working together and socializing, members would come to share values and a deep concern for each other. Two years later, while he felt that a real sense of community had developed, his earlier view seemed a bit idealistic. His rough estimate was that only half of Harbourside's members participated at all. Those who did participate he divided into two categories. The large majority did things that had been organized for them. Then there were the few who saw 'things that need doing' around the co-op and did them: people who pulled up weeds without being asked or who changed burned-out light bulbs. As someone who had thrown himself in wholeheartedly, he felt frustrated that so many others had not. But he still hoped to create the conditions through which others would develop a deeper commitment to the co-op as a community, as more than just a place to live.

Some Rewards of Involvement

The rewards of co-op involvement were various and often diffuse but nonetheless real for most members. Cumulatively, they made some members feel that the co-op was home, in a way that multiple housing rarely is. For others, the benefits did not balance the time spent, frustrations, and other costs of involvement.

One of the simplest rewards was the casual recognition accorded by members to others in the courtyard, elevator, or hallway. As Ken Lawrence of Windward put it:

> Co-op living seems to give me a satisfaction, in that I am recognized. When I come in the building, I see people that I know, and I say 'Hello' to them. It may be nothing more than a 'Hello' or 'Good morning', or 'How are things going?' If I meet them in the elevator, it's that.
>
> And I don't, necessarily, always initiate the discussion; it comes from others. [If I'm] absent in the hospital for a while, I come home, and people express their pleasure at seeing me back again. It's this recognition that satisfies the feeling that, I guess, we all *want*, to some degree (whether we'll get it or not). Being recognized is, I feel, perhaps, a basic yearning in all of us.

Certainly, people living in traditional neighbourhoods accord each other this sort of recognition. But many co-op members remarked on how important it was to them and how their co-op experience differed in degree from living in other kinds of housing in the city.

Another Windward member, Michael Lord, saw additional benefits flowing from casual recognition.

> Seldom will it be that I'll walk across ... from one side of the courtyard to the other, without at least two or three people – whose names I *may not* know – stopping and remarking about whatever

issue happens to be [current]. So, [there's] a kind of social under-current that causes you to realize that you're living *with* these peo-ple, and how their thinking and feeling *is* important. Because these are the people you'll have to rely on if things are going to get done.

So the more aloof you are, the more hostile the community you're guaranteeing for yourself. The more friendly you are with people – you're *moving* in the direction of assuring that people are going to be friendly when they see *you*. And that you're going to feel like you're living in a little village, or a little community – not feel like you're living in one isolated unit.

For Michael casual recognition expressed members' sharing of interests and understandings. Little by little it helped to create the feelings on which community identification is based. He stressed how different these feelings were at Windward from what he had felt at the other places in Toronto he had lived.

Mutual support was another of the benefits of involvement. At one level, such support meant occasionally looking after each other's children or lending the proverbial cup of sugar. Single mothers, especially, came to rely on each other to help out with child-minding. We cannot quantify how frequent such exchanges were or whether they occurred more often at these co-ops than in other multiple-housing projects. But many members remarked on how significant they were.

At a deeper level, adversity or personal tragedy showed how the co-op community could mobilize to support its members. Sharing in such experiences also helped reciprocally to strengthen the bonds of community. When a member of Harbourside drowned in early 1989, the community rallied around to help his wife and young children.

As soon as the death happened, it was like a small village. There were offers of food and babysitting, and support, and cars available. And there was a very successful wake, if you can call a wake suc-cessful – but it *was* – and it went on, and on. Like, for days, people would gather together and sit and drink – people that, maybe, wouldn't have a lot to do with each other, otherwise. You would sort of meet outside or in the courtyard – and it was cold, still – but there were clusters of people looking for each other. People began to talk about how happy they were to be here, because they realized that those big tragedies are easier to bear if you have a sense of friendship and community.

People weren't finished with it, and so someone suggested that we plant a tree. And, a few weeks ago there was a tree-planting ceremony, and *lots* of people came to it.

Participating together in the simple ritual and planting the symbolic tree also helped to deepen people's identification with Harbourside as a community. 'It's not finished, and ... people continue to speak about Reg and ask about Val, his wife, and [their] two kids ... they continue to be supportive to her on, you know, levels like babysitting and, occasionally, some food. It's not forgotten and I think it really changed something here.'

One of the more diffuse rewards of participation, as a highly involved Harbourside member told us, was

a sense of involvement in the community. You know what's happening, which is nice. And, for me, I've been home the past three years with the kids, working one day a week for the past two and half years. So when you're not out in the work world, it's nice to have some involvement where you have some interaction with adults. You know you're making decisions. You have a sense that, yes I can still do things. My mind isn't totally mush – mostly but not quite.

You know some meetings can be a drag, but also you can get a real bond with people. I think weathering some of the issues makes some of those bonds stronger and I think strengthens your involvement in the community.

Being empowered and gaining a sense of heightened control over one's own life often are pointed to as significant rewards of co-op participation.[9] These benefits often were said to accrue especially to the people at Windward and Harbourside who previously were least powerful, namely low-income people in general, women, and people with disabilities. In the last two categories, single mothers and people with disabilities who previously lived in institutions are particularly important. It is difficult to say, however, how many members actually were empowered by their co-op experience. The woman at Harbourside quoted above reflected on her own experience. 'You have an opportunity to learn some skills that you really don't get an opportunity to in other places, sit on committees, sit on a board, make decisions, learn about building problems and things like that which a lot of people ... never heard of.'

Another member of Harbourside, a single mother, told us how the security of living there had affected her life.

> To feel stability – for someone like me. I mean, I'm not very well educated; I'm a single parent; I come from a really working-class background, you know. I'm a woman ... blah, blah, blah.
>
> There are a lot of things that make it difficult for me to find security – anywhere – in terms of housing. And to actually feel secure in my housing situation gives me a base, that I didn't know I was missing .... I mean, you move from place to place, and you sort of think that that's going to happen for the rest of your life. The landlord sells it, or whatever .... You have no control ... And all of those things you assume are going to be part of your life forever. Once that hassle is gone, it really does change your life in a very fundamental way. Like, it is very different. It's great!

Her formal involvement with Harbourside included committee memberships and serving on the board of directors. But she also attended training courses and workshops on co-op management run for co-op members. As well, she served as one of Harbourside's representatives to a national co-op housing federation meeting. With the skills and experience she gained she went on to secure a job as coordinator of another co-op.

As we have said, the rewards of co-op involvement were real but somewhat diffuse. They were not as easy to pin down as the costs, such as spending three hours at a committee meeting. Nevertheless, for many members the advantages gained, which generally heightened their identification with the co-op as a community, led them to remain involved. As one Harbourside member wrote, 'I never suspected – much less imagined – how closely the co-op would come to resemble my notion of a home.'

Some Costs

Generally, our interviews showed that members considered time and emotional energy to be the most important costs of participation. Not surprisingly, competing claims on people's time and energy affected their ability and willingness to participate. For example, a recent president of the board of Harbourside co-op worked both as a private consultant and at a regular job. He worked shifts, which began to interfere with his ability to attend evening meetings. A single mother of three felt that she could not give much time to co-op activities. She thought that those who were much better off than she was must have more spare time. They were very active in the co-op but did not seem to understand the problems she and other single mothers faced. Others found that evening committee meetings were not enticing after a long day's work. In a written comment, one member said: 'Toronto is a stressful place to live. We all have to work too hard and too much and travel too long to work. Thus, we have little energy/time to devote to our community.'

As well, young co-ops have more organizational work to be done than well-established ones and their members often lack experience. Thus, they need more time from their members in the early stages. One member described to us his experience on Harbourside's first board of directors after it opened. 'We had learned a valuable lesson early on when we came here. We would sit up till 1:00, 2:00 in the morning when we would make the last decisions and get through the agenda, only to find out at the next meeting it was the wrong decision and we would have to do it again.' That board often met several times a week.

Another member of that board pointed out that 'a lot of committees were functioning with no policies or with something that was handed to them by the resource group and they never read it. They didn't know what it was about.' Contrasting 1988 with 1987, he went on:

> The board functions this year more like a management team. The board last year was really a fire department. It seemed like the whole year was consumed with one emergency that needed to be dealt with after the other. There wasn't any time to deal with the day-to-day. That fell really to the coordinator or to nobody at all because we had legal proceedings that didn't actually materialize but were threatening with the builder and so on. And there were problems with members and problems with non-existent policies and all of that. And now it seems that, at least organizationally, the co-op's on track.

A co-op's size also makes a difference in how much time it needs from its members. Very small co-ops (some have fewer than ten units) find it hard to afford professional maintenance services, for example. Everyone must participate, otherwise the co-op fails. Harbourside, with 54 units and fewer than 80 members, had a smaller pool to draw from than Windward with about 160 members.

Thus, time affected member participation in several ways. The scheduling of meetings and other events was an obstacle to people who worked shifts or had to study at the appointed times. Many people felt that they simply were too busy to devote much time to the co-op. To some extent the ages and sizes of the co-ops affected how much time they needed their members to donate. As well, if much time was required, members had to feel that it was being used productively. This was not always the case at Harbourside and Windward; thus some members became frustrated and discouraged.

More generally, members' involvement in the co-ops, both formal and informal, depended to some extent on how they evaluated the alternative uses to which their spare time could be put. Windward and Harbourside are downtown co-ops. Several co-op sector consultants pointed out that one way downtown and suburban co-ops differ is in the greater range of attractions competing for members' leisure time in the city. In some ways, they said, having forty people at a downtown co-op party may be more impressive than having a hundred at a suburban one. One summer recently, co-ops in suburban Scarborough organized a league of twenty-four baseball teams, complete with uniforms and trophies, while the downtown co-ops could not field a single team.[10]

Whether members spent their leisure time socializing in the co-op depended to some extent on how easy it was to go out. People with children and those who used wheelchairs were the most frequent participants in social events within the co-op. At Harbourside, 44 per cent of the respondents to our survey reported attending most or all social events organized by the co-op. Of these, 83 per cent had children living at home. At Windward, only 30 per cent said they attended most or all social events. A much larger percentage of members with disabilities (50 per cent) than others (25 per cent) attended these events. Furthermore, the extent to which members socialized within the co-op depended partly on the strength and number of their social ties outside the co-op. Those with lots of friends and family outside the co-op might have little interest in attending co-op events. As one Windward member pointed out, 'I didn't move into this building to make friends and use its activities.' Thus, she did not feel guilty about not attending social events. On the other hand, a Harbourside member said: 'We have a wonderful mix of neighbours. Many of them have become our good friends as well. I have found, for the most part, that there is great concern and caring for each other's well-being.' Another said he liked Harbourside, among other reasons, because there was usually something to do every weekend.

For some people, participation, especially on committees, had other costs as well. One was that committee work and other meetings often proved frustrating and even unpleasant. At Harbourside over the first year or so, many members found the frequent lengthy discussions of building deficiencies and financial problems frustrating. Conflicts over what course to follow, and who was responsible for the situation, made some people bitter. Winning occasionally could help people overcome this sort of frustration, according to one Harbourside member: '[I]f you lobby and present your case, and say things that you want to say, and try and be articulate – or even try and speak up – maybe, you'll get what you need ... I think it's a matter of people winning sometimes. That they actually change something that is bugging them, and they get some really positive results – or half-positive results – or, at least feel that they've been heard.'

People who did become very active, especially in leadership positions, sometimes felt that no one else appreciated their efforts. Or they felt that they had to do everything. Occasionally, this resulted in disillusionment or burn-out. In 1988, Enid Burton told us how she felt about chairing Harbourside's landscape committee.

> I was really disappointed. Really hurt. Out of all the hours that I'd put into this and I put a lot of hours in – I'm not just talking about meetings. I'm talking about all the extra things that were put in. Like the caring and the organizing and being inspiring and all that's involved and not one person out of that committee turned around and said, 'That was great!' I don't want people saying, 'Oh you're wonderful, you did a fabulous job.' I know I did a good job because it got done. But it would have been really nice if there was something other than criticism and greed.
>
> Okay, a lot of what's happening here and it probably happens at other co-ops too – you get certain people who end up doing all the work. And I've had a lot of discussions with friends about this. You get the people who care and you get people who don't give a damn ... So that means that the people who live here who care end up doing all the work and all the worrying.
>
> I'm not saying I do it all. I do a lot of it and I take the responsibility for it because that's what I feel a chairperson is. If you are responsible it's up to you to make things work. But a lot of people who don't give a damn – they want to be on the committee – a lot of people want to be on the landscaping committee because they don't feel they have to do anything.

Shortly thereafter she quit the committee.

Several members suggested to us that being a member of any community has a price, namely the loss of a certain degree of individual freedom. 'The "price" includes the need for everyone to participate in the life and activities of the co-op; it includes having to take responsibility for your unit ... in order to meet the agreed standards of the community; and it includes respecting the rules. Those who consider this "price" too high should not be living in a co-op.'

Giving up a small amount of individual freedom, however, was not necessarily a consequence only of participating or being involved in the co-op; rather it flowed from the nature of these housing co-ops. First, they consist of multiple housing; propinquity alone often affects individual freedom of action. Second, they are communities based on an explicit social contract. Being a member provides well-defined rights and privileges, but also obligations.

In sum, the involvement of Windward and Harbourside members generally seemed to depend on their rough-and-ready evaluation of its costs and rewards. But their evaluations changed over time, partly as a result of people's co-op experience and partly in response to other changes in their lives. Thus, involvement also varied in amount and intensity. The problem for the co-ops, as associations, then, was to find ways of generating and maintaining member involvement. Not surprisingly, this problem is a general one among Toronto housing co-ops.

Motivating Involvement

Mandatory Participation and the Cooperative Housing Federation of Toronto

'Member Participation: "Two of the dirtiest words in the co-op vocabulary." 'These two words stirred up more debate and strong feelings than any other issue in Toronto co-ops during the past several years (Co-operative Housing Federation of Toronto 1988b). Many co-ops debated participation issues and policies at great length. The Co-op Housing Federation of Toronto itself

staged several member forums at which people from different
co-ops discussed the question.[11]

The immediate reason for opening the discussion was the sub-
mission of two resolutions to the federation in late 1987 and early
1988. Both were put forward by co-op staff rather than members.
The first proposed that all penalties for non-participation be removed from the federation's model by-laws and policies for housing co-ops. The other resolved that co-ops should encourage equal
levels of involvement on the part of members. However, if some
members refused to live up to the defined standards then they
should be evicted.

The issue of mandatory participation raised a host of subsid-
iary questions. Is member participation vital for co-op operation
as such? Or are there differences among co-ops, perhaps according to size? If it is not really necessary, for example, to reduce
housing costs, is it essential for community building? How should
participation be defined anyway? Should allowances be made for
people's different levels of participation over time or in relation
to their physical abilities? How could a strict mandatory participation policy be enforced? Would the consequences of such enforcement be worse for co-ops than the cure? Would it lead to
little 'police states,' for example? How else could high levels of
participation be achieved?

In essence, the issue revolved around two related themes: the
co-ops' mix of goals and member incentives. We have discussed
the question of goals in chapter 4. If the chief (or even, exclusive)
goal is to provide affordable housing, then the main task simply
is to ensure that members pay their housing charges on time. But
if their social goals are taken seriously, then the question arises
of how individuals can be motivated to provide for the collective
good.[12] Do material or social (e.g., moral) incentives work better?
Should communities appeal to their members' (enlightened) self-
interest or moral obligations or to their desire for social recognition? What balance should be struck between reward and punishment, or at least the threat thereof?

As the federation pointed out, some co-ops have tightened
participation policies and enforcement. For example, some

threatened or began eviction proceedings, established fines or punishments, tracked participation by computer or through a regular 'audit,' required those with poor participation records to appear before committees, and so forth. A participant in one of the federation's forums declared: 'If nobody participates, the co-op fails democratically and as a community. No co-op tolerates members who choose to not pay. Why should a co-op tolerate members who choose to not participate?'[13]

Nevertheless, many other co-ops looked for ways to encourage involvement by making it more attractive and interesting. As another forum participant put it, 'The idea that a Co-op is a better family because of mandatory participation is not true. It is a better family because of a *willingness* to participate.'[14] Co-ops tried to promote participation, for example, by setting up welcome committees for new members, improving communication between the co-op and members, running co-op education programs, providing greater recognition for involved members, removing obstacles to participation by setting up child-care systems, and widening definitions of participation.

Although many co-ops made their own decisions, the mandatory participation issue remained unresolved at the federation level. Summing up some of the results of the discussions, the federation made four general suggestions. First, co-ops should think seriously about *why* they want members to participate. Then, they should widen the definitions of participation, e.g., to include involvement in the wider community. Third, co-ops should look at why members do not attend meetings. They should remove whatever obstacles stand in the way. Fourth, co-ops should become more open-minded about alternatives to the ways in which they do things. They should talk to their members to find out what *they* think.

Encouraging Participation at Windward and Harbourside

At Windward and Harbourside co-ops there was a range of opinion about how members should be motivated to participate. When surveyed in September 1989, 57 per cent of the Harbourside respondents thought there was too little participation; 54 per cent felt the co-op did not encourage participation sufficiently. At Windward, considerably more respondents (72 per cent) felt there was too little participation; 58 per cent thought there was not enough encouragement. About 40 per cent at each co-op thought that participation was encouraged sufficiently.

We did not ask directly on the questionnaire about mandatory participation policies. However, respondents were asked for further comments at the end of the form. Several people wrote that they favoured compulsory participation.

From those comments and our interviews we inferred that many of those who favoured some degree of compulsion felt that high levels of participation are necessary for the co-ops to operate. Since there always will be people who contribute very little voluntarily to the community, everyone else is burdened. Thus, participation should be mandatory and enforced.

Others recognized participation as a legal or moral obligation. All members signed occupancy agreements in which they agreed to contribute time to the co-op. Everyone, therefore, should live up to the terms of the contract. Most members, however, favoured encouragement over compulsion. They thought that the costs of enforcing a strict participation policy far outweigh its potential benefits. People are far more likely to get involved if they are made to feel comfortable and if their tasks are ones in which they are interested. Members should be invited to meetings. They should be made more aware of the range of alternatives open to them, besides committee membership. Established members might make themselves responsible for introducing newer ones to co-op affairs. By making committees run more efficiently, the co-op could help members feel that their contribution was worthwhile. As several people pointed out, if participation is felt to be rewarding in itself then people will continue to be involved. And, of course, the converse also is true.

Partly because Harbourside and Windward were young co-ops, the participation issue stayed fairly low on the agenda. They had many other, more-pressing issues to sort out, especially relating to finances and construction deficiencies. Also, as Dan Fast, Windward's coordinator, pointed out, compared with older co-ops they did have high levels of participation.

As in most housing co-ops, few of the early members of Harbourside or Windward had had co-op experience; thus the need for member education, some of which was provided by co-op resource group developers Lantana and Chris Smith Associates. Unfortunately, the co-ops' buildings cost so much to develop that neither firm had as much time or money left to devote to member education as it had planned; hence, both co-ops felt that more needed to be done.

Harbourside created a member development (later, member involvement) committee in 1986. This committee conducted surveys of members' abilities and interests. It tried more generally to encourage participation and to provide recognition for people who were trying to make Harbourside into a community.

In 1989 the committee decided to carry out a so-called social audit of the co-op, assessing how well Harbourside was meeting its goals.[15] Our proposal to carry out a survey of the co-op in September 1989, therefore, was welcomed. The member involvement committee assisted in publicizing and carrying out the survey. In late November, it organized a workshop in which some of the results were discussed. Although the survey showed generally high levels of satisfaction with Harbourside, the workshop's goal was to find ways of increasing it. While some suggestions had to do with the buildings and grounds, many focused on improving the co-op's social life and sense of community (see chapter 1).[16]

One step taken at Windward was to establish an education committee in December 1987 because it was felt that many members did not have sufficient knowledge about the workings of the co-op. Members also needed help in acquiring relevant organizational skills. Over the next year or so, the committee undertook a member education interest survey and provided members with some resource materials on participation. As well, it arranged for training workshops to be offered by the Co-op Housing Federation, e.g., on the operation of boards of directors. The education committee also collaborated with us in administering our survey in the fall of 1989.

When the mandatory participation issue arose directly at Windward, it provoked strong feelings but little action. Tom Norman described, in the quotation near the beginning of this chapter, how he had introduced a motion in early 1989 about attendance at general meetings. Essentially, he had asked Windward to consider if members should be required to notify the co-op when they could not attend a general meeting. (Bear in mind that such attendance is required in the by-laws and occupancy agreement.) If they did not, then they should suffer some undefined but commensurate punishment. The motion was defeated after what Tom felt was very little discussion. From his perspective, the lack of discussion was worse than the defeat. It showed how unwilling the co-op was to address the issue. But many other members saw his motion as coercive and perhaps were unwilling to entertain it for that very reason.

Co-op Social Functions and Member Involvement

One way to encourage member involvement at Harbourside and Windward co-ops was by organizing social events. These ranged from informal drop-in gatherings through wine and cheese parties and Christmas parties to the ceremonies at which the co-ops officially were opened. Such events are well known to help create or strengthen members' identification with and emotional attachment to their co-op. They can play an important role in the symbolic creation of community in several ways. One is to forge or intensify emotional bonds among people. A second is to foster identification with the co-op through symbolically significant activities. Another is through making places in the co-op symbolically meaningful. Naturally, some events work in more than one of these ways simultaneously. Yet, it is important to bear in mind that there is nothing automatic about this. Co-op social events can create or reveal fault lines in the community as well.

In 1988, an older woman who served on the Windward social

committee described to us a few of the events of the preceding year. The Christmas party particularly stood out for her.

> I [was] heavily involved in the social committee this year and we've had some really good social times together. I think our Christmas buffet supper, we had about 125 out to it. You know, people in wheelchairs and whole families and [others]. We did all the cooking – the social committee ... I don't know how we're going to do it this year. It was a lot of work, but it was fun. The spirit of that party, I hope it continues on.
>
> We've had maybe twelve people from South America in here. We had several families – Peru and [Chile] and [Uruguay]. Well, there was a bunch of them and none of them knew each other really till they got in here. And I guess they met maybe at the wine and cheese party in May or maybe at the ... I think it was at the barbecue in August. Fantastic. That was in the courtyard.
>
> So then at Christmas time they had started to get together and didn't tell any of us and they came in while we were having dinner and sang to us – about fourteen of them in sort of robes of their country. And one chap played some sort of an instrument and they sang carols of their country and then some of our carols. And every one of us I think came away that night with such a ... I never had such a feeling of community and ... good thoughts about everybody and there were people from all over the world there really. You know it was fantastic.

At Harbourside, pub nights were held regularly at the community centre but were only a moderate success. As one participant said: 'There were a diehard group of a dozen or so people who came – not a dozen every time – who came to most of them. [But] there were some nights when we didn't have more than maybe six or eight.' There were some members though (thought of as dissidents) 'who were conspicuous by their absence.' These events may have helped to strengthen ties among those who attended. At the same time, though, they allowed others to demonstrate their disaffection.

In August 1988, Harbourside staged its first Summerfest. Held in the courtyard, the festival filled an entire day. At 12:30 there was a parade of decorated bicycles, tricycles, and 'noisy plastic-wheeled things.' Then came the visit of a city fire truck especially for the children. Games and sideshows began at 1:30, followed by races – three-legged, four-legged, potato races, etc. From 5:00 to 6:30 there was a barbecue, then bingo until 8:00. Finally, the party began. The theme for the first few hours was the 'Summer of '68,' with music of the sixties and everyone invited to dress appropriately. The evening ended with a ' "Let Your Hair Down, Get Your Knees Up" hour of World Beat Music which we are calling a "global carnival," ' according to Harbourside's newsletter.[17]

Summerfest was a 'bigger success than we dared to hope,' wrote one of its organizers. 'On that day there was a real feeling of community spirit.' Not only did many people attend but the event actually made money – $55.62 plus a large number of left-over hot dogs. Yet only a few months later, the editor of Harbourside's newsletter lamented: 'Unfortunately it was the exception rather than the rule.' Participation in committees, turnout at general meetings and social functions all seemed dismally low to him. 'If it had always been like this it wouldn't concern me as much; however, it is the slide into apathy that is a cause for concern.'[18]

Unlike the ordinary apartment or townhouse development, Windward and Harbourside both had official openings. Windward's was especially interesting. Even though the co-op had been occupied since early 1987, the official opening did not actually occur until September 1988 (see Fig. 8.1).

On a sunny Saturday at 2:00, guests and members assembled near Windward's entrance. Guests included not only members' family and friends (and anthropologists), but also their alderman and member of parliament. Everyone had been given a name tag and a printed program outlining Windward's history and the day's events. A town crier, dressed in eighteenth-century garb, rang his bell and loudly proclaimed Windward open. The president of the co-op formally welcomed everyone. Then he introduced the board of directors and special guests. Representatives

Figure 8.1
The official opening ceremonies at Windward co-op in September 1988 encouraged member identification with the co-op.

of Lantana (the housing resource group), the architects, and CMHC all offered their greetings. After brief remarks on the history of Windward, the ribbon stretched across the portico was cut.

Tours of the building followed. Groups of guests were led by volunteer guides to visit the Waterview Room (the large meeting room), courtyard, laundry rooms on the second floor, an apartment in the main building, and another in the townhouses. The guides pointed out interesting features of the building, especially having to do with its accessibility. The afternoon concluded with a wine and cheese reception in the Waterview Room.

Several things about this function deserve mention. First, for members and guests alike the crucial focus of the events was on the corporate nature of the co-op. As a body, Windward co-op was shown to be more than just buildings or a group of residents. It had its own identity, which was attested to by the specially invited guests, by the formal introduction of its officers, and by the program that described its background and listed the awards it had won for accessibility. The official opening proclaimed this identity to the wider community. Second, the publicly recited history reinforced this proclamation of identity. It connected present success with past struggles to overcome a host of obstacles. By so doing, it proclaimed that 'we are those who made this project work, and we did it together.' Members who had not been part of that early history could share in it vicariously, thus strengthening their own sense of belonging. Third, by celebrating the co-op's physical facilities, the guided tours helped to reinforce people's attachment to the co-op as a community. Members could take pride in the appearance of the courtyard, whether or not they actually had been involved in the work of the landscape committee. They could take pride in the building's accessibility even if they had no disabilities. Finally, the tours changed the way in which people perceived the buildings. They marked off areas of the co-op as significant, whether for their appearance, good design, or utility. Thus, places that might have been taken for granted by members acquired new meaning through their celebration. Guests experienced the reality of the co-op through these marked places. For them it became a special place.

In all of these ways, and no doubt others, the official opening of Windward encouraged member identification with the co-op. It was fitting that this ceremony should have occurred more than a year and a half after the co-op actually had opened. By then they were ready to introduce themselves to the wider community.

Social functions did play a part in stimulating member involvement and identification with the co-ops. Not all were parties or celebrations. The memorial ceremony at Harbourside mentioned earlier in this chapter is a case in point. But these co-ops existed principally to provide housing near the downtown of a large city for people with many other interests and concerns. How significant an effect social functions had in general remains open to question.

Conclusion

Thus, both at Windward and Harbourside, while some steps had been taken, neither co-op really had grappled with the issue of participation. People were concerned about keeping up levels of participation. Most seemed to feel that encouragement works best. But there was concern, especially at Harbourside, that the same few people continued to do all the work.

As we have seen, Harbourside and Windward are located in a downtown area that provides many other attractive activities. They also were rather heterogeneous socially. We suspect that it always will be difficult for these co-ops to overcome the centrifugal forces separating members. It also seems likely that there always will be a few people who do far more than their share and many who do less.

One way of dealing with the issue of participation in these co-ops would be to try to ensure that these few people are not the same few people for years on end. Encouragement of member participation, which is the route both co-ops seem to favour over punishing shirkers, could then involve both organizational development – with attention to clear procedures and policies – and the creation of a positive environment in which meetings are reasonably pleasant and productive.

CHAPTER NINE

Taking Control

Making Newsletters at Harbourside and Windward

Edward was surprised by the way the Harbourside newsletter committee operated. As he told us in 1987, 'I came home from the first meeting depressed, thinking "This is not what I anticipated!" Because I work in the kind of business that I do [theatre production], I'm used to working with professionals – good writers, artists, editors, whatever, right on down the line. So I went to the newsletter meeting expecting that same sort of professional approach. Of course that was silly, when I think back on it, to have expected things to be that way!'

He brought his professional approach with him to that first meeting.

I walked in and my first suggestion was, 'I guess we should pick an editor and an art director and people who are going to write and people who are going to be in production.'

Instantly, the coordinator said (Edward uses a gruff tone of voice) 'This is a co-op. We don't do that in a co-op.' And I'm thinking, 'Oh, yes. What am I doing! I understand.' But actually I thought the coordinator was being pretty extreme. [The coordinator's view was] that we were all equal and that we couldn't even assume these specific responsibilities [of writer, art director, etc.]. He thought I was sort of creating a hierarchy in the newsletter. And when I think about it now, it probably wasn't the right approach at that time.

That experience was a real eye-opener for me. I suddenly realized that, yes, this is different. This requires a different approach from me and from everyone. Then I suddenly became more tolerant and realized that these people weren't professionals. These people had no experience. I realized that [their ideas] of what a newsletter should be were much different [from my own]. So I changed my attitude and decided this was going to be lots of fun. I started comparing it to the kind of things I'd worked on when I was a kid in high school. You know?

There was this other part of me that emerged from all of this. I thought, 'Well, for one thing, I have something to offer here.' I have some experience. If I can teach someone who wants to learn about this, then that's helping other people. I also have a fascination for newsletters and anything like that. I was interested in aspects of production that I usually don't do – the writing, editing, and so on – that answered some interests of mine.

It soon became apparent that if we got an issue out every couple of months we were doing well. There were problems with the budget and the realization that we didn't have the facilities to produce a 'slick' newsletter. And it didn't matter! I think [this experience] really helped me a lot because I learned to look at things through different eyes.

Later Edward moved to Windward where he planned eventually to join a different committee. Initially, though, he joined the newsletter committee because he felt he still had something to offer that he knew about. He was amused that Windward committee members followed pre-cisely the approach that Harbourside's coordinator had criticized!

At the first meeting all the people were trying to decide who should take what position – art director, editor, writers – all the things I had done [inappropriately at Harbourside]. (Edward laughs) I just sat there and felt really confused. Not only the [members] – I could think, 'Well, it's their first day' – but the people who were organizing this were suggesting this [approach]. The people from Lantana [the resource group that de-veloped Windward], this was their approach.

I found their approach rather offensive because I had already been conditioned at Harbourside in the other direction. I sat there and it was like 'Okay, we've got to produce!' [It was as if] this was a real money-making venture here: let's make it good, let's make it quick. So I found myself on the other side saying, 'Wait a second. Why do we have to do this?'

Unlike at Harbourside, people at Windward had experience with such work. At Windward, Edward found: 'There are professional editors, there are professional artists. [The newsletter] is almost as good as a professional production in some ways. Obviously, I mean, the writers aren't great and the kind of material that's going into it isn't the best. But it's better [than Harbourside's].' Windward's product was better but its process, Edward felt, was not. 'I should add that our newsletter committee is a fiasco. There are so many people who know so much about it that there's constant jockeying for positions. It's anything but cooperative! ... It's everything everybody dreads in a committee! (laughter). Just people trying to take control, not being able to agree and not being able to get along.'

Member Control

The phrase 'member control' has a pleasing ring, but which members, what abilities, what kind of control over what sorts of things?[1] Should decisions be made by consensus or majority rule? Should the co-op practise direct or a representative form of democracy? How can the rights of those in the minority be protected? 'If you were to picture a situation in which a tenants' association bought out the landlord of a housing project and set up their own administration you would have a picture of what we're about ... All co-ops have to grapple with the problem of ensuring that the members are able to control their organizations' (Tabuns 1986).

Democratic control by members often is said to be co-op housing's 'most attractive feature.'[2] In practice, it is also one of co-op housing's most elusive goals. Problems of member control arise for a variety of reasons. There is no landlord to complain to, or about. How able people are to control the organization may be in doubt. Members may have little expertise in needed areas such as finance. Some may try to dominate the co-op. Others refuse to do their share of the work. Democratic processes create losers, as well as winners. Control by consensus requires long, inefficient meetings.

Member control in co-ops rests on a principle of direct democracy. In this, co-ops differ markedly from most condominiums. There some property is owned in common but management generally is highly delegated, often to professional managers (Spronk 1988; Wekerle et al. 1980). But in co-ops, 'wherever possible, members should have the right to make the decisions affecting their lives or be able to intervene in decision-making that affects them. There is also the idea that as many people as possible should be drawn into decision-making bodies.'[3] One reason member control is difficult to achieve is that it presumes such a broad base of participation. As the last chapter showed, urban co-ops are doing well if they have even one member from 75 per cent of the households involved in any kind of committee work.

How can co-ops reconcile limited participation with the goal of direct democracy? How can members who do not participate in committee work or attend general meetings still be ensured a measure of control over their housing? How can people be sure that those who do exercise control act responsibly? This chapter explores possible answers to these questions.

First, we consider definitions of member control and democracy through the statements of people working and living in co-ops. Then we show how these ideas were put into practice and how they changed between 1986 and 1989 at Harbourside and Windward. In particular, we explore the social democratic vs the business orientations to creating community through member control in each co-op. We discuss the pros and cons of an emphasis on consensus or majority rule. The differences in the two co-ops' (and their coordinators') approaches to organizational development are shown to be greater in intent than in effect.

What Is Member Control?

The contrast Edward Quaglia drew between the newsletter committees at Windward and Harbourside is a familiar one. It exemplifies the social democratic and business frames of reference we discussed in our overview of the various goals of cooperative housing (see chapter 4). Member control in the social democratic model grows out of equivalence. Everyone is seen as equally able to participate on a committee. Expertise and experience are irrelevant or even detrimental.

This was the model in use at Harbourside when Edward joined the newsletter committee. But at Windward he found the business model predominated. Those with experience, for example as writers, were seen as the best people for the job. Decisions were made through competitive rather than cooperative give and take. There were winners and losers.

To some extent, Edward Quaglia's experiences in the two co-ops illustrate basic differences in modes of decision making. These differences were apparent between some committees within each co-op. Some Windward committees, for example, had members with a more social democratic outlook than the newsletter committee. But, at a very general level, they also characterized each co-op as a whole, perhaps reflecting differences between the resource groups that developed them and the make-up of the membership. Windward tended towards a business orientation while Harbourside was more interested in a social democratic one, especially in its first year.

Windward and Harbourside members tended to talk about member control in one of two ways. For some, member control should occur through consensus formation. For others, it should happen through majority rule. Both kinds of decision making took place in each co-op, but consensus played a more important role in Harbourside. This was partly because its smaller size made consensus formation more feasible. Furthermore, the resource group Chris Smith and Associates encouraged member selection and, later, member education for committee work along these lines.

Working to achieve consensus was a new process for some people who had no previous co-op experience. From the viewpoint of a young professional at Harbourside, the consensus process was unendurable. He attended one meeting of the maintenance committee and swore he would kill someone if he ever had to sit through another! Such meetings seemed endless and inconclusive. To him, they reflected weak leadership. Others favoured the consensus process because it seemed to work for the common good. 'It's hard to accept that getting your way is not the point,' said a Harbourside member. 'The point is that the cooperative does well.'

In contrast to consensus-based decisions, 'resolving things democratically creates winners and losers. Because in the end it comes down to a vote, and the other people feel they have *lost*. That's not a very positive feeling to have. So it's better if you can do things by consensus, I suppose, except that's pretty idealistic with a large number of households.' This Harbourside member recognized that freedom to express diverse opinions in meetings might not be enough. Often people must live with an outcome that does not take their views into account.

Others argued against consensus. They thought the formality of democratic process, including voting, protected members' rights. In particular, it seemed to protect the rights of those members least able to defend their views in the give and take of a consensus setting. Consensus 'is fine if you have a lot of really articulate, bright, nasty, strong people who tend to stand up for themselves. If you have people who aren't used to talking about what they think and who need some space and time in which to do it, you just lose them.'

The Windward member who made this comment played a watchdog role on a member selection committee that was experiencing difficulty. She tried explicitly to ensure that democratic process was followed and to protect such people against consensus. 'We don't have the kind of resources where we can afford to have a bad process.' In her view: 'People have to feel safe and comfortable going into a meeting or they're going to run away from being part of the decision-making process. That's [the problem] I addressed. I would go into meetings and I would demand that a very formal process be followed. I don't think it's particularly good in an overall sense for that to happen in decision making but it was needed. People were not being allowed to speak. I demanded that there be a "rules of order" process: every meeting, every question, every debate, every item. There would be none of this informal [business].' Whether her approach had its intended effect is debatable, however. Such a strict adherence to rules of order often deters those from participating who, in some sense, most need to be empowered.

The carrot as well as the stick could be used. The chairman of Windward's finance committee tried to accomplish through informal encouragement what the 'watchdog' member sought to achieve through parliamentary procedure. He told us that he 'took special pains to see that none of the long-standing members monopolized the discussions.' As chairman, he said: '[I did] my best to get the newer members to participate. At times I would purposely direct questions towards them, try to draw them out to express their ideas and expand upon them. [This was] not so much because I thought the idea was great, but more or less to get them used to the idea of entering into open discussion and not to be suddenly shut up like a clam because somebody's voice seems [in response to one of their suggestions] to be a little bit sharp.'

Despite such efforts to encourage less aggressive co-op members to play roles in controlling the co-op and to enforce their right to do so, not everyone wanted to participate in the decision-making process. 'When you talk about democracy you have to take into account that not everyone is going to buy into it.' The Windward member who made this point to us hoped that greater participation could be encouraged. But on balance, he concluded, 'the majority of the people who are at the meetings are making decisions, and that's democracy. But in a sense it's not democracy in that it could be a lot better.'

While attendance at general meetings 'could be a lot better,' it is important to realize that such improvement is unlikely. There will always be members who would rather leave management to others so long as they can continue to reap other benefits. For some people we interviewed, affordability and security of tenure were what housing co-ops should be about, not democracy or community. 'I wasn't really thinking about the sense of community,' one Harbourside woman told us. 'I was just looking for a nice place to live.' She was willing to do what was required of her, but did not seek a deeper involvement with the co-op.

This woman's sense of control over the co-op as a member

came from the general feeling that she could take action if she opposed a decision that affected her personally. But could she? Would she have? How would the rest of the co-op have responded? At a general level, the answers to such questions depend on many factors. Some have to do with the nature of the particular issues and with the individual's experience, personality, and so on. But others relate to the ways democracy and consensus formation work out in a particular co-op over time. In order to understand the interaction between coordinators, deeply involved members, and marginally or uninvolved members in managing a co-op, we looked at the history of member control at Windward and Harbourside during their first three years.

Harbourside: Beyond the 'Contras'

Harbourside residents' lack of experience with cooperative living was the biggest obstacle to member control from the summer of 1986 when people began moving in through the end of 1987. Only 4 per cent of those responding to our survey had lived in another co-op before joining Harbourside; 20 per cent had owned their own home or condominium unit. The rest had been tenants in private or public rental housing.

Inexperience led to high expectations about member control. Many people commented to us in 1987 that they saw the co-op as a place where everybody should participate and take responsibility as an 'owner.' They were disappointed when participation rates failed to measure up to their expectations. Those who did participate soon began to resent those who did not. At a time when about 60 per cent of Harbourside members served on committees, the wife of a man on the board of directors commented on his frustration: 'Those who don't participate drive him crazy because he's on the board and very active himself.' This sort of frustration paved the way for later divisions in the co-op.

In the co-op's first year, there was a tendency to regard the maintenance committee as the landlord. This, too, seemed connected to member's lack of experience with co-ops and the fact that most of them had been renters. One member expected the co-op to pay for a $3 part needed to fix his toilet. He was angry when the maintenance committee refused to reimburse him. Other young, able-bodied members called the maintenance committee for simple repairs that they could have done themselves. For example, there were calls to put a sliding door back on its track and change the washer in a leaky tap. The maintenance committee responded by trying to educate members so that they would know how to make minor repairs. Education sessions also encouraged members to develop the initiative to help themselves instead of calling on the committee.

A more serious legacy of members' history as tenants was their treatment of the board of directors, like the maintenance committee, as if it were their landlord. 'Complainers' emerged as a category in active members' interviews with us during 1987. Building deficiencies were a source of dissatisfaction for many residents, but the 'complainers' seemed to expect the board to be able to fix them. Failing that, some of the complainers said they would sue the co-op. To those sympathetic to the board, the complainers were naive in that they failed to recognize that suing the co-op would be suing themselves.

The relationship between complainers and the board was adversarial. The former saw the board as confrontational and unfair. Active co-op members expressed the view that the complainers would not help themselves and so could not take control over their housing in keeping with co-op ideology. As one board member noted: 'People need more education to convince them they can make a difference in their lives. The complainers have yet to get to this realization. They still see the board as doing things for them just like a landlord.'

Part of the problem, the coordinator felt, was that people moved into a co-op that was already set up for them. Resource groups took the burden of establishing committee structures off the new members. Ironically, though, this made it harder for the residents to understand the structure of member control in the co-op. The coordinator observed that 'people find themselves sitting on committees without knowing how what they're doing fits in.' Without a sense of how the co-op worked as a whole, members found it difficult to establish a sense of ownership of the co-op.

This coordinator played an important role in encouraging members to participate actively and develop a sense of control over the co-op. Deeply committed to member education, he saw his role as one of helping co-op members to 'build communities' and 'take charge.' He would have been delighted by the comment one woman made to us in a 1987 interview: 'I like having control over my environment, having some sense of power, not over other people but over my own life, over the direction it will take, a sense that my voice will make a difference. You don't get that in other kinds of housing!' This was exactly the kind of sentiment the coordinator tried to encourage. He contrasted his own style with that of other coordinators whom he saw as 'managers.' They soon recognized that there were only a few members of their co-op who were reliable and they became managers overseeing the co-op through the work of those few people. But Harbourside's coordinator followed a different path. He tried to encourage broad participation and minimize the gap between those likely to become the few 'reliable' ones and the others. As Edward Quaglia's account of the first newsletter committee meeting at Harbourside conveys, the coordinator favoured a social democratic model of member control. Giving everyone an equal chance to participate was far more important to him than the expertise, experience, or ability of the committee members.

Ironically, by mid-1987 the newsletter had a single editor. *Son of Sidelines* began to appear. First it supplemented, then replaced the official but irregular newsletter, *Harboursidelines*. At first the editor styled himself as a 'sort of editor' and the newsletter as an 'almost weekly.' But by September 1987 he was simply 'Editor' and *Son of Sidelines* had become *Harbourside's Newsletter*. Light-hearted and irreverent, *Son of Sidelines* amused many with its wry comments, pointed criticisms of non-cooperation, and cartoons from the 'Far Side' (see Fig. 9.1).

Not everyone found *Son of Sidelines* funny. One man called it 'Son of *Pravda*.' He felt it 'oozed hostility.' He was offended when the newsletter criticized non-participants as people who just

Dedicated to the Co-operative Lifestyle ?
No need to quit when you die.

Co-operative Funeral Service

Not ready to join the Co-operative Funeral Service ? Then it's time to start thinking about the next best thing. Run for the Board.

This year the elections will be held in January.

But before that there is-

Son of Sidelines
The Newsletter of Harbourside Co-op

Editor: D. Charlesworth   Vol 2 no 14   12 Nov 1988

GRUNT-THUTTOCK LASHES OUT
"Evict the Maggots"

Henry Grunt-Thuttock, local celebrity, hit out this week at what he called "The maggots in our community". Speaking to SoS, in what appeared to be an early start to his campaign for a seat on the Board, Grunt-Thuttock railed against people who put out garbage on the wrong days.

"Last weekend we had a bag of garbage put at the corner of Queens Quay and Stadium on Friday night, where it then sat for the weekend. The weekend before we had several bags sitting on Bishop Tutu", said an obviously irate Grunt-Thuttock.

"What is wrong with these people ? Are they so dumb that they cannot remember Mondays and Thursdays ?", he said. "They are maggots who should go and live at the garbage dump".

Warming to his theme, Grunt-Thuttock went on to wonder about the people who couldn't be bothered to tie their garbage bags properly. "Perhaps they have trouble with their shoe laces too", he said.

Figure 9.1   Light-hearted and irreverent, the Harbourside newsletter *Son of Sidelines* amused many with its wry comments. But some called it *Son of Pravda*.

wanted a nice place to live and so were 'Uppies' or not quite Yuppies. Already among those categorized as complainers, he felt the label of 'Uppie' added another layer of insult. 'So not only [does he put] me down, he further puts me down by saying I'm a Yuppie. I resent being a Yuppie. I resent being called an Uppie even more! (laughter). And I'm going to participate even less because he did that!'

The 'contras,' as the complainers became known, numbered perhaps half a dozen households. Tensions between them and the board increased. One couple, the Ashes, left the co-op after their request to move into another unit was turned down in a heated meeting with the board. They did not see themselves as complainers but as people who would take action when they had 'had enough.' They felt there was a sense of community developing at Harbourside but that they were not included in it. Furthermore, they felt that they were victimized by the majority in a way that would not happen if there were true cooperation and consensus. The majority, they said, should not always be able to change things and impose their decisions on other members.

By the end of 1987, some board members realized they were becoming too emotional about such issues. Other co-op members had started to see the board as an 'inner sanctum of power' and to some extent the board was beginning to see itself this way. Speaking of the meeting at which the board refused the Ashes' request to move to another unit, one member commented: 'Here we were like the cattle barons trying to keep the settlers from fencing in the grazing land. And I thought, "How stupid! This is ridiculous!" '

All but one member of the board were replaced in January 1988. The shift in power was less dramatic than this sounds. Four of the seven new members were spouses or family members of people on the previous board. Nevertheless, the emotional pitch of the board had been lowered. One former board member whose spouse was on the new board commented: 'With the old board there were tremendously long meetings, arguments, a sense of solidarity, but also a feeling of always being in a state of panic. Now things run much more smoothly.'

A new coordinator, beginning in the fall of 1987, added to this sense that co-op management was becoming routine. She favoured a businesslike approach to running the co-op and encouraged the board to keep its meetings to two hours instead of five. Committees also seemed to run more efficiently partly because of the new coordinator's influence and partly because members had had a year's worth of experience.

Yet there were several crises in 1988 that divided co-op members more seriously than any previous confrontations between 'contras' and the board. These concerned the budget, the subsidy policy, and landscaping. The fault lines that became obvious in the midst of these crises cut across the previous 'us/them' distinction between the involved members and the complainers. Inexperience, however, was still a problem, at least in so far as the budget dispute involved a board that had had little experience with co-op finances.

These disputes pointed to differences between so-called 'professionals' and others, some of whom had less education and fewer verbal skills. They gave voice to resentments felt by residents with very different time perspectives, and to tensions between members at different economic levels. We consider the budget and landscaping disputes in some detail in the next chapter. The dispute over Harbourside's subsidy policy was discussed in chapter 7. For now, the point is that while member control seemed to have become routine at Harbourside in 1988, *who* was controlling *whom* was a volatile question.

Burn-out began to be a problem. People who had served on committees for a year or more, especially those who had weathered one of the 1988 crises, were ready to 'put some distance between [themselves] and the co-op.' Some recognized that they were increasingly likely to view criticisms of their committee as personal attacks. As one burned-out member said, the co-op seemed to be in a transition stage: 'We know each other well enough to be irritated by things, but we don't have the bonds yet that give you a sense of tolerance for whatever the situation is.'

By 1989, the landscaping crisis had been forgotten by all but those closest to it. The new budget passed without any of the problems encountered the previous year. The subsidy policy issue was largely resolved. The fault lines that had been so clear in the co-op in 1988 were now covered over, at least for the time being.

Another new board was in power. Its strategy, in marked contrast to that of Harbourside's first board, was reactive. Rather than taking the initiative and acting, the board seemed to prefer to wait until members brought problems to it. But those who in 1987 would have hunted such a board down had withdrawn from the action. The most vocal 'contras' of the early days had either moved out of the co-op or fallen silent. Complaining itself could be seen as a kind of participation. Yet those who remained had stopped participating even to that extent. They had lost the sense that their concerns would be taken into account. Their withdrawal suggests that member control was no longer something in which this minority could share.

For most Harbourside members, however, participation seemed more possible than it had in 1987. One active member on subsidy was somewhat optimistic in speaking about less-involved people in her situation. 'People treat[ed] the board of directors as a landlord for the longest time until they finally figure[d] out that, oh yeah, they really *do* have control. Like, if something's not working there is a process. The process may not be that great, but there is a way to change what's going on besides this adversarial [feeling that] the board of directors has done this and we *have* to [accept it]. This authority figure [the board] can be challenged. That [recognition] takes a long time in a co-op.'

We asked if she felt that such a recognition of member control had taken place in Harbourside by 1989. She replied: 'It's happening. I do have conversations with people now where, if they don't like what's going on, they start to talk about how they can get it changed. [It used to be that they would] feel a need to have a *private* meeting so they can talk about it amongst themselves and then present it to the board – kind of like, you know, *aimed* at the board. I think that the general membership does have the power. If you lobby and present your case, and say things you want to say, and try and be articulate, and even try and speak up, maybe you'll get what you need.'

As an example of this process she spoke of the stairwell improvement committee. People who were not in what she called the 'core group' or 'power structure' came together to form a committee to paint and otherwise improve the Harbourside stairwells. Many of them lived in apartments rather than townhouses. For several reasons, such people had felt less attached to the co-op. It was important for them to see that they could win, even if they did not occupy powerful positions in the co-op. 'They made their case, they got quotes, they found stuff, and they lobbied. They got people out to a meeting. And they got the stairwells improved. I think they really felt [the process] worked for them. And it did! I mean, there are assets of a co-op – things that you can win – that cost money. They won something that cost money and that's a reward in anybody's language!'

Windward

In 1987, Windward Co-op's experiences with member control were similar to Harbourside's in some ways. Few (10 per cent) had lived in another cooperative. Three-quarters had come from rental housing. Although a history of volunteer work had been an important criterion for member selection at Windward, organizational expertise seemed lacking. The coordinator fumed: 'I don't know how you can interview everybody and make sure they're activists before you let them in the co-op, then find nobody who knows how to pick up a phone and organize two other people!'

Windward's building deficiencies were at least as big a problem as at the smaller co-op, and the financial situation that came out of the construction process was worse. By the summer of 1987, only six months after the first people had moved in, the co-op faced a 9 per cent rent hike in order to finance a $614,000 increase to the co-op's mortgage due to cost overruns in construction.

The tendency to regard the board of directors as the landlord was even stronger at Windward than at Harbourside. The board had been in place since 1982 when the project was incorporated. It seemed remote to many members. Although there were a couple of women on the board, its image among the members was one of 'businessmen in grey suits.' Communication between the board and the membership was poor. Minutes of board meetings were not distributed widely or posted in the co-op. The transition from a board charged with creating the co-op to one which represented people living in the co-op took place in mid-1987.

In June 1987, eighteen candidates came forward for the seven positions on the first board of directors to be elected by the residents. (Only five women ran for the board.) Many candidates expressed concern about the co-op's financial situation. Dealing with this situation had to be the new board's first task. As one candidate summed up the situation in his campaign brochure: 'I would hope that future Board Members will be able to deal with rather creative and exciting ideas and suggestions. Unfortunately, this will not be the case with our first elected Board of Directors. [Its] concern ... will be to deal with the serious problems at hand, which result from the unhappy experience which we have had with our builder.'

Candidates also stressed their commitment to openness. For example, one candidate wrote, in an implicit criticism of the previous board: 'I balk at heavy-handed power wielding by a select few, and prefer to negotiate in a reasonable manner until a consensus can be reached where the parties can come away with their self-esteem intact.'

Despite widespread grumbling about the board, the four men and one woman who ran as incumbents all were returned to office. But the presidency passed to one of the two new members. Both of these men had expressed concern during the 'all candidates meeting' with improving the social climate of the co-op. One, an Uruguayan immigrant, brought his skills as an accountant to the job. But in a speech at the all candidates meeting he emphasized his record of human rights work in Latin America and his devotion to freedom. He said that the co-op needed love. It needed an atmosphere of freedom without too many rules.

The other new board member promoted what we called in chapter 4 a 'new age' approach to community development in the co-op. In his campaign brochure, he wrote: 'Politically I carry no card. I respect differences of opinion ... I oppose exploitation, domination and violence. Philosophically, my beliefs take form in my Buddhist, atheist, mainstream/evangelical Christian, Pharisee, Jewish, new age friends.' As an expert in organizational development, he presented himself as a 'doctor' who could help Windward heal its internal problems. His election as president of the board seemed to promise a more open, closer relationship between the general membership and the co-op's key decision makers. But he had little chance to put his approach into practice.

In August, a particularly disgruntled member led twenty-one others in a challenge that accused the board of mismanaging co-op funds. They were concerned about the financial situation that had led to the 9 per cent housing charge increase. Trust funds, they felt, had been misappropriated. They feared that the co-op's agreement with CMHC had been violated by moving up the mortgage interest adjustment date. They called for an independent investigation of the co-op's financial situation. There was talk of demanding the board's resignation and even of suing its members. To discuss these issues, the dissident group requisitioned a general members' meeting at the end of August 1987. In the event, the board was cleared of allegations of mismanagement. The dissident group was reassured that 'almost all of the [Toronto co-op] projects commenced in 1985 went over budget. In every case but one, the bail-out that was arranged with CMHC was based on moving up the interest adjustment date.'4

The individual who launched the assault on the board remained convinced that the co-op, led by 'a few autocrats,' had breached its agreement with CMHC. But his supporters drifted away, reassured by the outcome of the meeting in late August. By 1989 this man was still unhappy with the way the co-op was run. But like the few 'contras' who remained at Harbourside, he no longer had a following nor did he seem to feel that he could make his opinion count in the co-op.

The realization that one member could effectively challenge the entire board's authority was initially threatening. The board saw him as an enemy and some even thought about trying to find a way to evict him. But later they accepted his right to intervene. As the president saw it, 'it was a very big growing period. It took a lot of energy and left a bitter taste in some people's mouths.' But on the whole it was incorporated in the co-op's history as a community-building experience. The Windward newsletter interviewed coordinator Dan Fast, who concluded: '[A]ll in all that whole episode with the special general meeting probably had a salutary effect since it let people in on what was going on. It's too bad it took so much time and caused a lot of wear and tear on people.'

Organizational development was something both Fast and the president were committed to, each in his own way. It seemed as if the board would be able to turn its attention to this once the crisis over the financial affairs of the co-op had passed. The president was re-elected for a second term in the spring of 1988. But little real progress was made in encouraging effective member control through committees. The board was so busy dealing with other problems as they arose that Fast's ideas for an organizational task force were continually pushed aside. In the summer of 1988, the coordinator concluded: 'This board ... has done literally no work at all in trying to build this sense of organization and where we're going and all that. It has essentially set its own agendas on the basis of simply reacting to whatever comes along from meeting to meeting without any goal setting. No planning. No nothing.' The board made little effort to establish better liaison with co-op committees. Fast wondered about Windward's potential for developing as a community: 'It could be that Windward will never really be able to go very far with anything just because people are not able to make the commitments of time and really throw themselves into this ... It could be that way. We haven't tried. That's the problem. One good [effort] for a year by the board of directors in that area and we'd know what our potential is.'

Lack of experience was beginning to have negative effects on member control in the co-op. Some committees never met. Many committee members had little if any organizational expertise. Chairs seemed unable to delegate responsibilities, and lost patience when committee members let them down. In Fast's view, they needed training in order to learn 'that if you find that the people don't show up to do whatever project you asked them to do, you don't go do it yourself, and you don't start screaming about it and quit. You keep coming back and get what you can.'

Ironically, some committees suffered from too much experience. The member selection committee, in particular, was becoming rigid by 1988. Most of the people on the committee had been together since 1985 or earlier. They did not share the tentative, uncertain approach that characterized other committees even after two years in operation. From the beginning, one Windward person commented: 'There was a self-assuredness about the committee ... They were in control. They had a lot of authority.' One committee member commented: 'It was difficult for us after the people moved in to accept the reduction in our authority. We used to have the same authority practically as the board of directors.'

The old guard on the member selection committee was unhappy that by 1988 the number of households on subsidy had climbed to 41 per cent from an initial 25 per cent. They took issue with the coordinator, who had increased the number of households receiving housing charge assistance in order to make full use of money that CMHC had allocated to the co-op for this purpose. They asked for direction from the board regarding subsidy quotas so that they would know how to process applications from potential new members. We discussed the content of this issue in chapter 7 where we dealt with mixing income levels in co-ops. Here, what is of interest relates to the place of member control in the committee's operations.

The board was slow to respond. Perhaps the seriousness of the situation was not apparent. Certainly, some board members were not eager to deal with the member selection committee's feeling that levels of subsidy should be reduced. As a result, the business of the member selection committee ground almost to a halt. It processed very few applications for co-op membership. Waiting-lists became too short. As Dan Fast remarked: 'They put these things on agendas from meeting to meeting. But they could never get any of it dealt with because there was this old guard sitting on the committee maintaining the majority vote. [They were] refusing to deal with any of these items because they were dissatisfied with the fact that the board had not [responded].'

Many co-ops have a rule that members may not serve on a particular committee longer than three years. Windward did not have such a rule. The chairman of the member selection committee felt overwhelmed by some of the long-serving committee members as well as by some of the newer ones. As one member said, 'the whole thing was out of control. That's the first job of a chairman, to control meetings and he obviously wasn't.' He submitted his resignation to the board, saying that he could not get any work done because of the old guard. Much to everyone's surprise, including some board members, the board dissolved the entire committee.

The disbanded committee requested a special board meeting and was reinstated with a board member assigned to serve a liaison/watchdog function. This was the person we mentioned earlier who attempted to ensure that the committee adhered strictly to parliamentary procedure so that no one member could bully others. The committee also had a new chair, someone who had served on the committee before. But by the fall of 1988, the chair had quit, partly for personal reasons but also because of continuing dissension in the committee. The board then appointed the 'watchdog' as interim chairman. She told us: 'I went to the first meeting not knowing if anybody was going to show up, of course. [Laughter.] Anyway, people did. And we talked. After that meeting more people resigned.' We asked her why. 'Why? It was reasonably clear that I felt, and the board felt, that changes had to be made. You know, a committee with this rocky a relationship with the board of directors and with this bad a performance was in trouble ... It was in trouble and not doing its job.'

The committee was isolated from and at odds with the rest of the co-op: 'I was struck at the kind of closed feeling of the meetings ... You know, like a body of people used to working together *taking on* a stranger. There were codes and a very definite subculture ... The committee had its own way of working *out* to the co-op, that was not integrated within the broader perspectives of other people in the co-op.'

To remedy this situation, the interim chair recommended a point system for member selection. This would encourage the committee to be more objective and accountable. But others on the committee disagreed with some of the weightings – the importance given to prior co-op experience, for example – and did not adopt the recommendation.

Elections in 1989 resulted in five new members of the board of directors and a new president. Generally, it was an inexperienced board but one open to new approaches. The two continuing board members expressed a commitment to work on the 'committee issue.' At last it seemed that Dan Fast's organizational development might take place and the board would establish closer ties with the other committees. By the summer of 1989 he was planning to resign within a few months and hand Windward over to another coordinator.

Fast reflected on the state of member control as he was about to leave Windward: 'If anything, I feel that members on the committees have become much more confident, in a way, about how things work. [It's] simply because they've seen that time goes by and nothing happens to surprise or shock them about the way things are supposed to work. You can go from month to month the way you're doing things and there are no repercussions. So it must be okay ... So in that regard, I think that there's been – I don't know if you can call it democracy, but sort of a feeling more at ease with [hesitates], with what it is they're a part of.' He continued: 'On the other hand, I'm more doubtful as to whether they understand how things are *supposed* to work here ... [N]one of the "training" happened at [the beginning], or whatever you would call it: "inculcation of co-op ways," or "respect for committee processes" or anything like that.'

Windward committees discovered things for themselves, developing their own ways of handling things in isolation from the board of directors. 'I think that makes it harder now for the board to go to them, especially a board that's wet behind the ears, and tell them what to do.' But Fast recognized that this was not really the board's task: 'all it has to do is sit down with them and listen to them and ... come to some sort of agreements with them so that everybody is making the board feel that they know what's going on. And the committees feel that they know what the board wants.'

Dan Fast left Windward in late 1989. He had delayed his departure for a year in hopes of achieving his organizational development goals. But, in his own estimation, over that year 'things just got worse.' Reflecting on his time at Windward, he felt good that the co-op 'never turned into a dictatorship' and that 'people's rights were generally protected.' Still, he wished he could point to a single organization in the co-op that did things right, got reports in on time, or worked as he thought it should.

Fast's views, however, were not necessarily widely shared by members of the co-op. For him organizing was 'a hobby' as well as a job. He approached the development of Windward from a different perspective than did most of its members. For them it was a place to live and a community of neighbours but not necessarily an experiment in social engineering.

Conclusion

How well has democracy worked in these co-ops over their first three years? Certainly government by the people has prevailed. But the degree of satisfaction with democratic process in the co-ops depends on *which* people one considers. It also depends to some degree on what people mean by 'democracy.' Is it direct democracy or a representative system of some sort? Which decisions should be delegated to representatives or staff? How can accountability be ensured? Should decisions be made by consensus or by majority rule? To what degree and how can the minority be protected from the majority? Perhaps because democracy as an ideal is highly charged emotionally but vague, its meaning is often contested. At Windward and Harbourside there was great agreement on the need for democracy, but less on just what the term meant.

Ironically, the means some members proposed to reach the goal of democracy were diametrically opposed. On the one side were those who believed in the necessity of stringent procedural safeguards, minutely spelled out rules and regulations. On the other were those who thought that 'true' democracy required the death of organization. A further irony was that elaborate bureaucratic rules and forms of organization might disadvantage precisely those members of the co-ops with less education and relevant experience.

We conclude that democracy worked well for active participants who supported and used cooperative ideology. They could encourage and, if need be, enforce egalitarian participation among those serving on committees. They could directly control much that affected the enjoyment of their housing. For those who actively but unsuccessfully opposed them and what they stood for, frustration and alienation were more likely outcomes. Such was the fate of the 'contras' at Harbourside and of the man who led a challenge to Windward's board alleging financial mismanagement. Of course, the possibility remains that such a challenge could be successful. A small group could capture the leadership of the co-op, in so far as it could take over the board of directors. Even dominating a powerful committee, as happened with the member selection committee at Windward, could pose a threat to cooperative member control. But these threats are hollow so long as the general membership retains – and uses – its voting rights.

Finally, the majority who were uninvolved or only moderately involved retained a fairly strong ability to assert their control. They contributed to decision making on those issues that excited them and could object to decisions made by the board of directors that seemed to run counter to their interests.

The effectiveness of these marginal participants, however, depends on the presence of adequate communication and organizational structures within the co-op. Members have to know what is going on. The procedures and policies to which they can have recourse must be in place. This is the area in which Harbourside and Windward both had serious shortcomings. They were especially evident at Windward where they were the focus of much concern but little action. At Harbourside, too, some serious policy issues (concerning guests and subsidies, for example) were swept under the rug. Factional disputes dissipated without resolving deeper issues.

Throughout the three years of our study, both co-ops' boards of directors were so caught up with concerns of the moment that long-range planning and development seemed a luxury. Perhaps it was. At both co-ops enough participants came forward to fill committees. Enough people committed to cooperative principles created a positive atmosphere on many of those committees. Turnover in committee membership did occur, sometimes with a nudge from the board. Given the other demands on board members' time and the nature of the co-ops as essentially residential communities, it was not surprising that work on organizational development would be low on the agenda.

The *product*, a clearly defined network of committees, is less important than a viable *process* of member control. Even Windward's coordinator was convinced that the process of participation, not the structure of the organization, created community. But further attention to the process of organizational development in both co-ops would be a safeguard. By late 1989, the two co-ops had informally achieved adequate member control. They were less successful in developing the policies and procedures that ensure this process will continue to work in the future.

CHAPTER TEN

Conflicts over Money and Space

Tearing Down the Barrier

Marie and Richard Victoire moved into an apartment as soon as Harbourside co-op opened in 1986. They became friendly with the Smiths who lived next door. A shared balcony made visiting easy. The architect's design called for a six-foot-high partition to be placed between their half of the balcony and their neighbour's half. The Victoires and the Smiths told the coordinator they did not want a barrier erected. But one day they came home from work to find the partition in place.

That night, the Smiths and Victoires tore down the barrier. They sent a strongly worded note to the coordinator. It was not very cooperative to ignore the explicit wishes of two member households, they complained. Moreover, the barrier itself discouraged cooperative living.

From the coordinator's perspective, the two couples had behaved arrogantly. The partition was co-op property, and not theirs to destroy. While the absence of a barrier might increase the balcony's value for the present occupants, future residents would probably prefer the privacy a barrier provided. What seemed cooperative for individuals in the short run was in conflict with the cooperative's long-run interests. The Smiths and Victoires had to agree to replace the barrier if either family moved out. This satisfied their desire to use the space collectively while meeting the co-op's need to protect future occupants' privacy.

Conflict over Use Values

The development and expression in action of people's social and personal requirements make spaces and things meaningful and potentially rewarding to them. These are the use values they can enjoy from their housing. Such values are not only intangibles, like prestige or having a lovely view. They can also be material, such as greater living space. Whether material or not, these values contrast sharply with the exchange values of housing, such as its ability to produce rents and its quality as an investment.

The idea that dwellings, including such exterior spaces as balconies and yards, reflect individual and community identity is well known.[1] But the investment of meaning in housing is no simple matter of reflection. It is filled with ambiguity, argument, contradiction, and competition. In cooperative housing the contested and reflexive qualities of this process become especially evident. Such conflict does more than express peoples' feelings about where they live. It also helps participants, like the Smiths, the Victoires, and the coordinator, to clarify what housing means to them. Through disputed decisions on such diverse issues as maintenance, budgets, landscaping, parking, pets, or internal moves, the tenant community of a co-op directly affects the use values its members realize from their housing.

In this chapter we present three different conflicts over use values. At Harbourside we consider two 1988 crises: the spatial expression of a landscaping dispute and the more verbal conflict over the budget. At Windward we look at conflict over internal moves in 1989. This brought the needs of individuals in conflict with each other. It also created tension concerning the goals of the co-op.

We note some implications of these three issues for the distribution of power among individuals, control over housing, ideologies of cooperation, the meaning of housing, and the reproduction of the cooperative community. Specifically, we explore (1) how conflict over housing helped people to define and to express certain social, cultural, and individual needs; (2) how at the same time people tried to make housing conform to those needs; and (3) how in so doing they discovered or changed what housing meant to them. We conclude that the use values of cooperative housing are social products. Several processes play a part in constructing them, conflict being especially important.

The theme of conflict over use values is particularly evident in cooperative housing for a number of reasons. First, as we have noted earlier, exchange values are largely eliminated as a consideration, at least internally, thus accentuating use value issues. Second, the social organization of a co-op makes it very clear that the realization of the use values of housing for individuals and households depends to a considerable degree on the actions of their neighbours. Third, the institutional structure of cooperative housing, with its emphasis on member participation, both encourages the expression of conflict among divergent interests and provides ways of mediating those differences. Finally, even within a housing co-op, the creation of use values reflects the broader society. At Harbourside and Windward, the idea of private property remained very important. Efforts to challenge or deny the hegemony of this concept within the co-op merely emphasized how dominant it was. They revealed how partial housing cooperatives are as communities, and how strongly attached many members continued to be to private property in a housing context.

Fighting over Flowers

Fights over flowers and conflicts over shrubbery may seem trivial. We suggest, however, that landscape disputes can reveal a great deal about problems of cooperative communities. Flowers and shrubs are not simply things people fight *about*. They are, if one is not too literal, things people fight *with*. So conflicts about landscape are evident in practice rather than only in what people say. They have a dynamic spatial reality which in turn relates to the social construction of the co-op.

Landscape is more than just a setting for social action. It becomes part of that action in practice. As such, the conflicts over landscape presented here illustrate three points: (1) that tensions between conflicting use values, especially those pitting individual needs against those of a community, can be expressed in landscape; (2) that conflicts among members at different income levels can be extrapolated from the landscaping process; and (3) that ideas of private property remain important. We offer some evidence for these three points, organized (appropriately enough) in spatial terms. First, we look at the landscaping of Harbourside's communal or courtyard space, next at the flower-beds in individual front yards, and finally at a cooperative project to plant shrubbery in the front yards and the courtyard.

Courtyard: Conflict over Use Values in Communal Landscaping

The three residential wings of Harbourside co-op shelter a communal courtyard. It is bordered on the fourth side by an expanse of green cement which the neighbouring artists' co-op installed in lieu of a lawn. Each townhouse has a patio and each apartment has a balcony. These are either private or shared with one neighbouring household.

Fences demarcating the patios and balconies were critical design features. They marked, as they did in the Swiss co-ops Roderick Lawrence (1989: 98) studied, 'the interface between private/personal and collective/social domains.' Despite the cooperative ethos, these boundaries were important. The neighbours who tore down the barrier on their balcony were required to replace it.

Each townhouse also has a patch of front lawn which can express the household's individuality, within limits. The Harbourfront waterfront redevelopment corporation oversaw the co-op's landscaping plans, regulated what kinds of trees and shrubs could be planted, and prohibited individuals from planting vegetable gardens.

The courtyard was mud when we began our study. Harbourside residents hoped the courtyard would become the kind of informal meeting ground that seemed appropriate to cooperative living. But in the beginning the landscaping of the communal space was more of a battleground pitting different residents against each other. First, the relative importance of expenditures on interior and exterior space was contested. In the fall of 1986, everyone agreed that the co-op should buy and install sod in the courtyard. But when it became clear that there was enough money for either sod or laundry tubs, the lawn seemed less important. It was going to be winter soon. So members voted to install laundry tubs in the townhouse basements rather than lay sod in the courtyard. Second, conflicts emerged between active and passive recreational use. For example, the next summer when the grass was in and planned flower-beds were outlined in orange spray paint, some members with children objected. They complained that the proposed flower-beds were too big and would cut into play space. Playground equipment was similarly contested. The playground, it was feared, would reduce green space for the use of other residents. Members argued that the planned sandbox would attract cats from all over the neighbourhood. A related issue concerned pets from the neighbouring co-op who preferred to relieve themselves on grass rather than their own co-op's green cement. Finally, to some, the semipublic space of the courtyard seemed an extension of the semiprivate townhouse patios. Without patio access to the courtyard, apartment dwellers on the third floor of the co-op expressed the feeling that they had no place in the courtyard and felt uncomfortable there.

Park benches were installed to improve the situation and encourage informal socializing. But a gap between townhouse and apartment people remained. In our survey, we asked, 'Do you think apartment residents feel as much a part of the co-op community as people in townhouses?' No matter where the respondents lived, 70 per cent said that apartment dwellers felt somewhat or much less part of the co-op.

Front Yard: Income Differences, Commitment, and Conflict

As in private housing, the flower-beds between the front door of each townhouse and the street allowed Harbourside residents to display their individuality. And as in private housing, some residents devoted considerable time and money to these flower gardens. Others did not. Members sometimes saw this difference as being related to income. One single mother on subsidy brought up the subject of flowers to support her view that richer members of the co-op sometimes made 'foolish assumptions' about poorer members:

One person who is very well off and has [his] garden full of flowers says to me, 'aren't you going to plant flowers and things like that?' Well, I can't afford them. In truth I can't. Still [this person] says, 'Well you need some flowers there.' I said, 'I certainly do. Then why don't you give me some? These flowers out there, I cannot afford them!' [So] they think I'm not a very good co-op member because I have not put flowers over there, and I feel I can't.

Similarly, she objected to items in the newsletter criticizing residents of her wing of the co-op (see Fig 10.1). Such criticisms, she felt, indicated faulty assumptions on the part of more affluent members: 'Sometimes in the newsletter there are things like ... people over in [that wing] don't take good care of their front yards. And that includes me. And I said, "Well, wait a minute. It's not that we don't take good care of our front yard. I mean some people can afford flowers. Some people cannot afford flowers." I don't feel that kind of remark should be there.'

Differences in front gardens went beyond disputes about income levels to reveal a theme that has come up in our discussions of disability, participation, mixing incomes, and democracy. This conflict over flowers reflected members' different priorities. In many ways, it was more about commitment than the ability to pay. Some of the subsidized members kept very attractive and profusely flowered front gardens, and so did some of the members paying full rent. There was tension and conflict between these people and those who did not tend their gardens.

Richer and poorer members who were themselves strongly committed to the cooperative form of housing, and to Harbourside in particular, seemed to use flowers as a visible, symbolic measure of commitment to the co-op (see Fig. 10.2). This was couched in terms of 'pride of place.' Its proponents were not all people with middle-class incomes. Those less concerned with keeping a flower garden included richer members who were plan-

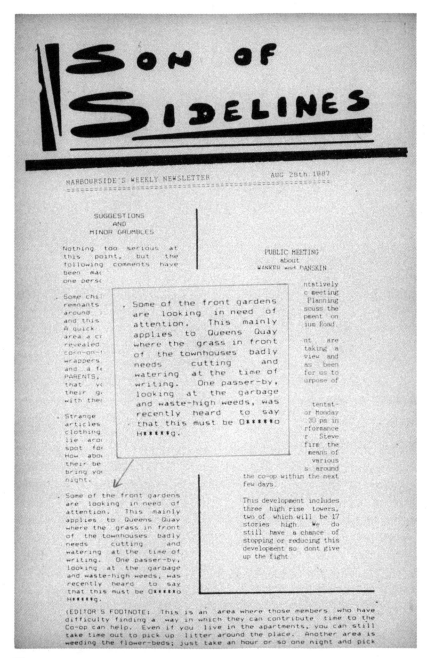

Figure 10.1

Son of Sidelines criticized members for neglecting their gardens. Conflicts over gardens reflected members' different priorities.

Figure 10.2
Harbourside members who were strongly committed to the co-op seemed to use flowers as a visible, symbolic measure of their commitment.

ning to move once they had saved a nest egg and poorer members who hoped to move or who did not care particularly about Harbourside. The woman quoted above preferred to construe the others' concern with planting flowers as insensitivity to her poverty. In fact, her bitterness about the flowers seemed symptomatic of her own lack of commitment to the co-op. She was talking at the time about leaving Harbourside. A few months later she did.

Front and Back: Private Property, Self-Interest, and Shrubs

A landscaping crisis occurred in the spring of 1988. It involved conflicts over use values between individuals, as well as between members and the co-op. The ambiguity of cooperative landscaping as at once collective and private property was especially evident.

The co-op's landscaping committee decided to plant all 274 of the shrubs planned for the front yards and the courtyard at once. This meant a large financial investment. Mass participation from co-op residents was essential to plant everything promptly. To plant less, the committee felt, would have been discriminatory or unattractive. It would have been unfair if only every second yard had been done. Alternatively, if only a couple of shrubs had been planted in each yard the co-op would have seemed sparsely landscaped.

The distribution of the shrubs was decided in cooperative fashion by a committee with participation from the membership at large. But leadership was needed for the actual planting, and the leader, Enid, became a target for criticism. She told us how hard she had worked preparing for the planting day. She wrote and distributed memos, spent hours on the phone, and dealt with the nursery.

The night before the big event, she arrived home late. 'It was about quarter to eight. I'd come home by way of ... well, I'd left school, gone to the chiropractor, left there, got some groceries, left there and went to the daycare, picked up the kids and came home. I put away the groceries and I was just about to start feeding the children.' At this point in her hectic evening, another member of the landscape committee knocked on her door. Could she have her shrubs? She wanted to get a start on the planting that night.

'I said "No",' Enid explained.

'Why not?' asked her visitor.

Enid recounted the rest of their conversation. In this encounter the theme of tensions between the interests of individuals and the community arises again that also was expressed in conflicts about landscaping the courtyard. She remembered replying, 'Well, because there's 200 shrubs under [the tarpaulin]. They're all bundled up. It will take hours to sort them out and I can't do it now.'

'Do you mean you can't do it or you won't do it?'

'I can't. I'm not willing to do it now. We haven't had our supper yet.'

'Well, let me do it.'

'You can't.' Enid said this because she knew what the job would involve. This made the other woman angry.

'She was absolutely furious with me and said who did I think I was to put myself in front of the co-op. I was flabbergasted ... I was upset.'

Those who earlier had invested their own money in planting shrubs in their front yards, including Enid herself, resented attempts by others to deny them their share of co-op bushes on planting day. The similarity between this conflict and the fight over flowers discussed earlier should be obvious. Enid commented, that despite her limited income 'last year I spent maybe $200 on [shrubs]. I knew what I wanted and I wanted them in. I couldn't wait for this [mass planting]. But I knew there were evergreens coming and so I was just going to put in [my share of] the evergreens and take two burning bushes. So I got right to the end of the [planting] day, and there were my two burning bushes sitting there. I managed to not let them be taken anywhere else. Somebody on the landscape committee said, "I'm going to put these across the window."'

Enid remembered how the conversation went from there:
'Those aren't going in front of your window. Those are for my garden.'
'You've got enough in yours.'
'I've got plenty in mine because I went out and bought them. If you want more in your bed go out and buy them the way I did.'
'Oh, well, I live in the apartments. And I told the apartment people I'd look out for their interests. I'd make sure that they had a good show outside the door.'
'You're missing the point,' Enid said, 'Totally missing the point.'

The shrubs were explicitly co-op property bought with co-op money and planted with cooperative labour. But, ironically, reliance on cooperative labour contributed to people misconstruing the shrubs as potentially their own personal property. If Harbourside had been a condominium, for example, it might have hired a landscaping company to plant the shrubs, thereby avoiding the individual participation that made co-op members see the shrubs as a contestable resource. As it was, shrubs became private goods to be competed for – my 'rosebushes, my burning bush' – or to be defended by particular interest groups, such as the apartment dwellers who designated one of their number to 'look after their interests and ... make sure they had a good show outside the door.'

On planting day, there were heated arguments. According to Enid, people kept saying 'How come they get this many shrubs?' 'How come she gets all these?' Enid exclaimed, 'They're not *hers*. ... Why is it all so *personal*?'

Pay Now or Pay Later: Fighting over a Budget

To explore why it is 'all so personal' and to gain a different perspective on the issues of self-interest and commitment evident in these spatially expressed conflicts about landscape, we turn to another contentious area of co-op life. A budget dispute that took place at Harbourside co-op in 1988 provides our second example of conflict in the social construction of use values and of the effects of this process on cooperative housing.

Each year the co-op adopted a budget proposed by its board of directors which based its proposal on the work of the finance committee, and then submitted it to the membership at a general meeting for approval. In 1988, a dispute arose over how much to increase housing charges in view of the co-op's continuing problems with building deficiencies.

When Harbourside opened in 1986 there were many such deficiencies. Although most of them were remedied there continued to be problems, especially with wet basements in the townhouses. As well, repairs to hallways and stairways leading to the apartments already were necessary after only two years because the contractors had used cheap materials. Concerned about long-term maintenance of the co-op, the board of directors hired consultants to do a technical audit. The consultants recommended that the co-op put aside an additional $12,000 per year beyond the $15,000 per year required by CMHC as a reserve fund. To do this would have required an increase of 8–10 per cent in housing charges.

The board proposed a 5 per cent increase as a compromise from the original 8–10 per cent they thought necessary. But at the general meeting many members became upset. They demanded that an ad hoc budget committee be set up, which, eventually, recommended a 3 per cent rise. In the end, members agreed to a 4 per cent increase as a compromise. The dispute was serious and bitter although a difference of 1 per cent meant only $5–10 per month for those paying full market housing charges and nothing for those receiving rental subsidies. What does this dispute say about the social construction of use values in cooperative housing?

As in the flower dispute, initially the best way to account for the sides people took seemed to be in terms of differences in income or their relation to the housing market. Those receiving rent subsidies favoured the raise; those paying full market rent opposed it. This breakdown helps up to a point but it fails to account for some people, especially in the full rent category who also favoured the increase. It also misses the differences of meaning and perspective that informed people's actions.

As we pursued this topic with co-op residents the depth of feeling became obvious. Many were disappointed and even exasperated to find how different their views and feelings were from those of their neighbours. After two years of working to form a community (albeit a partial one) of like-minded people they discovered the depths of their differences. Some members evidently felt so uncommitted they refused to spend an additional $5 a month for the long-term good of the co-op. Those who opposed the increase felt the others were asking them to subsidize the co-op's future. They did not expect to be part of that future, so felt the increase was unfair.

One resident proposed to us that political attitudes underlay the differences. 'My feeling is that the ones on the left are really so strongly committed and so strongly believe in what the co-op is all about that they tend to be overeager to try and persuade the other group and the other group ... is simply not willing to listen ... to the philosophical arguments.' A member of the other group, she said, was likely to respond: 'I don't have any investment – a long-term investment in this project. I'm not getting anything out of it. And therefore I'm not putting anything more than I absolutely have to into it.'

More than politics was involved. Implicitly, she divided the co-op into the philosophically committed and those whose commitment rested on material grounds. For the latter, in her view, the *lack* of exchange value in their housing made them unwilling to commit themselves. She went on to add a third group: ambivalent people who thought of the co-op as being theirs and treated it as if it were a home they owned, yet refused any long-term commitment to it. She suggested the complexity of people's views by comparing them to those of homeowners who take good care of their property, yet who intend to sell and move on in a few years. Ironically, to clarify members' motives she had to draw her analogy from market housing. Yet exchange value considerations were mostly irrelevant within the co-op.

Other residents divided the co-op into 'professionals,' who

opposed the rent increase, and others. Our self-categorized non-professionals characterized the professionals as better educated, more experienced financially, and better able to argue their points in meetings, but also as more mobile and uncommitted to the co-op. At the general meeting in which the ad hoc budget committee (made up of professionals) presented its alternate proposal, the professionals argued that their 3 per cent increase represented 'fiscal responsibility.' Their opponents, they said, had based their budget on 'neighbourly love.' Trying to capture the rhetorical high ground of responsible, tough-minded concern for the co-op, the professionals managed only to infuriate everyone else.

Some co-op members focused on how commitment seemed to depend on people's time perspective, which itself varied with economic power. They tended to associate strong commitment to the co-op with a long time perspective and weak economic power. But they recognized that these dimensions did not always reinforce each other.

Those who favoured the increase did so for different reasons. Some expected to reside at Harbourside for the foreseeable future because they were on subsidy and had few options. Others, both people on subsidy and some who could afford to buy a house, were committed ideologically and emotionally to co-ops and to this one in particular. Some of those who paid full rent did have only a short time perspective. If, for example, they were living in the co-op to save for a down payment on a house, then they were not concerned with what the co-op would be like ten or twenty years on.

Internal Moves and Security of Tenure

Security of tenure is one of the key use values in cooperative housing. It allows for the kind of commitment evident on one side of the budget dispute. It helps to make the cooperative seem like home and encourages a sense of ownership. Like many co-op goals, the significance of security of tenure is seldom considered in the abstract. But its contested meaning became very apparent in a dispute over policy regarding internal moves at

Windward. The dispute expressed divergent feelings about the co-op as home.[2] It also helped to shape those feelings, as one person's right to security of tenure endangered another's and as neighbours became rivals for each other's units.

What obligation does the co-op have to provide appropriate housing for its members? This was the central issue underlying a number of conflicts in Windward co-op. Most cases arose partly as a result of the pressure for housing in Toronto. But they revealed other pressures. Questions of need, responsibility, justice, and greed all entered into the issue. A few examples illustrate the kind of problems that arose over internal moves.

Two young women joined Windward as room-mates sharing a two-bedroom unit. A year later, one of them married. She and her new husband wanted to keep the two-bedroom apartment. The other room-mate then applied to the co-op for a one-bedroom unit. What priority, if any, should she be given on the waiting-list?

A husband and wife lived in a two-bedroom apartment. The couple split up. Was the co-op obliged to find housing for both members? A relationship developed between two co-op members, each a single parent in a two-bedroom apartment. They wanted to live together. Should the co-op give them priority for a larger unit?

Subletting and the modification of some Windward units for people with mobility impairments complicated the issue. For example, a couple, the Trevors, moved into a one-bedroom modified unit because nothing bigger was available. The man used a wheelchair, but over time his mobility increased. After an operation he needed only a cane. The Trevors wanted a bigger apartment. They saw an opportunity to move when another member left to live with a man outside the co-op. She did not want to relinquish her Windward unit in case the relationship did not work out. So she sublet to the Trevors.

They in turn sublet their modified one-bedroom unit to a non-member with no mobility impairment. Time passed. The woman who had sublet to the Trevors decided to stay with her new partner. She gave up her apartment, which the Trevors were able to keep. That left an able-bodied man in a modified apartment. But he had joined committees and was participating actively in the co-op. No one wanted to throw him out. So the member selection committee waived its rules and let him stay even though he was not at the top of the waiting-list for a unit and had no disability.

Chains of people moved within the co-op, and some could bypass or rise to the top of the internal waiting-list. This troubled the president of Windward's board of directors. He wondered at what point the co-op should say, 'We will have a structure that kind of gives the necessary keel – the rudder or stability – that says that we know what the rules of the game are.' Alternatively, he wondered if the board should just throw up its hands and say, 'It doesn't matter. The first one to the pipe with the most kids wins the biggest unit!'

Sublets arose more often at Windward than at Harbourside. But a somewhat similar issue at Harbourside arose from the presence of long-term guests. If they began to take an active part in co-op affairs, they could hope to be accepted as members. Even though it was against the rules, they could jump over others on the external waiting-list and 'get in through the back door.'

There was another important difference between the two co-ops that made internal moves much more contentious at Windward. At Harbourside, household size was not a factor in allocating units to members, except for those who received subsidies to reduce their rent below 30 per cent of their gross income. A single person could live in a four-bedroom townhouse if he or she could pay for it. This was not the case at Windward. The membership policy adopted in 1986 required that unit size be appropriate to household size. This was not a luxury apartment building but social housing. There had to be at least two individuals in a two-bedroom apartment, three-in a three bedroom, and so on. In 1989, members whose household size had diminished were under pressure to move out of their large units. They defended themselves, saying their compliance with the policy at the time they moved in was what counted, not the subsequent changes in their household composition. But a faction in the co-op felt these people had to make their units available to members whose household size had grown and who needed more space. Members who had married within the co-op and whose combined households needed the space were especially vocal. The story of Brian and Maureen Yardley is a case in point.

Brian was a single parent with shared custody of two daughters when he moved into Windward. Maureen's husband died soon after they joined the co-op, leaving her with two daughters. Brian and Maureen met on the landscaping committee, fell in love, and were married in the co-op courtyard. In interviews with us, people spoke of their wedding as one of the first moments of shared community. It seemed to bring the whole co-op together. But the demands that the co-op then placed on them and that they placed on the co-op proved divisive.

Brian and Maureen each had a two-bedroom apartment. Both of them received some housing charge assistance. At first they planned to move to British Columbia and build a log cabin in the forest. They gave notice that Maureen would move out of her apartment. Her parents would sublet the other unit because they needed a place to stay in Toronto for a few months. Then Maureen discovered she was pregnant and all their plans changed.

Instead of moving, they wanted to hold on to both units. But new members were ready to move in to Maureen's apartment. Furthermore, the board of directors insisted that if they were one household they had to live in one unit. The Yardleys were very upset. As one person summed up the situation, 'It was going to be too stressful having them and this passle of children all in one two-bedroom apartment.' Brian and Maureen decided to separate.

At this point, the coordinator arranged for Maureen to sublet another unit in the co-op. But within a few weeks it became apparent that she and her husband were back together. The member selection committee then went to the board. The committee insisted that Maureen be made to live with Brian in his two-bedroom unit. The Yardleys explained that they wanted to keep both units so they could store Maureen's furniture in one. The girls were too little to sleep in one unit while the parents slept in the other. Using the second unit for storage was the only way the whole family could be together.

The board relented and gave them three months to get back into one unit. By that time, Maureen had had a baby boy. Her sublet ran out. The Yardleys had to live in his two-bedroom apartment with their baby, her two daughters, one of his daughters full time and another part time. Brian hired a lawyer who said the co-op was in violation of municipal by-laws. By law, his family had to have a larger unit.

On the recommendation of the member selection committee, the Yardleys were placed at the top of the waiting-list for a three-bedroom unit. But there was little turnover of these larger units. As a three-bedroom sublet ended, Yardley considered hiring a private investigator to determine if the principal occupants were entitled to keep their unit. Did the man's children really live there?

At this point, a three-bedroom unit became available. But then the Yardleys let the co-op know they were separating. They wanted the member selection committee to allow Maureen, her children, and the baby to move into the three-bedroom unit. Brian and his daughters would keep his two-bedroom apartment. But as two households the Yardleys were no longer much larger than others on the waiting-list. Another couple that had come together within the co-op and had similar housing needs protested. The Yardleys should not be at the top of the waiting-list if they were splitting up.

At the meeting, the member selection committee debated the issue for hours. Eventually, a decision was made to give the Yardleys only the three-bedroom unit. Thus, their priority on the waiting-list was retained, as if they still were a very large household. And by the same logic they could not keep Brian's unit. Allowing Maureen the three-bedroom apartment seemed the best option partly because it was the only one that would keep open the possibility for reconciliation in the marriage.

As our study came to an end, Brian had agreed to move into the three-bedroom with Maureen and all the children. But he planned to apply immediately for another internal move. The internal waiting-list for a two-bedroom was empty at that time. So Brian hoped to get the first two-bedroom that became available – his own.

The co-op clearly put pressure on the Yardleys, at times intruding into their personal lives. The Yardleys and others put pressure on the co-op generally and on specific individuals. The conflict generated by such pressures was a factor in one family's decision to leave.

Tom Norman had helped to found the co-op and had invested a great deal of time and emotional commitment in the place. He and his wife left partly because of the intrusion of the collectivity (which he called the macrocommunity) into the private domain of their home. When their children left home they were under pressure to give up their three-bedroom apartment overlooking the lake. During our final interview, Tom commented: 'I guess that when you're in a single family dwelling, although you can be very involved, very committed, when you close the door that's where the macrocommunity ends. In Windward, to some extent, the macrocommunity is also part of the microcommunity. That becomes a problem.'

The households that were 'underhoused' – that is, who had too many members for the size of the unit – complained loudly. The co-op had to find a unit for them in order to comply with city density regulations. Those that were 'overhoused' had no such leverage. But they did have strong opinions on the issue. Some were full of anguish at the thought of losing the apartments that had become their homes. An older woman worried that if her spouse died she would have to move to a smaller unit: 'What's the incentive in that situation to care for your apartment? Like everyday I clean the sink. I use Comet and I clean between the taps so there's no build up. I want it to stay nice. You put a lot of money into drapes, or whatever. It's like a home, you know. There's no incentive if you can just go in there until so-and-so leaves and then you have to move into another one.'

This woman took great pride in maintaining her home and secondarily in maintaining the building that was the extension of that home. But more than the co-op at large, her unit was her home. As such she felt, the unit should not be redefined as common property to redistribute on the basis of others' need. One board member defended these people's positions: 'I think that we provide people with a *home*, not with a *unit*. We cannot solve the housing problems of Metro Toronto. People's units should be their homes for as long as they want to stay there.'

But other board members disagreed: 'Maybe I'm too much of an idealist. But the reason we're in a housing co-op is that we're looking for some sort of justice in housing. The single mother who is in an abused situation and really short of cash ought to be able to live decently. Okay. So is that where it stops? We've got [single mothers] in. But we're still going to have this retired couple with an extra bedroom used as a den sitting up on a seventh- or eighth-floor corner overlooking the lake. They're in one room and they've got one room as a guest room and one room as a den! That's fantastic stuff. And, okay, they may have been the original builders and stuff like that, but where does it stop? The justice has obviously stopped and someone is now sitting where it was!'

The only thing people generally agreed on was that the situation was out of hand. Tom Norman commented:

> If you looked at any other housing situation [this] doesn't happen. You know, you don't have households combining and splitting and recombining and manipulating. It has been a very chaotic kind of existence.

> A rather uninvolved Windward member said she had heard about the Yardleys as two people in the co-op trying to live together, then splitting up, then getting back together, and how the co-op was *scrambling* to accommodate these decisions that these people made in their personal lives. I thought it was a bit much. It's like anywhere else. If you make the decision to split up and you can't both afford to find housing you have to cope with that ... If my relationship ended and one of us had to move, I wouldn't expect them to house both of us and subsidize one of us because now we couldn't afford [the housing charges]!

Yet our survey found that nearly half the respondents (47 per cent) felt that a household that grows or shrinks after several years in the co-op should *always* be rehoused in a different-sized unit if possible. Only 4 per cent replied that such rehousing should never take place.

As in the landscaping episode, greed seemed to feed the frenzy of internal moves. In Tom's view, 'People start thinking, "Well, this person's getting all this stuff and that person's getting all that stuff. Why can't I ask for something that normally I wouldn't be asking for?" ... People who bitch and complain are getting what they want ... I think there has been a negative spin-off from these combinings and jumping the waiting-list ... The co-op is allowing people *not* to have to take a lot of responsibility for their situations. When push comes to shove, who's responsible here, really? Is it the co-op? No. It is the people involved.'

It seems obvious that the co-op could not keep up with the rapidly changing housing requirements of its members. Moreover, the cost in terms of conflict between households with competing interests was great. The conflict highlights competing use values bound up in the notion of security of tenure. These include the right to stay in one's unit as 'home' versus the right to stay in the co-op whatever the changes in one's household or home life.

Conclusion

The conflicts presented here show how much neighbours could affect the use values of each other's housing. Not only the co-op community as a whole, but individuals able to exert power within that community, could directly affect how use values were defined. Thus, they could affect the present and future rewards that others would derive, both materially and emotionally, from living there.

Yet, clearly, the ideologies established within co-ops were not hegemonic in the wider society. Housing cooperatives were only a limited and relatively recent part of residents' experience so the ideologies of the wider society continued to inform their thinking. Even for those who were strongly committed to cooperation as a counter-ideology the meaning of housing as private property remained significant. So did personal gain.

In a number of ways, the conflicts also showed the importance of institutional structures in the social construction of use values. First, the co-op's structure of committees and decision-making processes mediated and at times exacerbated the conflicts. It allowed divergent interests to be expressed and choices made. This was particularly evident in the budget dispute which was fought out in the meetings of regular and ad hoc committees. In the case of the internal moves conflict, however, the member selection committee and board of directors imposed rules and forced choices on households, entering areas that might better have remained private.

Second, associated with this structure is an ideology of co-operation, community responsibility, justice, and 'neighbourly love.' Regardless of the strength of anyone's commitment to this ideology, it provided rhetorical resources for and constraints on residents' ability to advance their perspectives and interests in all the conflicts. Construction, propagation and manipulation of this ideology were themselves issues and importantly affected the co-op.

Third, the rhetoric of the co-op movement emphasizes taking control of one's housing. People who did take control of their housing seemed likely to be people who would assert themselves in other ways. They might fight for control over the shrubs in the yard, argue over a few dollars as a matter of principle, or try to take over their neighbour's larger apartment. The potential for conflict along these lines exists from the beginning of a co-op's life. But, as the internal moves conflict particularly shows, this strain inherent in co-ops can become worse over time.

The cases also show how conflict helped to *define* use values for individuals and groups, not merely express them. In the landscaping dispute, residents came to terms in a practical sense with the meaning of private and cooperative property. In the budget dispute it is especially evident that participants were conceptually refining their own visions of the cooperative. The dispute over internal moves reflected a struggle to define housing need and the relative entitlement of individuals to space. We conclude by dealing with each of these in turn.

The fights over flowers and shrubs point to the property-based source of fundamental tensions in cooperative housing. Co-ops are not communes. The cooperative housing movement retains a strong orientation toward private property at the same time as it emphasizes the power of collective action. This tension can be positive in the context of community formation, as when members view maintenance or security in the co-op as being as important as if it were their private home. Yet it can also have negative effects. Some of the problems this tension causes are particularly evident when one considers them, as we have done here, quite literally on the ground. Competing use values of playgrounds and pets, flowers as a measure of commitment to the co-op or as discrimination on the basis of income, and the shrubbery war with which we concluded the landscape section, all reflect the ambiguities of yard space in a housing co-op as both private, and not so private, property.

Because of the budget dispute, residents tried to conceptualize the make-up of the co-op and how that affected people's positions. They came to understand better what the co-op meant to them, what their own goals and needs were, and how those needs could be met in it. For some, its uses were relatively restricted. It was a good place to live, pleasant, convenient, cheap enough so that some could save for a down payment on a house. For others it meant not only shelter but the diffuse values of family and community, a physical and social setting in which to grow old together, and in which to enjoy the social support they had found so conspicuously absent in other forms of housing.

The conflict over internal moves was a struggle over the entitlement of individuals as co-op members to appropriate housing. In a sense, the conflict arose because membership is vested in people not property. In a condominium a member household owns a particular unit. Changes to the household are irrelevant. Yet in these co-ops members have rights in the *co-op* not to a particular unit. Thus, both husband and wife are equally entitled to housing if their marriage breaks up.

Windward's policy matching unit size to household size met co-op housing goals concerning justice while jeopardizing others concerning security of tenure. The value of housing those in need came into conflict with the value of making the co-op unit a home. As Dan Fast, Windward's first coordinator, remarked: 'It's only in co-ops that you're always talking about justice.'

CHAPTER ELEVEN
Conclusion

We have argued that giving citizens more control over the conditions that affect their lives would improve the quality of urban life. Not all aspects of the quality of life necessarily would benefit equally. Still, as Neighbourhood Watch programs and community-directed schools, for example, show in areas like security and education, citizen involvement can make a difference.

The quality of life depends on more than the availability of clean water and air, neighbourhood amenities, adequate food, or a feeling of personal security. To us, it also requires enlargement of the area of human freedom and dignity. The march of enormous institutions, governmental and private, that control large sectors of people's lives often seems relentless. Alienation follows. Thus, we value institutions of community control especially as sources of activism and liberty, hence as sources of human dignity. Freedom implies not only freedom from want and oppression but also freedom to create and to take responsibility for one's creations. These spiritual benefits are in many ways at least as important as the more material benefits that might flow to citizens.

Participatory democracy allows citizens to gain control while also promoting the general good. It entails the realization that other people's interests and needs are deeply rooted and cannot be wished away. Inevitably, therefore, it involves conflict over values. Such conflict, while sometimes tiresome, expresses the healthy diversity of a complex society.

Citizen participation, of course, can take many forms. There is a wide range, at the lower end of which citizens are merely informed about alternatives or passively watch decision makers at work. People do participate in civic affairs, at least in a weak sense, even by watching city council meetings on cable television.

At the upper end of the range citizens are involved in actually formulating goals and making important decisions. Beyond the formal political arena, citizen engagement in the crucial areas that affect daily life empowers people who have been the takers of decisions made by others. It allows people mutually to work out local solutions to their needs and problems as they perceive them. Thus, it holds out the hope of meeting those needs more fully.

In housing, as we have argued, the diversity of needs has been poorly met by much of what is available. The Canadian and American dream of homeownership has faded for all too many families. The 'typical' household, for whom so much of the housing built since the Second World War was designed, comprises perhaps only one-quarter of all households. Thus, the availability of housing alternatives has become ever more necessary. The co-ops we have described represent one kind of alternative. While far from perfect, they clearly have raised the level of housing satisfaction of most of their residents.

We think that the model co-ops offer, of member involvement and democratic control, is of general value. In contemporary society it is rare to find institutions that do not enforce sameness. Housing cooperatives allow for the expression and coexistence of differences. By fostering involvement, co-ops encourage members to deal with and meet the diversity of their housing needs.

Evaluating Harbourside and Windward

The co-ops described in this book were built as a response to housing problems. They held out the possibility of solutions, at least for a few, to two kinds of problems affecting thousands of households in Toronto. They sought to provide alternative housing that was affordable to low- and middle-income residents. And they addressed some needs poorly met by conventional rental housing. These included the need for housing appropriate to non-traditional households – especially single parents and households in which one or more members had a disability. The need for security, control, and sociability also often was not met by ordinary housing.

How well have Harbourside and Windward met these objectives? Has each co-op become, as the promotional film promised, 'more than just a place to live'? Have the new neighbours come to feel at home? We think they have.

This is not to say that these co-ops became everyone's ideal home. Some members would much rather have lived elsewhere. Even some who were fairly content hoped to buy their own houses one day. But for many these co-ops were deeply rewarding. Those who were most satisfied seem to have been people with appropriate expectations, high levels of involvement, and a sense that they could make things happen in the co-op.

The economic benefits of co-op housing were attractive, but the non-monetary rewards seemed even more important to the people we interviewed. These non-economic rewards are the use values of housing. They are what housing means to people as 'home' and as a place connected to a community. These differ to some extent from person to person. Conflicts arose as co-op members created and defended different use values associated with their housing. They had to negotiate with each other, persuade, achieve consensus, or take a vote. As in any democratic process, there were winners and losers.

In the next sections we reflect on the process of democratic member control as the key to what success these co-ops have achieved. We consider first *how* member control worked in the co-ops. Then we evaluate how *successfully* it worked.

How Did Member Control Work?

The social organization of housing cooperatives is founded on the principle of democratic member control. This is both a goal and a process. While the co-ops shared an organizational structure built around this principle, each developed differently. The people in the co-ops and the issues they wrangled with shaped each place. Internal moves became a source of conflict at Windward but were not controversial at Harbourside. There the budget was disputed because of different views about the future. At Windward, financial questions focused on the past. The practical working out of issues, small and large, over three years made each co-op quite different as a place to live.

We have tried to convey some of those differences throughout the book, and we will summarize them in the next section. But for the moment we want to consider how they arose. The exercise of democratic member control in these co-ops, we found, was a continual process of give and take. In part, this was an expression of conflict – and agreement – about the use values of housing. It also involved negotiation of the practical meaning of democracy. Learning to take control over housing was a crucial element in the symbolic construction of community.

For the residents, taking control began with the member selection process. Choosing members to form the hoped-for community of like-minded people competed with the requirement that the co-op be heterogeneous. Discrimination on such grounds as ethnicity or education was not allowed. But it was important to be discriminating in other ways. Ambiguity and subjectivity entered into decision making. Committee members could not be sure they were accepting people who would make good co-op members, yet they had always to aspire to that goal. They controlled who joined the co-op, but they tried to admit people who would take active roles in controlling their own housing. They felt responsible for these people: new members had better participate. And they felt responsible for choosing neighbours who would not detract from their own quality of life in the co-op.

Members became aware, sometimes painfully, that enjoyment of the use values of cooperative housing depends on one's neighbours. Rejections particularly revealed negotiation over the meaning of use values in housing. What did it mean to say that someone would not make a 'good neighbour'? Reaching selection decisions around these and other highly charged phrases helped membership selection committee members create an image of what each co-op should be like. Rejections, however difficult some were to make, helped clarify these images.

Ability and willingness to participate in democratic member control was an important criterion for membership in both co-ops, but especially at Windward. The mandate that at least 25 per cent of the co-ops had to be low-income households cut across this criterion, for the poorest applicants often lacked apparently necessary middle-class skills. Both co-ops included more households on subsidy than the required 25 per cent. By 1989, subsidized households amounted to more than 40 per cent of both co-ops. The selection process may well have creamed off those low-income people who expressed an interest in participation and who had the skills to do well in a interview. It also favoured those people with physical disabilities who had experience with volunteer work and who seemed likely to play active roles in running Windward.

We found that participation rates and informal involvement reflected neither income nor disability differences. If the selection process was biased in favour of middle-class skills, these were made use of once a member moved in without regard to income or physical differences. Both co-ops were run by a casual mixture of people receiving housing charge assistance and paying full rent. Similarly, at Windward people with physical disabilities served on the board of directors and committees. There seemed to be no quotas, even informally.

Mixing incomes and trying to ensure that both richer and poorer members would play active roles in controlling their housing contributed to the vitality of the co-ops. It meant a mixture of attitudes, backgrounds, family types, and so on. This contributed to the lively negotiation of sometimes competing use values as new neighbours tried to sort things out democratically. These sorting-out processes form the substance of many chapters in this book. Examples include the subsidy issues in chapter 7, the newsletter production process in chapter 9, and the three conflicts that make up chapter 10.

While some members, regardless of income or physical ability, participated actively in co-op democracy, a central problem remained. Clearly, not everyone would participate. While member participation differentiates co-ops from other kinds of housing and the obligation to participate is part of the membership agreement, universal participation is an unrealizable goal. It may not even be desirable. In Windward's and Harbourside's first three years, between half and three-quarters of the members participated in co-op committees and activities at any time. That was enough to fill committees, run the co-op, and involve many members in informal activities. It left plenty of people available, if not always willing, to play active roles in the co-ops in the future.

Democratic member control, we feel, could operate effectively in these co-ops without universal participation in practice. The opportunity to participate, however, had to be present. Participation also had to seem attractive. Greater organizational development in both co-ops would ensure turnover of committee membership and continuity of process.

Democracy is a highly charged term emotionally. It also is vague. Many of the issues at Harbourside and Windward expressed the different meanings that participants attributed to democratic control. The relative rights of individuals and the co-op as a whole were contested in many issues, ranging from the selection process, through modifications for people with disabilities, alternatives to participating on committees, the role of subsidized members in deciding on housing charge increases, and the tearing down of a barrier between two apartment balconies.

Even when there was agreement on the need for democracy, divergent means of attaining that goal were evident. Some favoured consensus. Others argued for majority rule. The 'contras' at Harbourside and those involved in the financial challenge to the board of directors at Windward (see chapter 9) became frustrated and alienated through participation in democratic processes based on majority rule. At Windward, differences became apparent between those who felt that detailed rules and procedures safeguarded democracy and those who felt organization inhibited 'true' democracy.

How well democratic member control works in a co-op, we feel, will depend on *how* it works. At Harbourside and Windward, member control operated on an issue-by-issue basis. There rarely seemed to be time to reflect on democratic processes more abstractly. Decisions on urgent repairs, internal moves for members crowded into units, and even social events took priority. This is not surprising. What is more, the processes in place in both co-ops did work. Even marginal participants could have their say. Their effectiveness in joining issues in future, however, is likely to depend on the existence of communication and organizational channels that neither co-op had a chance to elaborate in its first three years.

How Successful Was Member Control in the Two Co-ops?

Differences between the two co-ops over time reflected the diversity that citizen control encourages, as well as physical differences in the design and size of the two projects.

The physical forms – Harbourside's townhouses and courtyard, Windward's full accessibility – reflected residents' particular needs. But the buildings also *created* certain needs, as, for example, at Harbourside where there were differences between apartment dwellers' views and those of people in the townhouses. People in apartments felt removed from the rest of the community because of their physical isolation from the courtyard.

Harbourside became a fairly tightly knit community, partly because of its size and layout but also because of the gregarious personalities of some key members. There was a related curiosity about fellow members that some saw as nosiness and prying. Member control sometimes became a question of peer pressure, as the landscaping dispute in chapter 10 illustrates.

Windward, with almost twice as many units, was less cohesive. But there people saw their neighbours as less invasive as well. For many residents, the co-op was not much different from an ordinary apartment building except for two crucial differences: members ran it and the building was accessible.

The integration of people with disabilities, which the fully accessible building made possible, shaped the new neighbours' experiences. As chapter 6 indicates, the mixing of people with and without physical disabilities at Windward was a success story. A measure of this success, we feel, was that social interaction among and between able-bodied people and those with disabilities was neither intense nor avoided. It was just 'normal.' Some people with disabilities were among the leaders of the co-op. Others played no active role in member control.

Those who were active, however, tended also to be the most satisfied with life at Windward. The co-op could meet their expectations for independent living integrated into a larger community partly because they helped it to do so. Of course, not every active participant with a physical disability was satisfied with the co-op for the entire three year period. Tom Norman, whose story we present in chapter 8 and elsewhere, helped found the co-op. He left eventually partly because he felt a victim of democratic control. His neighbours' needs seemed to win out over his own in the end.

One goal of cooperative housing has been to create mixed-income residential communities. In order to make co-ops attractive to middle-income people, everyone benefited financially from living in the co-ops instead of other forms of rental housing. As we describe in chapters 2 and 7, the financial structure of co-ops under section 56.1 of the National Housing Act benefited all members, whatever their income. The mortgage interest reduction grant reduced all housing charges in the co-op to the low end of market rents charged for similar housing in the neighbourhood. Further housing charge assistance was available in the form of subsidies to reduce a household's rent to 30 per cent or less of income.

The success of the co-ops as mixed-income communities was evident in the little difference that income differences made. This success, we feel, stemmed from member control backed by a mandate to include low-income households. Income was sometimes an issue – as when subsidy policies were debated in both co-ops – but people did not take sides mainly along income lines. Those most active in the co-op included people on deep subsidies and the relatively well-to-do. The selection of lower-income people with the skills to play leadership roles in the co-ops may have contributed to the success of mixed-income member control.

Participation in the co-ops shaped communities out of people from diverse backgrounds and income levels. This shaping could take place because members had been selected to some extent on the basis of shared attitudes. They believed in their own ability to control and improve their housing. Experience in the co-ops then developed – or in some cases, discouraged – that belief in practical ways.

As housing for low-income households, the cooperatives we studied were, for many, 'heaven' compared with the alternatives. But their attractiveness as housing for middle-income renters also should be underscored. Much of this attractiveness has to do with use values centring around 'home' and 'community,' quite apart from the financial benefits co-ops provided. In the housing crisis that beset Toronto at the time of our study, there were few breaks for middle-income people. Security of tenure and control over one's housing, not to mention affordability, were difficult to obtain for ordinary renters. The kind of housing that co-ops like Harbourside and Windward provided was especially welcome. There, young families, retired couples, single mothers, self-employed writers, and quadriplegics just out of hospital, among many other kinds of households, could become new neighbours and find 'more than just a place to live.'

A Final Vignette

Finally, we offer a story that summarizes much of what we found to be most positive about both Windward and Harbourside.

Before Ken moved to Windward, he was in some sense imprisoned by his surroundings. The accessibility of the building freed him physically. Participation in the co-op freed his spirit. Although Harbourside lacked Windward's accessibility features, its potential for empowering and enlivening those who lived there was as great.

Elizabeth and Ken were in their early sixties when they first spoke to us in 1987. They had led active lives. Because of Ken's work as a forester with the government, they had lived in many towns in northern Ontario. But about ten years after they married, Ken began to suffer from rheumatoid arthritis. In the mid-1960s, they moved to Toronto and settled in a large apartment in the west end. Elizabeth remembered it fondly: 'We were very comfortable. It was a safe place. We had a big three-bedroom apartment, two bathrooms, an eat-in kitchen, and our three daughters were with us. Gradually the eldest moved out ... and the other two were married from there.'

Then for Ken the apartment became a prison. He retired from the forestry service in the early 1980s and spent all day at home. He felt unwell and depressed. Broadloom carpet and narrow doorways made it hard for him to get around the apartment in a wheelchair. Elizabeth remembered: 'He couldn't move. If I'd go out and leave him sitting at the dining-room table, he'd still be sitting there when I'd get home. I'd have to go out and shop. I'd come home – say it was in the winter – he'd be sitting in the dark. It was just terrible. Bad for him. Bad for us both.'

They heard about Windward through their daughter, who lived in another Toronto co-op, and her husband, who had been involved in the International Year of the Disabled. Ken and Elizabeth applied, were accepted, selected a unit, and specified the modifications they needed. They moved in on 30 December 1986, before the building was completed. They planned to stay. As Elizabeth put it six months later, 'We plan to stay because I don't know of anything better for Ken and me if we want to be together.'

The adjustment was not easy. Elizabeth could hardly believe how little storage room they had compared with the spacious old apartment. The lack of stores in the area was an inconvenience. They missed their friends. But she enjoyed serving on the social committee. Ken joined the finance committee and became its chairman. Elizabeth thought this was 'great for Ken because he hadn't done anything for two years and he's really enjoying it.' But it was also a lot of work and Ken wondered if he had taken on too much.

We met Ken in 1987, but he chose to let Elizabeth be interviewed alone that first year. By the summer of 1988 when it was time for the second interview, Ken and Elizabeth both wanted to talk. The changes Ken described had a special poignancy when compared with the quality of his life a few years earlier. He spoke like a statesman, carefully reflecting *on our questions and composing eloquent replies.: 'You ask what I think is the major change in the co-op [in the past year]. First of all, looking at that from the perspective of its impact on Elizabeth and me, I would say that the major change in our lifestyle is that we've come to enjoy and appreciate some of the aspects of cooperative living ... We have a feeling of greater involvement in the community. This involvement has added a new dimension – How can I describe how we feel about it? Words like "greater involvement" [convey] how this has made our lives more enjoyable.'*

In 1988, Ken was elected to the board of directors. Through co-op participation he had found new meaning in his life. *'We had become somewhat staid in our habits [before joining the co-op]. Especially myself, not so much Elizabeth. But here I look forward to each new day because I know I'm going to be caught up to some small degree in the affairs of this particular community.'*

By 1989, Elizabeth and Ken were clearly thriving in the co-op. Elizabeth had made several close friends. One was a woman whose husband also needed considerable care. Another used a wheelchair herself. Some of her friends were much younger than Elizabeth. She delighted in their babies and said she was glad not to be in housing for seniors only. Elizabeth and Ken had learned a lot about interacting with people with disabilities. As white, middle-income earners, they also enjoyed the mix of people's incomes and backgrounds at Windward.

Elizabeth told us: *'It's a real mixed bag in here and I've found it most interesting. I've really enjoyed it. I really enjoy the people from Uruguay. And my neighbour across the hall is from Chile. You know, colour, background, I mean it's worked out quite well.'*

The mixing of incomes reminded them of the communities they had enjoyed living in up north. As Ken said, *'Your next-door neighbour can be a millionaire and the one of the other side can be living on welfare in small communities.'* And Elizabeth added,*' Maybe that's why I loved it there, because it was exactly the same thing [as Windward] as far as income [mixing].'*

Ken concluded our final interview by saying:

I'm sure as anthropologists one of the questions that you'll try to answer, and perhaps will answer, after your examination of the co-op[s] is: 'What is it about a co-op that makes it attractive to people? Why do people want to live such a style of life?

As for myself, in partial answer to that question, there are a lot of things physically about the building and the surroundings that are appealing. And that means a lot.

There are things that happen in here that tend to take the edge off your enjoyment of the co-op. You become more aware, after a period of time, of the unpleasant characteristics of people ... I think, somehow or other, you become more aware of what you consider the unpleasant characteristics of individuals [in co-ops]. And the reverse is true too, that you become more aware of the very pleasant characteristics and the good points about them.

But I think the thing in a co-op that really attracts me to it is – one way or another co-op living seems to give me a satisfaction in that I am recognized ... In the other apartment, there were few people that you got to know. In small-town living if you stayed long enough in a neighbourhood, you'd get to know everybody. [The co-op] is something like that.

Ken took satisfaction from his service to the co-op as a member of the board, but he did not seek recognition for this. What he wanted, and found, in the co-op was recognition as a neighbour.

Living at Windward Co-op: A Survey of Members about Goals and Satisfaction

This survey is part of the study we are doing to understand better how co-ops deal with the problems facing them in the first few years of their existence and how satisfied co-op residents are with their housing.

Please answer all of the questions. If you wish to comment on any questions or qualify your answers, please use the margins or a separate sheet of paper. Your comments will be greatly appreciated.

You may be assured of complete confidentiality. The questionnaire has an identification number for distribution purposes only. This is so that we may check your name off the mailing list when your questionnaire is returned. Your name will never be placed on the questionnaire.

'Co-operative Housing in Toronto,' the research project of which this survey is part, is supported by McMaster University, York University, and the Social Sciences and Humanities Research Council of Canada.

Please return this questionnaire to the Co-ordinator's office in the envelope provided. Thank you for your co-operation.

Please answer the following questions by CIRCLING THE NUMBER next to the appropriate category.

1. In general, how satisfied are you with living at this co-op? (1) Very dissatisfied; (2) Fairly dissatisfied; (3) Neither dissatisfied nor satisfied; (4) Fairly satisfied; (5) Very satisfied

2. During the time you've lived here, has living in this co-op become better or worse? (1) Much worse; (2) Somewhat worse; (3) About the same; (4) Somewhat better; (5) Much better

3. How committed do you feel to the co-op? (1) Not committed at all; (2) Fairly uncommitted; (3) Neutral; (4) Fairly committed; (5) Strongly committed

4. How long do you intend to live at this co-op? (1) As short a time as possible; (2) About a year; (3) A few years; (4) More than 5 years; (5) The foreseeable future

Listed on the right below are some possible sources of *satisfaction* or *dissatisfaction* with the co-op. Please WRITE THE NUMBERS of the *3* that are most important to you as sources of satisfaction *and* then the *3* that are most important to you as sources of dissatisfaction.

SOURCES OF SATISFACTION		1 Your own unit
5. __ Most important		2 The co-op's location
6. __ Second most important		3 The co-op's buildings and grounds
7. __ Third most important		4 Neighbourhood amenities
		5 The people at the co-op
SOURCES OF DISSATISFACTION		6 Affordability
8. __ Most important		7 Participating in the co-op
9. __ Second most important		8 The way the co-op is run
10. __ Third most important		9 Sense of community
		10 Security of tenure
		11 Other (please specify)

Now we would like to ask you some questions about what you think this *co-op's goals* should be. For each of the following CIRCLE THE NUMBER of the category that best expresses how strongly you agree or disagree with the statement. (1) Strongly disagree; (2) Disagree somewhat; (3) Neutral; (4) Agree somewhat; (5) Strongly agree

11. Providing affordable housing should be one of this co-op's major goals.   1   2   3   3   4   5

12. A high priority for the co-op should be making members feel that their tenure is secure.   1   2   3   4   5

13. High-quality, well-maintained housing should be one of this co-op's main goals.   1   2   3   4   5

14. One of the co-op's main goals should be to house people of different economic levels, social backgrounds, disabled and able-bodied.   1   2   3   4   5

15. This co-op should make it a priority to house people who really are in need.   1   2   3   4   5

16. Developing a genuine sense of community is one of the most important goals this co-op should have.   1   2   3   4   5

17. One of this co-op's principal aims should be to encourage members to take control over their own housing.   1   2   3   4   5

18. The co-op should be run in a completely democratic fashion. For example, all major issues should be debated and decided at general members meetings.   1   2   3   4   5
19. The co-op should strive to have almost everyone participating in co-op activities and community life.   1   2   3   4   5
20. The co-op should do all it can to help members upgrade their skills and training.   1   2   3   4   5
21. One of the co-op's chief goals should be to support its members when they are going through a difficult period.   1   2   3   4   5
22. The co-op should be actively involved in important neighbourhood issues.   1   2   3   4   5
23. This co-op should actively support and participate in the wider co-op housing sector.   1   2   3   4   5

The next questions ask you to think about the *actual characteristics* of this particular co-op and neighbourhood.

How would you rate the following aspects of the *neighbourhood?* For each item, please CIRCLE the appropriate number. (1) Very bad; (2) Poor; (3) Adequate; (4) Good; (5) Excellent

24. Transportation   1   2   3   4   5
25. Neighbourhood facilities   1   2   3   4   5
26. Density/Congestion   1   2   3   4   5
27. Noise levels   1   2   3   4   5
28. Security   1   2   3   4   5
29. Other local services   1   2   3   4   5

How would you rate the following aspects of your *housing?* For each item, please CIRCLE the appropriate number. (1) Very bad; (2) Poor; (3) Adequate; (4) Good; (5) Excellent

30. Co-op's exterior appearance   1   2   3   4   5
31. Common rooms   1   2   3   4   5
32. Courtyard   1   2   3   4   5
33. Construction of building   1   2   3   4   5
34. Cleanliness of co-op   1   2   3   4   5
35. Security of building   1   2   3   4   5
36. Layout of your unit   1   2   3   4   5
37. Size of your unit   1   2   3   4   5
38. Privacy of your unit   1   2   3   4   5
39. Noise level in your unit   1   2   3   4   5

40. How often do you or other members of your household use the court-

yard? (1) Almost never; (2) About once a month; (3) Several times a month; (4) Several times a week; (5) Every day

41. How much have you been affected personally by building deficiencies in this co-op? (1) Not at all; (2) Slightly; (3) Moderately; (4) Considerably; (5) A great deal

42. Please compare your present sense of security (eg., from theft, vandalism, and assault) today with your sense of security when you first moved here. (1) Much less secure now; (2) Somewhat less secure now; (3) About the same; (4) Somewhat more secure now; (5) Much more secure now

43. Is your monthly housing charge (1) Much more than you can afford? (2) Somewhat more than you can afford? (3) Approximately what you can afford? (4) Somewhat less than you can afford? (5) Much less than you can afford?

How would you rate the following aspects of the *co-op as a community?* For each item, please CIRCLE the appropriate number. (1) Far too little; (2) Too little; (3) About right; (4) Too much; (5) Far too much

44. Neighbourliness   1   2   3   4   5
45. Mix of economic levels   1   2   3   4   5
46. Ethnic mix   1   2   3   4   5
47. Privacy   1   2   3   4   5
48. Member participation   1   2   3   4   5
49. Conflict   1   2   3   4   5
50. Democracy   1   2   3   4   5
51. Leadership by Board   1   2   3   4   5
52. Leadership by Coordinator   1   2   3   4   5

53. Which one of the following statements seems to you to most accurately describe this co-op?
    (1) People in this co-op can't agree on anything.
    (2) There are more differences than similarities among people's opinions in this co-op.
    (3) There are a lot of different opinions here, but some basic agreement about important issues.
    (4) There are more similarities than differences among people's opinions in this co-op.
    (5) This is a community of like-minded people.

54. Some members are taking unfair advantage of this co-op. (1) Strongly disagree; (2) Disagree somewhat; (3) Neutral; (4) Agree somewhat; (5) Strongly agree

55. In my opinion some nonmember residents and guests are taking unfair

advantage of this co-op. (1) Strongly disagree; (2) Disagree somewhat; (3) Neutral; (4) Agree somewhat; (5) Strongly agree

56. Do you think that the member selection process has chosen the right kind of people for this co-op? (1) Almost never; (2) Seldom; (3) About half the time; (4) Often; (5) Almost always

57. Do you feel the co-op encourages members sufficiently to participate in committee work? (1) Far too little; (2) Too little; (3) About the right amount; (4) Too much; (5) Far too much
If you have not served on any committees, please go on to #60.

58. Please list the committees (including the Board of Directors) on which you've served in the co-op.

COMMITTEE   YEAR

59. In general, has your committee experience been (1) Strongly negative? (2) Somewhat negative? (3) Neutral? (4) Somewhat positive? (5) Strongly positive?
Please go on to #61.

60. If you have not served on any committees, which of the following is your main reason? (1) Too busy; (2) Not physically possible; (3) Not encouraged to join; (4) Dislike co-op participation; (5) Dislike committee work; (6) Haven't got around to it; (7) Other (please specify) _____

61. Do you think that general members' meetings usually are (1) Uncomfortable and unproductive? (2) Uncomfortable but productive? (3) Comfortable but unproductive? (4) Comfortable and productive?

62. Do you think that members have a sufficient say in making decisions at general meetings? (1) Far too little; (2) Too little; (3) About the right amount; (4) Too much; (5) Far too much

63. To what degree do you feel you can really influence what happens in the co-op? (1) Not at all; (2) Slightly; (3) Moderately; (4) Considerably; (5) A great deal

64. In general, do you feel your involvement with the co-op has increased or decreased over time? (1) Decreased substantially; (2) Decreased somewhat; (3) Remained the same; (4) Increased somewhat; (5) Increased substantially

65. About how many social events organized by the co-op do you attend each year? (1) None; (2) A few; (3) About half the events; (4) Most; (5) All

66. How many of the people you usually socialize with are residents of this co-op? (1) None; (2) A few; (3) About half; (4) Most ; (5) All

67. If there is a change in the size of a household that has been in the co-op for several years, do you think it should be rehoused in a different sized unit if possible? (1) Never; (2) Only if it is a special case; (3) Only if it needs a larger unit; (4) Only if it needs a smaller unit; (5) Always

68. Do you think the co-op should allocate funds for extra parking spaces? (0) No; (1) Yes

69. How much influence do you think Windward's disabled members have in running the co-op? (1) Far too little; (2) Some what too little; (3) About the right amount; (4) Somewhat too much; (5) Far too much

70. Do you think the number of disabled members in the co-op is about right? (1) Far too few; (2) Too few; (3) About the right number; (4) Too many; (5) Far too many

71. In social terms, how do you think the able-bodied and the disabled members of the co-op generally interact? (1) Very poorly; (2) Poorly; (3) Adequately; (4) Well; (5) Very well

72. The co-op intrudes too much in my personal life. (1) Strongly disagree; (2) Disagree somewhat; (3) Neither disagree nor agree; (4) Agree somewhat; (5) Strongly agree

If you are *NOT* disabled, please go to #81.

Please rate how well the following meet your needs. Please CIRCLE THE APPROPRIATE NUMBER. (1) Very bad; (2) Poor; (3) Adequate; (4) Good; (5) Excellent

73. Accessibility of your unit   1   2   3   4   5
74. Modifications to your unit   1   2   3   4   5
75. Courtyard & common rooms   1   2   3   4   5
76. Entries, exits & halls   1   2   3   4   5

77. Compared to other accessible housing, how does the fact that Windward is a *co-op* affect your satisfaction with living here?
(1) Co-op makes housing much less satisfactory.
(2) Co-op makes housing somewhat less satisfactory.
(3) Co-op makes no difference in housing.
(4) Co-op makes housing somewhat more satisfactory.
(5) Co-op makes housing much more satisfactory.

78. Please indicate the extent of your mobility. (1) Ambulatory; (2) Paraplegic; (3) Quadriplegic; (4) Wheelchair dependent (not paralysed)

79. Do you have other special needs related to the following? Please circle *ALL* the numbers that apply. (1) Speech; (2) Vision; (3) Hearing

80. Do you require attendant care? (1) None; (2) Low; (3) Medium; (4) High

Finally, we would like to ask a few questions about you to help interpret the results statistically.

81. What type of housing did you live in before you joined this co-op? (1) Private rental; (2) Own private home (incl. condo); (3) Other housing co-op; (4) Non-profit housing (eg Cityhome, OHC); (5) Other (please specify) _____

82. If you could live in any type of housing, what would be your ideal? (1) Private rental; (2) Own a private house/condo; (3) Housing co-op; (4) Non-profit housing; (5) Other (please specify) _____

Listed below on the right are some reasons why members *joined* the co-op. Please WRITE THE NUMBERS of the reasons that were most important for you.

83. __ Most important

84. __ Second most important

85. __ Third most important

1 Limited availability of other housing
2 Affordable housing
3 Location
4 Friends or relatives lived here
5 Guaranteed security of tenure
6 Co-op lifestyle
7 Accessibility
8 Control over housing
9 Other (please specify)

86. When did you move in to the co-op? _____(month/ year)

87. Is your unit an apartment or a townhouse? (0) Apartment; (1) Townhouse

88. What size is your unit? (1) 1 bedroom; (2) 2 bedroom; (3) 3 bedroom; (4) 4 bedroom

89. What are your current monthly housing charges? $___

90. Have you moved within the co-op since becoming a member? (0) No; (1) Yes

Why are you *staying* at the co-op? Below on the right are some possible reasons. Please WRITE THE NUMBERS of the reasons that are most important for you.

91. ___ Most important
92. ___ Second most important
93. ___ Third most important

1 Limited availability of other housing
2 Affordable housing
3 Location
4 Friends or relatives live here
5 Guaranteed security of tenure
6 Co-op lifestyle
7 Accessibility
8 Control over housing
9 Other (please specify)

_____

94. Your gender: (0) Female; (1) Male

95. When were you born? 19___

96. In what country were you born? _____

How many children do you have *living with you (including part time)* in each of the following age groups? Please write the number in the space provided. If the answer is 'NONE', please write '0'.

97. ___ Under 5 years of age
98. ___ 5 to 12
99. ___ 13 to 18
100. ___ 19 to 24
101. ___ 25 and over

102. Do you share your unit with any other adults? Please circle *ALL* the numbers that apply. (1) Spouse or partner; (2) Parents or siblings; (3) Roommates; (4) Others (please specify) _____; (5) No other adult present

103. At present, are you (1) Employed (paid) part time? (2) Employed (paid) full time? (3) Employed (unpaid) at home full time? (4) Unemployed? (5) Full time student? (6) Retired?

104. Please describe your usual occupation. (If retired, please describe your usual occupation before retirement.)
POSITION: _____
BRIEF JOB DESCRIPTION: _____

_____

105. Please indicate the highest level of education that you have completed (e.g. grade 11, 2 years community college, etc.).

_____

106. Finally, which of these broad categories describes your total household

income before taxes in 1989? (1) Less than $10,000; (2) $10,000 to $19,999; (3) $20,000 to $29,999; (4) $30,000 to $39,999; (5) $40,000 to $49,999; (6) $50,000 or more

Is there anything else you would like to tell us about the co-op? If so, please use this space for that purpose. Any comments (positive or negative) or suggestions you wish to make will be appreciated.

To ensure confidentiality, a typed summary of comments will be prepared for the co-op. Please rest assured that no one at the co-op will see your handwritten comments.

THANK YOU!
YOUR CONTRIBUTION TO THIS EFFORT
IS VERY GREATLY APPRECIATED

Notes

1 Since our major concern in this book is the description of two specific alternative housing projects rather than a neighbourhood, we use the phrase 'urban quality of life' in a deliberately naive way. Lyon (1987) is concerned with community and the quality of life in contemporary cities. He discusses methods for studying community quality of life at some length (143–251). Pacione (1988) gives an up-to-date survey of public participation at the neighbourhood level, especially in relation to the range of ways in which participation can occur. Hall's (1988: 242) magisterial history of urban planning in the twentieth century includes a fascinating chapter on influential planners who 'contributed to planning theory the idea that men and women could make their own cities.'

2 Many of the same arguments in favour of local control have been made for at least the past thirty years (e.g., Jacobs 1961; or from a very different standpoint, Sennett 1970). Such arguments still are fresh. Ironically, although they have been made many times they still retain their force today.

3 For example, see 'Housing Folly Shuts Out Average Earner' (1990).

4 The distinction between use values and exchange values can be traced to Aristotle. It also is employed by Adam Smith and, especially, by Marx. For Aristotle, economics is the science of household management. 'The art of household management is not identical with the art of getting wealth, for the one uses the material which the other provides' (*Politics* 1256a). The art of getting wealth is the realm of exchange values. The chief economic problem is the selection of ends, not of means. It focuses on the central question of human thought and ac-

tion – the nature of the happy life. The use value of an article or service derives from its being productive of an individual person's good. For Aristotle, use values are subjectively defined and transitory, for example, because of sudden shifts in human desires and motives.

More generally, in the traditional sense 'use value' refers to things or aspects of the world that can be useful to someone. This view leads in two different directions. Either it can lead toward an examination of the thing itself, following an older, essentialist view that things have 'natural' uses. Or it can lead toward a consideration of why and how the thing can be useful to someone (i.e., in relation to the needs or wants of particular people in a particular setting). In this sense, the idea rests on a relativistic conception of needs, which must be understood as largely socially and culturally constructed. The idea of use value thus implies a certain conception of human needs and wants, what they are, how they arise, what determines them, how they relate to people's experience.

For us, the more important point is that the term 'use value' is interesting precisely because it *connects* a slice of the world with culture – in this case, the contemporary, urban North American culture of a mixed-income new neighbourhood. Values, cultural definitions, language, social and cultural processes all are important for carving out a slice of the world. Why does the slice have the very qualities and boundaries that it does? How did it come to be defined in the way that it is? Conflict over use values implies a concern not only with things or ideas but also with social process, power, and ideology.

5 Logan and Molotch (1987) use the phrase 'the urban growth machine' to describe the powerful forces behind these contemporary patterns; see also Molotch (1976), Logan (1978), Molotch and Logan (1985), Molotch and Vicari (1988). Some useful Canadian works include Lorimer (1978), Bettison (1975), Magnusson and Sancton (1983), Higgins (1986), Hellman (1987), and Frisken (1988). See Stone and Sanders (1987) and Fainstein et al. (1986) for several U.S. case studies. Goldberg and Mercer (1986) provide an important corrective to the tendency to view Canadian cities as essentially the same as American ones through a carefully documented comparative study of cities in the two countries.

6 See also Harvey (1973, 1985) and Castells (1983) for other recent approaches to the conflict between interests based on exchange and use value in contemporary urban settings.

7 The summary of the book's themes comes from pp. xiii–xiv. The exam-

ples referred to in the rest of the paragraph come from chapters 1–11. See also Hayden (1981, 1984).

8 So far, relatively little research has been conducted in the cooperative sector and it remains to be seen how well cooperatives meet social housing goals. Sources in English include Andrews and Breslauer (1975), Chouinard (1989a, b, c), Schiff Consultants (1982), Selby and Wilson (1988), Spronk (1981, 1988), Wekerle (1988), and Wekerle and Novac (1989). Selby (1989) is a useful bibliography on Canadian cooperative housing.

9 This description is reconstructed from our notes of the meeting. The remarks quoted directly are not necessarily verbatim records but we have tried to be as accurate as possible.

10 Two disclaimers are necessary at this point. First, because of our focus on a limited number of themes, we have deliberately not tried to provide equal coverage of both co-ops on all of them. Nor have we dealt with all matters that arose at the co-ops during the period of our study. Second, we focus mostly on themes internal to the co-ops. Thus, we have not described changes in the neighbourhood at any length.

Chapter 2

1 Frisken (1990) provides a useful discussion of the interplay of provincial and municipal interests in planning for the Greater Toronto Area.

2 'Flipping' refers to real estate speculation. Properties are purchased for rapid resale in a rising market. The meaning of 'reform' in the Toronto context is discussed by Caulfield (1988).

3 See also Lorimer (1983), Lorimer and MacGregor (1981), Higgins (1986).

4 See Smith (1987) and Mills (1988) for somewhat different views of the relation between urban restructuring and the 'new' middle classes.

5 In Ontario, the idea of affordable housing generally relates the proportion of income spent on shelter to the distribution of income. In other words, to be 'affordable' housing should not require expenditure of more than 30 per cent of income for the lower 60 per cent of households. In early 1990, 60 per cent of households in Metro Toronto had incomes of $55,800 or less.

6 Clearly, this depends on the composition of the household. Family households and single persons would be rated differently. In addition,

suitability (or appropriateness) for households with children would consider distance above ground level.

7 Similar newspaper stories on this topic appeared constantly during this period, e.g., 'Housing Cheaper [sic], Royal Bank Reports' (1989), 'Few Toronto Families Qualify for Mortgages' (1989), 'Housing Folly Shuts Out Average Earner' (1990), and 'Families in Toronto, Vancouver Pay 60% of Income to Carry Home Costs' (1990).

8 'Housing Cheaper, Royal Bank Reports' (1989). House prices in Metro Toronto were expected to average about $289,000 in 1990. A first-time buyer, putting 25 per cent down and paying 30 per cent on a mortgage, thus would have needed $72,250 in cash and an income of $90,000 a year. For comparison, the median household income was approximately $42,000. See 'Home Harder to Buy in Toronto, Vancouver' (1990).

In the event, however, the housing market began to fall in early 1990. High interest rates, concern about the then impending goods-and-services tax, overbuilding of condominium units fuelled by speculation, and the beginnings of a sharp recession all severely affected the housing market. Sales dropped dramatically, later followed by prices. By the end of June 1990, the average cost of a home in Toronto had dropped to about $250,000 ('Resales of Houses Take 28.9% Plunge' [1990]). Further declines continued into early 1991 when falling interest rates encouraged buyers to return to the market.

9 Condominium conversions or luxury upgrades in buildings containing four or fewer units are exempted from current provincial legislation on conversions. Such small buildings have been a major source of low-cost housing. As a result, according to the Social Planning Council of Metro Toronto, over 2,100 apartments disappeared from the rental stock between 1985 and mid-1989; see 'Action Needed to Stem Loss of Apartments, Groups Say' (1989).

10 The first quote is from 'Rent Controls Clearly Necessary When You Look at Other Cities' (1989); the second is found in 'Inexpensive Rental Housing Now Toronto's Rarest Breed' (1988).

11 'Housing: A Slippery Treadmill' (1989).

12 See, among many other examples, 'Our Rental Rate Still Country's Lowest' (1988), 'Apartment Vacancy Rate Reaches Critical Stage in Vancouver, Toronto' (1989). With a weakening housing market in 1990, vacancy rates rose to around the 1 per cent level again.

13 'Inexpensive Rental Housing Now Toronto's Rarest Breed' (1988)

14 On the other hand, at the high end of the rental market by the end of

1990 landlords were offering inducements to lure prospective tenants. At the same time, affordable apartments were not available unless 'you know someone who can get you on top of a waiting list' (quoted in 'Rental Vacancies Set 7-Year High in Toronto' [1990]).

15 'Housing: A Slippery Treadmill' (1989)

16 'Metro's Rental Crunch Leaving Its Mark on Neighbourhoods' (1988)

17 For international comparisons see 'Metro IS World-CLASS – in Rents' (1989).

18 Miron (1988) provides the best discussion of this issue.

19 'Cuts "Beyond my control" Says Minister' (1989: 7)

20 See Miron (1988) for the best and most complete analysis of factors influencing changes in the demand for housing in Canada in the postwar period. In general, while household size has been declining for at least the past 100 years the number of households has increased. Postwar changes in household formation can be attributed to a variety of factors including the baby boom, increased longevity, changes in marriage patterns, rising divorce rates, increased household income and wealth, government programs affecting housing, and more diffuse changes in values and expectations. All of these factors have affected the demand for housing.

21 However, it was only with amendments to the National Housing Act in 1964 giving the federal government a direct role that large numbers of public housing units began to appear. Prior to 1964 only 12,000 units had been constructed. Today, there are more than 250,000 units, built mostly between 1964 and 1973. Public housing represents less than 3 per cent of Canada's total housing stock.

22 Hulchanski and Drover (1987) discuss the effects of several attempts at financial restraint on the part of the Canadian government between 1973 and 1984. They are concerned particularly with the shifting pattern of housing subsidies and their distributional impacts.

23 A recent example is the Killarney Gardens co-op in Vancouver. It is a rehabilitation project on land provided by the City of Vancouver on a long-term lease. CMHC has guaranteed the co-op's mortgage. Otherwise, there is no federal government assistance. ('Killarney Gardens Co-op: Co-op Gets underway without Federal Funds' [1989])

24 In a series of papers, Chouinard (1989a, b, c) interprets changes in co-operative housing policy in terms of the development of the state in Canada, local experience of the state, and class struggle.

25 CMHC (1983: 1–4) describes the difficulties found by the government in

the 1973 program and how the 1978 amendments were supposed to correct them.

26 In 1988, amendments to the National Housing Act renumbered the various sections. Thus, the section that instituted the 1973 co-op program was changed from section 34.18 to section 61. Section 56.1 became section 95. We retain the older numbering because these are the terms our informants used.

27 The economic rent consists of the monthly mortgage payment at market rates plus operating costs.

28 This innovative financial instrument was developed by the Co-operative Housing Federation of Canada for the Canadian market. The index-linked mortgage is a loan whose interest rate provides a fixed real rate of return combined with a variable rate which is adjusted periodically in accordance with changes in the rate of inflation. For evaluation of this program see CMHC (1990b).

29 'CHF Lobbies Government for More Housing Co-ops' (1989: 1). The 1990 federal budget allocated $5.8 million for new non-profit co-ops, an increase of 5 per cent over 1989. About 1,600 new units were produced.

30 'CHF Welcomes Continuing Co-op Housing Commitment' (1991)

31 Ironically, co-ops were the smallest proportion of social housing allocations in 1989, 26.6 per cent (CMHC 1990a, Table 12).

32 'Federal Gov't Cuts Co-op Housing Funds' (1989: 1)

33 The earlier parts of this history are briefly described in McMillan (1987). She also compares the social characteristics of residents of different public housing projects with each other and with the general population of Toronto.

34 Through the Residential Rehabilitation Assistance and Neighbourhood Improvement Programs created by the 1973 amendments to the National Housing Act (Sayegh 1987: 484–514).

35 'Original St Lawrence Project Passes Test of Time' (1988) for this quote and the next paragraph

36 'Metro Housing Plan Aims Subsidy Funds at Small Households' (1989)

37 From 1984 to 1988, Metro Toronto Housing Co Ltd built about 380 units per year ('Toronto Doubles Non-Profit Housing Target' [1989]).

38 For example, the policy announced in August 1988 required that 25 per cent of new housing in all municipalities must be for low- and moderate-income groups. Earlier, the province had amended the Ontario Planning Act to allow it to intervene in municipal land use planning. Predictably, there were screams from all sides; see 'Ontario Imposes

New Housing Policy' (1988). The policy, however, did allow for non-profit housing to be included. Representatives of the non-profit sector felt that it would ensure a better mix of housing in communities; see 'Province Calls for New-Home Construction' (1989).

39 'MP Defends Co-op Housing for the Poor' (1988)

40 By early 1991, 118 co-ops with more than 11,000 units belonged to the Co-operative Housing Federation of Toronto.

41 'Co-op Funds Cut in Half, Group Says' (1989).

42 See, for example, 'Neighbors Fear Project Would Be Ghetto' (1987); 'Neighbors Vow They'll Battle Plan for High Park Co-op' (1988); 'Minister Blasts Foes of Low-Cost Housing' (1988); 'Cooperatives' Bad Image Is Undeserved' (1989).

43 See, for example, 'Ontario Housing Statement Called Misleading' (1989); 'Ontario Starts Allocating Funds to Non-Profit Housing Groups' (1988); 'Non-Profit Housing Help Set' (1988); 'Hosek Moves on Low-Cost Housing' (1989). See also Ministry of Housing, Ontario (1989).

44 '6,400 New Housing Units to Get Ontario Backing' (1989)

45 At the time of writing, it was not clear how many units would be built, how many would be 'affordable,' or how many would be social housing. See, for example, 'Pledge for Housing Units Would Meet Olympic Needs in 1996 Bid, Eggleton Says' (1990) and 'Should Have Seen CN Letter before Games Bid, Councillors Charge' (1990).

46 'End to Housing Crisis Likely in Next Decade, New Minister Says' (1989). In early 1990, vague plans were announced to create a new town to the east of Metro Toronto on provincially owned land. As much as half of the housing might be affordable. See 'New Town of Seaton Will Feature Affordable Housing for 30,000' (1990) and 'Ontario NDP, Tories Doubt New Community Will Be Built by Grits' (1990).

47 'Province Calls for New-Home Construction' (1989)

Chapter 3

1 In using the term 'disability' we follow Cluff's (1982) usage. She defines disability in functional terms building on the United Nations definition of disability as applying to 'Any person unable to ensure by himself or herself wholly or partly the necessities of a normal individual and/or social life, as a result of a deficiency, either congenital or not, in his or her physical or mental capabilities.' The functional categories of disability relevant to Windward are non-ambulatory, semi-ambulatory, and co-

ordination disabled. We refer to people as having mobility impairments or disabilities almost interchangeably. We recognize, however, that more precisely, impairment refers to 'an interference with the normal structure or function of the body,' disability is 'a reduction in functional ability resulting from an impairment,' and a handicap is 'the social and/or environmental consequence to the individual of the impairment and disability' (World Health Organization classifications cited in Medicus Canada 1981: 2).

2 Daly co-op in Ottawa is like Windward in that it is a barrier-free building housing both able-bodied and mobility-impaired members. Some, like Prairie Housing co-op in Winnipeg and L'Auberge Co-op in Ottawa, specialize in housing people with physical (and/or mental in the case of Prairie co-op) disabilities (Weston 1979a). Some regular apartment buildings that are not cooperatives provide integrated, fully accessible environments for disabled and able-bodied residents (e.g. Glenwood Court Apartments in Thunder Bay, Ontario) (Coalition of Provincial Organizations of the Handicapped 1984: 104–30).

3 'Harbourfront's History Marked by Controversies and Bickering' (1987)

4 Dale (1990: 84, 86) suggests that interest from the development fund actually accounted for only a very small part of programming expenses. For example, in 1988 Harbourfront spent more than $13 million on programming expenses. However, only $867,845 of that came from interest on the development fund.

5 'Harbourfront's History Marked by Controversies and Bickering' (1987)

6 See also, for example, 'This Time, There's Hope for Harbourfront' (1987).

7 'End Involvement in Development on Waterfront, Ottawa Is Urged' (1989)

8 'Harbourfront, City Agree on Tentative Deal' (1989) and 'Toronto Council Supports End to Waterfront Freeze' (1989)

9 'Ontario Declares Indefinite Freeze on New Harbourfront Building' (1989).

10 'Toronto Seeks Cap on Island Airport Flights' (1989). The City of Toronto tried several times to get the courts to prevent airport expansion but without much success. See also 'Judge Rules Airport on Island Can Expand' (1990). Some of the history of the Toronto Harbour Commission is discussed in relation to current issues in Steering Committee on Matters Related to the Board of Toronto Harbour Commissioners (1989).

11 In May 1990, a federal-provincial agreement was announced that would take all land development out of Harbourfront Corporation's hands. This scheme proposed that the city would get the additional parkland and cash it had earlier agreed to. Harbourfront's cultural activities would be supported by income from an endowment fund set up by the federal government. Finally, four condominium projects caught in the various freezes would be allowed to go ahead. But the projects would be moved to different sites, away from the water's edge. Less positive was the proposal to sell off the remaining development sites rather than leasing them. See 'Harbourfront Can No Longer Develop Land by Lakeshore' (1990) and 'Quick Solution a Costly One for Harbourfront, Mills Charges' (1990).

In August 1990, the royal commission recommended again that Harbourfront Corporation should get out of the development business. It also proposed that the Harbour Commission should be restricted to managing the port. No longer should the Harbour Commission act as a developer and landlord.

In late November 1990, Darcy McKeogh, appointed by the federal government to resolve Harbourfront's problems, issued his report. He called for turning it into a non-profit cultural organization whose commercial assets should be disposed of. After paying debts of some $50 million, about $80 million would be left for an endowment fund. Income from the fund would underwrite Harbourfront's activities. See 'Ottawa Moves to Implement Harbourfront Restructuring Plan' (1990), 'Harbourfront to Cut 45 Jobs' (1990). Although the report seemed definitive, it was immediately rejected by the Toronto City Council; see 'Which Two Will Be Axed?' (1990).

By early 1991, Harbourfront Corporation had been dismantled to create three new bodies: a non-profit organization to run cultural and recreational programs; a charitable foundation to manage Harbourfront's endowment; and a federal corporation charged with selling off most of Harbourfront's assets to developers. A three-year plan was established to try to provide some stability at least for the short term; see 'Harbourfront Unveils 3-Year Plan' (1991).

12 'Hearings Open with Attacks on Harbourfront' (1989)

13 'This Time, There's Hope for Harbourfront' (1987)

14 Housing issues along the entire waterfront are discussed in Royal Commission on the Future of the Toronto Waterfront (1989).

15 These lots remained undeveloped in early 1991.

16 Medicus Canada (1982: 112ff.) found that 'It is those projects in which the disabled had an active role in the planning and development process which have proven to be most successful.'

17 This report presents a useful series of drawings and a checklist contrasting institutional and homelike design principles. While the architectural definitions of normalization focus on the housing needs of severely and profoundly retarded adults, the design principles are useful guides for thinking about the integration of people with other special needs.

18 'If the comparison of costs between barrier-free design resulting in independence and employment of the handicapped and the cost of segregating this sector of society, forcing them to be dependent on the community were made known, politicians as well as planners would opt for complete integration by means of barrier-free design' (United Nations Expert Group Report on Barrier-Free Design 1975, quoted in Canadian Organizing Committee 1981: 6).

Chapter 4

1 As noted previously, in 1988 section 56.1 was changed to section 95.

2 This points up one of the weaknesses of the survey design. Respondents did not have to choose among or rank the various goals. Most of the goal items were worded in such a way as to spread out the responses, however.

3 The concept of 'communitas,' as opposed to 'structure,' has been explored extensively by Victor Turner (1974: 237–8, emphasis in original). He argues that in societies of all levels of complexity a 'contrast is posited between the notion of society as a differentiated, segmented system of structural positions ... and society as a homogeneous, undifferentiated *whole* ... The second model, communitas, often appears culturally in the guise of an Edenic, paradisiacal, utopian, or millennial state of affairs, to the attainment of which religious or political action, personal or collective, should be directed. Society is pictured as a communitas of free and equal comrades – of total persons.'

Chapter 5

1 It is important to note that Windward and Harbourside may not be representative of Toronto area co-ops because of the kind of people they attracted. Given their prime location on the waterfront and relatively high cost, they attracted, according to the consultants involved,

higher-income and 'more-sophisticated' people than would ordinarily apply to join co-ops.

Chapter 6

1 DeJong (cited in Boschen 1984) observes that traumatically rather than congenitally disabled people tend to be the ones who initiate lobbying for accessible accommodation, individually managed attendant care arrangements, etc. This occurs because of expectations established before they become disabled.

2 The yacht clubs were relocated the following year as plans to develop the site with high-rise apartment buildings proceeded.

3 These figures come from our survey of the members in September 1989. Among members with disabilities, the response rate to the survey was 74 per cent. Grouping respondents by disability, 16 per cent were ambulatory, 26 per cent paraplegic, 21 per cent quadriplegic, and 29 per cent were confined to a wheelchair for other reasons.

4 The FOKUS project, a Swedish scheme for integrated housing begun in 1964 as a private project then taken over by government, has been influential in shaping North American approaches to integrated housing. But 'the first of its kind in the world' was a three-storey collective house at Hans Knudens Plads in Copenhagen built in 1959. All 170 apartments were adapted for the disabled, but disabled people represented only one-third of the residents, the remainder being nursing staff from a nearby hospital and the general public (Tate and Lee 1983: 91).

5 For other examples see also Medicus Canada (1982) regarding Sir Douglas Bader Towers in Edmonton, and Cluff and Cluff (1982) for Doug Saunders apartments in Toronto. Although not an evaluation, Robson (1986) provides a useful description of a six-person unit for quadriplegics within Creekview co-op in Vancouver.

6 Her view is supported in the literature. See Goldman (1978: 186), who comments on the difficulty people with disabilities have finding accessible housing that is suitable for married couples.

7 It should be pointed out that our survey aimed to include the entire population of members of the co-ops, rather than a sample. Therefore, our statements about differences among subgroups of members properly speaking apply only to the survey respondents. No statistical inferences can be made from the responses of the respondents to the entire population of the co-ops.

8 The need for attendant care for married people was highlighted in a Toronto newspaper article, 'The Hidden Price of Being Disabled' (1989). The prospective bridegroom who needs attendant care 'is adamant when he says he doesn't want his wife ... to become his attendant. "I can't imagine having a typical family quarrel and then asking her to help get me ready for bed," he said.'

Chapter 7

1 This comment is reminiscent of Jane Jacobs's (1961) influential advocacy of neighbourhood diversity.
2 Logan and Molotch (1987: 167ff.) sum up the political realities that ensured low-income housing projects would be constructed away from better neighbourhoods and planned high-rent developments in the United States.
3 Initially, the requirement was only 15 per cent but it had been increased to 25 per cent by the time Windward and Harbourside's contracts were drawn up.
4 For descriptions of this formula and how the 56.1 mortgage interest assistance works see CMHC (1981, 1983).
5 Financial data from Harbourside come from an article in the co-op's newsletter prepared by the coordinator to educate members (Hawthorn 1988).
6 The term of Harbourside's mortgage was five years. CMHC will adjust the amount of its assistance in accordance with the interest rate at which the mortgage is renewed. Steeply rising or falling interest rates, then, could have considerable effect on the amount of assistance available to the co-op.
7 See chapter 3 for discussion of developments after the section 56.1 program was terminated.
8 The response rate for Harbourside as a whole was about 70 per cent. But the response rate was better for non-subsidized members than among those on housing charge assistance. Respondents included thirty-six out of forty-three non-subsidized members (84) and only eighteen · out of thirty-five subsidized members (50 per cent).
9 For a 'Not in My Backyard' response to plans for a ninety-eight-unit rent-geared-to income co-op in Toronto's St Lawrence area see 'Neighbours Fear Project Would Be Ghetto' (1987).
10 There was also a concern, which we have not gone into here, that the Revenue Canada statement would provide proof only after the fact.

That is, it would provide information for a particular year's earnings only some months after the year was over.

11 The increase in the cost to the co-op of mortgage payments theoretically could be offset by savings the co-ops make in operating costs due to member participation.

Chapter 8

1 Pacione (1988) is an excellent review of forms of public participation in urban neighbourhoods. See Monti (1989) for recent research on resident management of public housing projects in the United States. Arnstein (1969) and Pateman (1970) are important earlier sources on forms of participation and participation in the workplace, respectively.

2 For a comparison of a co-op and a condominium project in terms of organization, see Spronk (1988); see also Wekerle et al. (1980).

3 'Co-operatives Not Everyone's Cup of Tea Although They Do Have Many Advantages' (1989).

4 We employ 'involvement' as a cover term occasionally to include formal participation on committees and meeting attendance as well as less formal kinds of social interaction within the co-ops.

5 That is, first we added the number of meetings attended by each household member. Then we divided that number by the product of the number of members in the household and the number of meetings held. For example, suppose that the Smith household has two co-op members, each of whom attended three of the five meetings held during 1988; then $(3 + 3) / (2 \times 5) = 0.6$ or 60 per cent attendance.

6 A quorum at Harbourside is 50 per cent plus one of the members.

7 At Harbourside, it proved difficult to get adequate and comparable lists of committee memberships because the co-op's operations were considerably more decentralized than Windward's.

8 Of respondents with disabilities, 35 per cent reported increased involvement whereas 28 per cent of the non-disabled gave this response. Only 25 per cent of people with disabilities said their involvement had decreased compared with 33 per cent for the non-disabled.

9 We discuss member control of co-op affairs more specifically in the next chapter.

10 This was not simply a consequence of there being other things to do downtown, of course. Differences of class and values come into play. The same consultants pointed out that suburban co-ops tend to be over-

whelmingly working class while downtown co-ops socially are much more diverse.

11 See, for example, the Co-op Housing Federation's newsletter of March 1989, which reports on a member forum ('Member Participation' [1989]).

12 Much of the history of social philosophy is concerned with this issue. Erasmus (1977) provides a very useful discussion of utopian experiments in terms of this question. Kanter (1972) is the standard source on the importance of member commitment for the success of utopian (in this case, nineteenth-century American) societies. She discusses in detail how community practices, including incentives, affect levels of member commitment.

13 'Member Participation' (1989: 2)

14 Ibid.

15 The notion of social audits comes from attempts in recent years to make business more accountable to the public. The social consequences of business operations are the subject of the social audit. As used among Toronto housing co-ops, however, the term refers to a process in which the co-op spells out its goals and then tries to assess how well it is reaching them.

16 However, at the time of writing (June 1990), there had been no follow-up by Harbourside to the survey results or the goal-setting workshop.

17 'It's All Happening This Saturday' (1988)

18 'A Great Day ...' (1988) and 'Harbourside in 1989' (1989)

Chapter 9

1 'Control' as a psychological concept has been defined in several ways in the literature. For example, Langer (1983) talks about it as a 'mindful process of mastering,' while other writers deal with efficacy (White 1959), internal versus external control (Lefcourt 1982), or process versus decision control (Tyler, Rasinki, and Spodick 1985). In the literature on citizen participation, control has been taken to be an important goal of participation (e.g., Arnstein 1969). Our use of the term reflects primarily a concern with outcomes, as well as with perceived control. Mark Francis's (1989: 158) portmanteau definition of control of public places is useful: 'Control is the ability of an individual or group to gain access to, utilize, influence, gain ownership over, and attach meaning to a public place.'

2 'Co-operatives Not Everyone's Cup of Tea Although They Do Have Many Advantages' (1989)
3 Ibid.
4 Memo from Windward's board of directors to all members, 18 August 1987

Chapter 10

1 The idea that houses can be seen as containers of the individual self is especially clear in the work of Clare Cooper Marcus (Cooper 1974) and in Duncan's (1982) edited collection on housing and identity. Historically, homes have become increasingly expressive of the individual (Rybczynski 1986). The influences of community as well as individuality are evident in the furnishings of one's home, especially the more public living areas (Csikszentmihalyi and Rochberg-Halton 1981). Both individuality and community stamp their mark on places, as contrasted to 'placeless' buildings and spaces (Relph 1976). For a review of literature related to contemporary housing and identity in America see Hummon's (1989) and other chapters in Low and Chambers' *Housing, Culture, and Design* (1989). For an exploration of the changing meaning of yards see Kenneth Jackson's *Crabgrass Frontier* (1985: 54–61).
2 Like Hummon (1989:224), we are interested in the as yet poorly understood 'contradictions and conflicts people may experience through identification with home.'

References

'A Great Day ...'1988. *Summerfest News, The Final Edition.* Harbourside Co-op, August

'Action Needed to Stem Loss of Apartments, Groups Say.' 1989. *Toronto Star,* 24 June

Andrews, H., and H. Breslauer. 1975. *Cooperative Housing: A Case Study of Decision-Making in Design and User Satisfaction.* Toronto: Centre for Urban and Community Studies, University of Toronto

'Apartment Vacancy Rate Reaches Critical Stage in Vancouver, Toronto.' 1989. *Globe and Mail,* 28 November

Arnstein, S. 1969. 'A Ladder of Citizen Participation.' *Journal of the American Institute of Planners* 35: 216–24

Bacher, J. 1985. 'Keeping to the Private Market: The Evolution of Canadian Housing Policy. 1900–1949.' PhD dissertation, McMaster University, Hamilton, Ont.

– 1986. 'Canadian Housing "Policy" in Perspective.' *Urban History Review / Revue d'histoire urbaine* 15 (1): 3–18

Baird/Sampson Architects. 1987. *Harbourfront 2000: A Report to the Futures Committee of Harbourfront.* Toronto: Harbourfront

Besruky, E. 1984. *Housing, Support Services, Components of Independent Living: Ontario.* Vol. 6 in *The Canadian Disabled Housing Survey.* Ottawa: Coalition of Provincial Organizations of the Handicapped (COPOH) and CMHC

Bettison, D. 1975. *The Politics of Canadian Urban Development.* Edmonton: University of Alberta Press

Boschen, K. 1984. 'Residential Choice and Control Among Spinal Chord Injured Young Adults.' PhD dissertation, University of California

Bradbee, C. 1989. 'Harbourfront: The Making of a Neighbourhood.' Unpublished paper submitted to the Royal Commission on the Future of the Toronto Waterfront, Toronto

Canada Mortgage and Housing Corporation (CMHC). 1981. *The Co-operative Housing Program*. Ottawa: CMHC

- 1983. *Section 56.1 Non-Profit and Cooperative Housing Program Evaluation*. Ottawa: CMHC
- n.d. [1986]. *The Federal Co-Operative Housing Program*. Ottawa: CMHC
- 1986a. *A National Direction for Housing Solutions*. Ottawa: CMHC
- 1986b. *Annual Report*. Ottawa: CMHC
- 1990a. *Canadian Monthly Housing Statistics*. Ottawa: CMHC
- 1990b. *Evaluation of the Federal Co-operative Housing Programs: Draft Report*. Ottawa: CMHC

Canadian Organizing Committee. 1981. *Architectural Accessibility: Directions for Action*. Vol 1. International Year of Disabled Persons

Canadian Paraplegic Association. 1974. *Research Study on Integrated Housing for the Severely Physically Disabled*. Montreal: CMHC

Carroll, B.W. 1989. 'Post-War Trends in Canadian Housing Policy.' *Urban History Review / Revue d'histoire urbaine* 18 (1): 64–74

Castells, M. 1983. *The City and the Grassroots: A Cross-Cultural Theory of Urban Social Movements*. Berkeley: University of California Press

Caulfield, J. 1988. ' "Reform" as a Chaotic Concept: The Case of Toronto.' *Urban History Review / Revue d'histoire urbaine* 17: 107–111

'CHF Lobbies Government for More Housing Co-ops.' 1989. *From the Rooftops* 16(3): 1. Ottawa: Co-operative Housing Federation of Canada

'CHF Lobby Succeeds.' 1988. *CO-OPservations* 37(Fall): 1. Ottawa: Co-operative Housing Foundation of Canada

'CHF Welcomes Continuing Co-op Housing Commitment.' 1991. *From the Rooftops* 18 (1): 1. Ottawa: Co-operative Housing Federation of Canada

Chouinard, V. 1989a. 'Class Formation, Conflict and Housing Policies.' *International Journal of Urban and Regional Research* 13 (3): 390–416

- 1989b. 'Explaining Local Experience of State Formation: The Case of Cooperative Housing in Toronto.' *Environment and Planning D: Society and Space* 7: 51–68
- 1989c. 'Social Reproduction and Housing Alternatives: Cooperative Housing in Postwar Canada.' In M. Dear and J. Worch (eds.), *The Power of Geography: How Territory Shapes Social Life*, 222–237. London: Unwin Hyman

Cityhome. 1990. *An Evaluation of the 40/40/20 Targeting Plans under the 1986 Non-Profit Program, Draft Terms of Reference*. Toronto: City of Toronto Housing Department, Cityhome

Cluff, A., and P. Cluff. 1982. *Cost and Design of Housing for Disabled Persons – Case Studies*. Ottawa: CMHC

Cluff, P. 1982. *Accessible Residential Communities: Issues and Solutions.* Ottawa: CMHC

Coalition of Provincial Organizations of the Handicapped (COPOH). 1984. *The Canadian Disabled Housing Survey.* Vol. 6. Ottawa: COPOH

Cohen, A. 1985. *The Symbolic Construction of Community.* London: Ellis Horwood and Tavistock

Communitas, Inc. 1981. *Housing for Disabled Persons – Options, Problems, and Possibilities.* Ottawa: CMHC. (Published in 1982 as Part 2 of 'Two Studies of Housing for People with Disabilities.' Ottawa: CMHC)

'Co-op Funds Cut in Half, Group Says.' 1989. *Toronto Star,* 29 April

Cooper, C. 1974. 'The House as a Symbol of the Self.' In J. Lang et al. (eds.), *Designing for Human Behavior,* 130–46. Stroudsburg, Pa.: Dowden, Hutchinson and Ross

Co-operative Housing Federation of Toronto. 1988a. *The Circuit* 10, no. 2

– 1988b. 'Member Participation.' *Federation Findings: A Co-op Management Memo* 8: 1

Co-operative Housing Foundation of Canada. 1985. *Directory of Housing Co-ops.* Ottawa: CHF

'Cooperatives' Bad Image Is Undeserved.' 1989. *Now* (Toronto), 19–25 January

'Co-operatives Not Everyone's Cup of Tea Although They Do Have Many Advantages.' 1989. *Toronto Star,* 30 July

Cox, K., and A. Mair. 1988. 'Locality and Community in the Politics of Local Economic Development.' *Annals of the Association of American Geographers* 78: 307–25

– 1989. 'Urban Growth Machines and the Politics of Local Economic Development.' *International Journal of Urban and Regional Research* 13: 137–45

Crewe, N., and I. Zola (eds.). 1983. *Independent Living for Physically Disabled People.* San Francisco: Jossey-Bass

Csikszentmihalyi, M., and E. Rochberg-Halton. 1981. *The Meaning of Things: Domestic Symbols and the Self.* Cambridge: Cambridge University Press

'Cuts "Beyond My Control," Says Minister.' 1989. *CO-OPservations* 40 (Summer): 7. Ottawa: Co-operative Housing Foundation of Canada

Dale, S. 1990. 'Pier Pressures.' *Toronto Life* 24 (6): 46–9, 71–87

Desfor, G., M. Goldrick, and R. Merrens. 1988. 'Redevelopment on the North American Water-Frontier: The Case of Toronto.' In B. Hoyle, D. Pinder, and M. Husain (eds.), *Revitalising the Waterfront: International Dimensions of Dockland Redevelopment,* 92–113. London: Belhaven Press

– 1989. 'A Political Economy of the Water-frontier: Planning and Development in Toronto.' *Geoforum* 20: 487–501

Donninson, D. 1967. *The Government of Housing.* Harmondsworth: Penguin

Donninson, D., and C. Ungerson. 1982. *Housing Policy.* Harmondsworth: Penguin

Duncan, J. (ed.). 1982. *Housing and Identity.* New York: Holmes and Meier

'End Involvement in Development on Waterfront, Ottawa Is Urged.' 1989. *Globe and Mail,* 31 August

'End to Housing Crisis Likely in Next Decade, New Minister Says.' 1989. *Globe and Mail,* 4 August

Erasmus, C. 1977. *In Search of the Common Good: Utopian Experiments Past and Future.* New York: Free Press

Fainstein, S., N. Fainstein, R. Hill, D. Judd, and M. Smith (eds.). 1986. *Restructuring the City.* New York: Longman

'Families in Toronto, Vancouver Pay 60 per cent of Income to Carry Home Costs.' 1990. *Globe and Mail,* 23 March

'Federal Gov't Cuts Co-op Housing Funds.' 1989. *From the Rooftops* 16 (2): 1. Ottawa: Co-operative Housing Federation of Canada

'Few Toronto Families Qualify for Mortgages.' 1989. *Globe and Mail,* 13 June

Francis, M. 1989. 'Control as a Dimension of Public-Space Quality.' In I. Altman and E. Zube (eds.), *Human Behavior and Environment, vol. 10: Public Places and Spaces,* 147–72. New York: Plenum Press

Franck, K., and S. Ahrentzen (eds.). 1989. *New Households, New Housing.* New York: Van Nostrand Reinhold

Frisken, F. 1988. *City Policy-Making in Theory and Practice: The Case of Toronto's Downtown Plan.* London, Ont.: Department of Political Science, University of Western Ontario

– 1990. 'Planning and Servicing the Greater Toronto Area: The Interplay of Provincial and Municipal Interests.' Toronto: Urban Studies Program, York University, Working Paper No. 12

Gerecke, K. 1989. 'The New Vocabulary/The New Toronto.' *City Magazine* 10 (4): 20–5

Goldberg, M., and J. Mercer. 1986. *The Myth of the North American City: Continentalism Challenged.* Vancouver: University of British Columbia Press

Goldman, F. 1978. 'Environmental Barriers to Sociosexual Integration.' *Rehabilitation Literature* 39 (6–7): 185–9

Gottdiener, M. 1985. *The Social Production of Urban Space.* Austin: University of Texas Press

Hall, P. 1988. *Cities of Tomorrow: An Intellectual History of Urban Planning and Design in the Twentieth Century.* Oxford: Basil Blackwell

Harbourfront. 1978. *Harbourfront, Site History.* Toronto: Harbourfront Corp

'Harbourfront Can No Longer Develop Land by Lakeshore.' 1990. *Globe and Mail*, 1 May

'Harbourfront, City Agree on Tentative Deal.' 1989. *Globe and Mail*, 2 June

'Harbourfront to Cut 45 Jobs.' 1990. *Globe and Mail*, 29 November

'Harbourfront Unveils 3-Year Plan.' 1991. *Globe and Mail*, 26 February

'Harbourfront's History Marked by Controversies and Bickering.' 1987. *Globe and Mail*, 21 April

'Harbourside in 1989.' 1989. *Son of Sidelines*, 8 January

Harvey, D. 1973. *Social Justice and the City*. London: Edward Arnold

– 1985. *Consciousness and the Urban Experience*. Baltimore: Johns Hopkins University Press

Hatch, R. 1989. 'Foreword.' In K. Franck and S. Ahrentzen (eds.), *New Households, New Housing*, ix–x. New York: Van Nostrand Reinhold

Hawthorn, L. 1988. 'Mortgage, Mortgage Interest Reduction Grant and Housing Charge Assistance Summary or We're All in This Together.' *Son of Sidelines*, 4 November

Hayden, D. 1981. *The Grand Domestic Revolution: A History of Feminist Designs for American Homes, Neighborhoods, and Cities*. Cambridge, Mass.: MIT Press

– 1984. *Redesigning the American Dream: The Future of Housing, Work, and Family Life*. New York: W.W. Norton

'Hearings Open with Attacks on Harbourfront.' 1989. *Globe and Mail*, 11 April

Hellman, C. 1987. *The Milton-Park Affair*. Montreal: Vehicule Press

Higgins, D. 1986. *Local and Urban Politics in Canada*. Toronto: Gage

'Home Harder to Buy in Toronto, Vancouver.' 1990. *Globe and Mail*, 11 January

'Hosek Moves on Low-Cost Housing.' 1989. *Toronto Star*, 26 February

'Housing: A Slippery Treadmill.' 1989. *Globe and Mail*, 26 January

'Housing Cheaper, Royal Bank Reports.' 1989. *Globe and Mail*, 14 September

'Housing Folly Shuts Out Average Earner.' 1990. *The Globe and Mail*, 26 March

Hulchanski, J., and G. Drover. 1987. 'Housing Subsidies in a Period of Restraint: The Canadian Experience.' In W. Van Vliet (ed.), *Housing Markets and Policies under Fiscal Austerity*, 51–70. Westport, Conn.: Greenwood Press

Hummon, D. 1989. 'Housing, Home, and Identity in Contemporary American Culture.' In S. Low and E. Chambers (eds.), *Housing, Culture and De-*

sign: A Comparative Perspective, 207–28. Philadelphia: University of Pennsylvania Press

'Inexpensive Rental Housing Now Toronto's Rarest Breed.' 1988. *Globe and Mail*, 4 June

'It's All Happening this Saturday.' 1988. *Summerfest News* (Harbourside Co-op), August

Jackson, K. 1985. *Crabgrass Frontier: The Suburbanization of the United States.* New York: Oxford University Press

Jacobs, J. 1961. *The Death and Life of Great American Cities.* New York: Random House

Johnson, B. 1982. *A Sense of Being: An Evaluation of the Accessible Features of Auberge Cooperative.* Ottawa: CMHC

Jones, B. 1990. 'An Uneasy Certitude in Urban Political Economy.' *Urban Affairs Quarterly* 25: 524–31

Jones, D., and J. Turner. 1989. 'Housing and the Material Basis of Social Reproduction: Political Conflict and the Quality of Life in New York City.' In S. Low and E. Chambers (eds.), *Housing, Culture, and Design: A Comparative Perspective*, 13–29. Philadelphia: University of Pennsylvania Press

'Judge Rules Airport on Island Can Expand.' 1990. *Globe and Mail*, 31 March

Kanter, R. 1972. *Commitment and Community.* Cambridge: Harvard University Press

'Killarney Gardens Co-op: Co-op Gets underway without Federal Funds.' 1989. *From the Rooftops* 16 (3): 3. Ottawa: Co-operative Housing Federation of Canada

Laidlaw, A. 1977. *Housing You Can Afford.* Toronto: Green Tree Publishers

Langer, E. 1983. *The Psychology of Control.* Beverly Hills: Sage

Lawrence, R. 1989. 'Translating Anthropological Concepts into Architectural Practice.' In S. Low and E. Chambers (eds.), *Housing, Culture and Design: A Comparative Perspective*, 89–113. Philadelphia: University of Pennsylvania Press

Lefcourt, H. 1982. *Locus of Control: Current Trends in Theory and Research*, 2nd ed. Hillsdale, NJ: Erlbaum

Logan, J. 1978. 'Growth, Politics, and the Stratification of Places.' *American Journal of Sociology* 84: 404–15

Logan, J., and H. Molotch. 1987. *Urban Fortunes: The Political Economy of Place.* Berkeley: University of California Press

Lorimer, J. 1978. *The Developers.* Toronto: James Lorimer

– 1983. 'Citizens and the Corporate Development of the Contemporary Canadian City.' *Urban History Review/Revue d'histoire urbaine* 12: 3–9

Lorimer, J., and C. MacGregor (eds.). 1981. *After the Developers*. Toronto: James Lorimer

Low, S., and E. Chambers (eds.). 1989. *Housing, Culture and Design: A Comparative Perspective*. Philadelphia: University of Pennsylvania Press

Lyon, L. 1987. *The Community in Urban Society*. Philadelphia: Temple University Press

Magnusson, W., and A. Sancton. 1983. *City Politics in Canada*. Toronto: University of Toronto Press

McMillan, S. 1987. 'Forty Years of Social Housing in Toronto.' *Canadian Social Trends*, Winter: 24–30

Medicus Canada. 1981. *Data Handbook on Disabled Persons in Canada*. Ottawa: CMHC

– 1982. *Housing Needs and Problems of Disabled Persons*. Ottawa: CMHC

Melnyk, G. 1985. *The Search for Community: From Utopia to a Co-operative Society*. Montreal: Black Rose Books

'Member Participation.' 1989. *The Circuit* 11 (2). Toronto: Co-operative Housing Federation of Toronto

'Metro Housing Plan Aims Subsidy Funds at Small Households.' 1989. *Globe and Mail*, 17 February.

'Metro IS World-CLASS – in Rents.' 1989. *Toronto Star*, 29 January

'Metro's Rental Crunch Leaving Its Mark on Neighborhoods.' 1988. *Globe and Mail*, 8 June

Mills, C. 1988. ' "Life on the Upslope": The Postmodern Landscape of Gentrification.' *Environment and Planning D: Society and Space* 6: 169–89

'Minister Blasts Foes of Low-Cost Housing.' 1988. *Toronto Star*, 10 June

Minister's Advisory Committee on the International Year of Shelter for the Homeless. 1988. *More than Just a Roof: Action to End Homelessness in Ontario*. Toronto: Ministry of Housing

Ministry of Housing, Ontario. n.d. [1985]. *Assured Housing for Ontario, a Summary*. Toronto: Ministry of Housing

– n.d. [1986]. *Your Guide to Ontario's Housing Programs*. Toronto: Ministry of Housing

– 1986. *Annual Report 1985/86*. Toronto: Ministry of Housing

– 1989. *Annual Report 1988/89*. Toronto: Ministry of Housing

Miron, J. 1988. *Housing in Postwar Canada: Demographic Change, Household Formation, and Housing Demand*. Kingston and Montreal: McGill-Queen's University Press

Molotch, H. 1976. 'The City as a Growth Machine.' *American Journal of Sociology* 82: 309–32

Molotch, H., and J. Logan. 1985. 'Urban Dependencies: New Forms of Use and Exchange Value in U.S. Cities.' *Urban Affairs Quarterly* 21: 143–69

Molotch, H., and S. Vicari. 1988. 'Three Ways to Build: The Development Process in the United States, Japan, and Italy.' *Urban Affairs Quarterly* 24: 188–214

Monti, D. 1989. 'The Organizational Strengths and Weaknesses of Resident-Managed Public Housing Sites in the United States.' *Journal of Urban Affairs* 11: 39–52

'MP Defends Co-op Housing for the Poor.' 1988. *Toronto Star*, 11 October

'Neighbors Fear Project Would Be Ghetto.' 1987. *Globe and Mail*, 10 December

'Neighbors Vow They'll Battle Plan for High Park Co-op.' 1988. *Toronto Star*, 23 November

Nelson-Walker, R. 1981. *Planning, Creating and Financing Housing for Handicapped People*. Springfield, IL: Charles C. Thomas

'New Town of Seaton Will Feature Affordable Housing for 30,000.' 1990. *Globe and Mail*, 29 March

'Non-Profit Housing Help Set.' 1988. *Toronto Star*, 26 October

Olson, M. 1965. *The Logic of Collective Action*. Cambridge, Mass.: Harvard University Press

'Ontario Declares Indefinite Freeze on New Harbourfront Building.' 1989. *Globe and Mail*, 14 December

'Ontario Housing Statement Called Misleading.' 1989. *Globe and Mail*, 27 February.

'Ontario Imposes New Housing Policy.' 1988. *Globe and Mail*, 24 August

'Ontario NDP, Tories Doubt New Community Will Be Built by Grits.' 1990. *Globe and Mail*, 30 March

'Ontario Starts Allocating Funds to Non-Profit Housing Groups.' 1988. *Globe and Mail*, 26 October

'Original St Lawrence Project Passes Test of Time.' 1988. *Globe and Mail*, 18 July

'Ottawa Moves to Implement Harbourfront Restructuring Plan.' 1990 *Globe and Mail*, 28 November

'Our Rental Rate Still Country's Lowest.' 1988. *Toronto Star*, 28 November

Pacione, M. 1988. 'Public Participation in Neighbourhood Change.' *Applied Geography* (UK) 8: 229–47

Pateman, C. 1970. *Participation and Democratic Theory*. Cambridge: Cambridge University Press

Peck, M.S. 1988. *The Different Drum: Community Making and Peace.* New York: Touchstone Books

Planning and Development Department, City of Toronto. 1985. *Toronto Neighbourhoods, the Next Ten Years.* Toronto: Planning and Development Department

– 1986a. *Living Room II.* Toronto: Planning and Development Department

– 1986b. *Trends in Housing Occupancy.* Toronto: Planning and Development Department, Research Bulletin 26

– 1987. *Assisted Housing, Options for Private Sector Involvement and Section 36 Guidelines.* Toronto: Planning and Development Department

Planning Department, Metropolitan Toronto. 1987a. *Housing Trends, 1976–1986.* Toronto: Planning Department, Metropolitan Plan Review, Report No. 3

– 1987b. *Housing Intensification.* Toronto: Planning Department, Metropolitan Plan Review, Report No. 4

'Pledge for Housing Units Would Meet Olympic Needs in 1996 Bid, Eggleton Says.' 1990. *Globe and Mail,* 26 January

Poulin, A. 1984. *Le Choix des membres-locataires dans les coopératives d'habitation locative au Québec.* Montreal: Ecole des Hautes Etudes Commerciales

Pratt, G. 1986. 'Against Reductionism: The Relations of Consumption as a Mode of Social Structuration.' *International Journal of Urban and Regional Research* 10: 377–99

– 1987. 'Class, Home and Politics.' *Canadian Review of Sociology and Anthropology* 24: 39–57

'Province Calls for New-Home Construction.' 1989. *Globe and Mail,* 18 July

Pynoos, J., R. Schafer, and C. Hartman. 1973. *Housing Urban America.* Chicago: Aldine

'Quick Solution a Costly One for Harbourfront, Mills Charges.' 1990. *Globe and Mail,* 2 May

Reid, B. 1989. 'The Corporate City Revisited (1945-1989).' *City Magazine,* 10 (4): 16–19

Relph, E. 1976. *Place and Placelessness.* London: Pion

'Rent Controls Clearly Necessary When You Look at Other Cities.' 1989. *Toronto Star,* 7 May

'Rental Vacancies Set 7-Year High in Toronto.' 1990. *Globe and Mail,* 24 November

'Resales of Houses Take 28.9% Plunge.' 1990. *Globe and Mail,* 17 July

Robinson, J., T. Thompson, P. Emmons, and M. Graff, with E. Franklin. 1984. *Towards an Architectural Definition of Normalization.* Minneapolis:

University of Minnesota Center for Urban and Regional Affairs, School of Architecture and Landscape Architecture

Robson, M. 1986. 'Creekview Co-op.' *Rehabilitation Digest* 17 (4): 3–5

Rose, A. 1980. *Canadian Housing Policies: 1935–1980.* Toronto: Butterworth

Royal Commission on the Future of the Toronto Waterfront. 1989. *Housing and Neighbourhoods.* Toronto: Royal Commission

Rybczynski, W. 1986. *Home: A Short History of an Idea.* New York: Viking Press

Saunders, P. 1986. *Social Theory and the Urban Question,* 2nd ed. New York: Holmes and Meier

Sayegh, K. 1987. *Housing: A Canadian Perspective.* Ottawa: ABCD-Academy Books

Schiff Consultants. 1982. *Housing Cooperatives in Metropolitan Toronto: A Survey of Members: A Report.* CHF Research Bulletin No. 2. Ottawa: Co-operative Housing Foundation of Canada

Schwartz, D., R. Ferlauto, and D. Hoffman. 1988. *A New Housing Policy for America: Recapturing the American Dream.* Philadelphia: Temple University Press

Selby, J. 1989. *A Bibliography on Co-operative Housing in Canada.* Co-operative Housing Foundation of Canada, Research Paper No. 4. Ottawa: CHF

Selby, J., and A. Wilson. 1988. *Canada's Housing Co-operatives: An Alternative Approach to Resolving Community Problems.* Co-operative Housing Foundation of Canada, Research Paper No. 3. Ottawa: CHF

Sennett, R. 1970. *The Uses of Disorder.* New York: Vintage Books

'Severe Housing Shortage Exacts a Heavy Social Cost.' 1988. *Toronto Star,* 3 July

Short, J. 1989. *The Humane City: Cities as if People Matter.* Oxford: Basil Blackwell

'Should Have Seen CN Letter before Games Bid, Councillors Charge.' 1990. *Globe and Mail,* 31 January

Simmons, J., and L. Bourne. 1989. *Urban Growth Trends in Canada, 1981–86: A New Geography of Change.* Toronto: Centre for Urban and Community Studies, University of Toronto, Major Report No. 25

Simon, J., and G. Wekerle. 1985. *Creating a New Toronto Neighbourhood: The Planning Process and Residents' Experience.* Ottawa: CMHC

– 1986. 'Development of the New Urban Neighbourhood.' *Plan Canada,* April: 46–51

'6,400 New Housing Units to Get Ontario Backing.' 1989. *Globe and Mail,* 9 December

Smith, N. 1984. *Uneven Development*. Oxford: Basil Blackwell

– 1987. 'Of Yuppies and Housing: Gentrification, Social Restructuring, and the Urban Dream.' *Environment and Planning D: Society and Space* 5: 151–72

Social Planning Council of Metropolitan Toronto. 1984. *A New Housing Agenda for Metropolitan Toronto*. Toronto: Social Planning Council

– 1985. *Housing: The Faces behind the Need*. Toronto: Social Planning Council. Discussion Paper on Social Policy, No. 2

Spronk, B. 1981. 'Condominiums, Co-operatives, and the Home Ownership Dream.' *Canadian Journal of Anthropology* 2: 91–100

– 1988. 'Management by Democracy vs. Democracy by Management: A Housing Co-operative and Condominium Compared.' In J. Andre and D. Laycock (eds.), *The Theory and Practice of Co-operative Property*, 131–44. Saskatoon: Centre for Co-operative Studies, University of Saskatchewan

Statistics Canada. 1981. *Census of Canada*. Ottawa: Statistics Canada

– 1989. 'Statistics Canada Issues New Poverty Lines.' *Perception* 13 (1): 39–41

Steering Committee on Matters Related to the Board of Toronto Harbour Commissioners. 1989. *Persistence and Change: Waterfront Issues and the Board of Toronto Harbour Commissioners*. Toronto: Royal Commission on the Future of the Toronto Waterfront, Publication No. 6

Stone, C., and H. Sanders. 1987. *The Politics of Urban Development*. Lawrence: University Press of Kansas

Tabuns, P. 1986. 'Commentary: Co-operative Structure and Ideology.' *From the Trenches*, June: 10–15. Toronto: Co-Action

Tate, D., and T. Lee. 1983. 'Learning from Methods Used in Other Countries.' In N. Crewe and I. Zola (eds.), *Independent Living for Physically Disabled People*, 88–112. San Francisco: Jossey-Bass

'The Hidden Price of Being Disabled.' 1989. *Toronto Star*, 26 April

'This Time, There's Hope for Harbourfront.' 1987. *Globe and Mail*, 31 October

'Toronto Council Supports End to Waterfront Freeze.' 1989. *Globe and Mail*, 15 July

'Toronto Doubles Non-Profit Housing Target.' 1989. *Globe and Mail*, 18 February

'Toronto Seeks Cap on Island Airport Flights.' 1989. *Globe and Mail*, 17 November

Turner, V. 1974. *Dramas, Fields, and Metaphors, Symbolic Action in Human Society*. Ithaca, NY: Cornell University Press

Tyler, T., K. Rasinki, and N. Spodick. 1985. 'Influence of Voice Satisfaction with Leaders: Exploring the Meaning of Process Control.' *Journal of Personality and Social Psychology* 48: 72–81

Vaughan, C. 1987. 'Shoring Up Harbourfront. What Went Wrong? Can It Be Fixed?' *Toronto Life* 21 (8): 54–61

Vogel, R., and B. Swanson. 1989. 'The Growth Machine versus the Antigrowth Coalition: The Battle for Our Communities.' *Urban Affairs Quarterly* 25: 63–85

Wekerle, G. 1988. 'Canadian Women's Housing Cooperatives: Case Studies in Physical and Social Innovation.' In C. Andrew and B. Milroy (eds.), *Life Spaces: Gender, Household, Employment*, 102–40. Vancouver: University of British Columbia Press

Wekerle, G., R. Dragicevic, R. Jordan, I. Kszyk, and M. Sorenson. 1980. 'Contradictions in Ownership, Participation and Control: The Case of Condominium Housing.' In C. Ungerson and V. Karn, (eds.), *The Consumer Experience of Housing: Cross-National Perspectives*, 170–191. Westmead, England: Gower

Wekerle, G., and S. Novac. 1989. 'Developing Two Women's Housing Cooperatives.' In K. Franck and S. Ahrentzen (eds.), *New Households, New Housing*, 223–43. New York: Van Nostrand Reinhold

Wekerle, G., and J. Simon. 1986. 'Housing Alternatives for Women: The Canadian Experience.' *Urban Resources* 3: 9–14

Weston, J. 1979a. 'Homes without Handicaps.' *Habitat* 22 (3): 34–9

– 1979b. 'The Co-op Solution.' *Habitat* 22 (2): 26–37

'Which Two Will Be Axed?' *Globe and Mail*, 12 December 1990

White, R. 1959. 'Motivation Reconsidered: The Concept of Competence.' *Psychological Review* 66: 297–333

Yarrow, G. n.d. [1989]. 'On What It Takes to Be a Community.' *Windward Breeze* 2 (3): 7–10

Young, D. 1987. 'Commentary: The New Organizational Model: Throwing the Baby Out with the Water.' *From the Trenches*, June: 10–15. Toronto: Co-Action

Index